The streets of St. Louis

Jessica Whitfield

The Streets of St. Louis
Jessica Whitfield
2Real4TV Publishing

Published by Jessica Whitfield, St. Louis, MO
Copyright ©2021 Jessica Whitfield
All rights reserved.

No part of this publication may be reproduced, stored in a retrieval system, or transmitted in any form or by any means, electronic, mechanical, photocopying, recording, scanning, or otherwise, except as permitted under Section 107 or 108 of the 1976 United States Copyright Act, without the prior written permission of the Publisher. Requests to the Publisher for permission should be addressed to Permissions Department,

Limit of Liability/Disclaimer of Warranty: While the publisher and author have used their best efforts in preparing this book, they make no representations or warranties with respect to the accuracy or completeness of the contents of this book and specifically disclaim any implied warranties of merchantability or fitness for a particular purpose. No warranty may be created or extended by sales representatives or written sales materials. The advice and strategies contained herein may not be suitable for your situation. You should consult with a professional where appropriate. Neither the publisher nor author shall be liable for any loss of profit or any other commercial damages, including but not limited to special, incidental, consequential, or other damages.

Names, characters, businesses, places, events and incidents are either the products of the author's imagination or used in a fictitious manner. Any resemblance to actual persons, living or dead, or actual events is purely coincidental.

Cover and Interior design: Davis Creative Publishing Partners, DavisCreative.com

Jessica Whitfield

The Streets of St. Louis

ISBN: 9781737422501 (paperback)
       9781737422518 (ebook)

   2021

Dedication

This book is dedicated to everyone who lost their life to the streets of St. Louis, including my only brother Steven Joseph Whitfield Jr. Just like many young brothers his life was cut short before he had the opportunity to realize his full potential. We all should value life and think twice before taking it away from each other. Put an end to the blood and tears that flood the streets of St. Louis.

Acknowledgment

No experience or work is complete without the help of many people who provide support and encouragement. Thank you to my family and friends who pushed me to see this through.

Table of Contents

The Porch 1
Off The Porch 12
In The Streets 26
Sudden Death 37
Blood Brother 44
Mr. St. Louis 50
Back In The Trenches 60
Back To The Basics 69
Homesick 79
Home Sweet Home 87
Block Monsters 98
The Chase 106
Caught Up 119
Ruff Love 131
High Speed 142
Hit The Gas 151
Head On Collision 161
Bros Before Hoes 170
Babymama Vs Babydoll 178
No Game Plan 186
Changing The Game 193
Game Time 199
Team Player 205
Switchin Up 212
Cut Throat City 222
Loyalty And Lust 232
A Dirty Game 242
Playing Dirty 253
Shameless 260
Heartless 267
Fight To The Death 277
Two Ways Out 286

THE PORCH

"Stay in nis yard and out the damn street. These niggas drive crazy out hurr. Don't leave off this front," my mama said leaving me and my lil brother Chucky outside alone for the very first time. Chucky was eight and I was nine. My pops got my mama pregnant right after she had me so we only like eleven months apart. She felt like it was really no need to supervise our bad asses long as we stayed together rather than branching off an doing our own thing. That way we could basically just watch each other.

"Who is that nigga walkin down na street bruh? Whyda fuck we can't leave off the front porch but he can?" Chucky asked as the lil boy who was clearly our age walked alone towards us from down the street. So we went to the edge of the yard hoping he would tell us who he was but all the lil nigga did was came up to me, pushed my head, then ran down the street to the store at the end of the block.

"Man I know Mama said we can't leave off the front but chu should've just punched that nigga then ran back over hurr," Chucky said as we watched him run in the store.

"It's cool. He gotta come back this way cuz his house down thurr," I said pointing to the other end of the street but still watching the store. "Thurr that nigga go!" I said anxiously as he walked out the store heading back towards us like nothing happened.

"And he walkin on nis side of the street! He prolly finna do it again. You gone punch em soon as he get up hurr?" Chucky asked, anticipating my response.

"Hold on, get back!" I told Chucky as the lil nigga approached us again. I walked right up to him then hit him right in his jaw. We started fighting right then and thurr.

"Mama Dashon fightin nis boy!" Chucky yelled as my mama came to the door.

"What in the hell is yall doin?" she yelled, pulling us away from each other. "Whurr the hell is yo mama lil boy?" my mama asked as she took a firm grip of the lil boy's arm.

"She at home," he said with his head down taking a deep breath.

"OK, well we finna go to your house right now so we can let her know you out hurr fightin. What is your name?" my mama asked the boy as he continued to catch his breath.

"My name Chad my house right thurr," he said pointing to the house down the street. So we walked to the house, smelling a strong aroma of weed the closer we got.

"Chad, what the fuck you done did?" his mama yelled as she came to the door already sensing it was an issue.

"Hey, my name Rayshell. This my son Dashon," my mama said introducing us both.

"We live right thurr down the street. I left him an his lil brother Chucky outside on the front porch and next thing I know I'm hearin all kinds a commotion. I come outside an both a they asses all in na damn grass fightin," my mama explained, pointing to me and Chad.

"Now Chad, whyda fuck would you go down ner fightin somebody when you was sposed to be goin to the fuckin store? I should smack the shit outta yo ass. Say sorry," his mama yelled as she put the blunt she was smoking out in the ashtray on her porch.

"Man sorry," Chad said holding his head down.

"That's why yo ass gone be in na damn house instead a makin friends you wanna fight? Ok, you gone look stupid as fuck in nis house all summer too," his mama continued, still tempted to smack the shit outa his ass despite that dry ass apology he gave.

"Well I think they can be friends. Yall just need to learn howda communicate without fightin. You're always welcome to my house if you wanna be friends okay," my mama said to Chad, feeling a lil sympathy for him cuz he clearly just wanted some new friends but didn't really know how to express it.

"Can my lil brother Theo come too?" Chad asked, warming up to the idea after all.

"Yeah, Dashon got a lil brother too an yall was jus settin a bad example for him cuz if he see yall fightin, he gone think he supposed to fight yo lil brother. But neither one of yall need to be fightin each other cuz yall don't even got no reason to. Just be friends an get along, it'll be better for everybody trust me. Everybody jus play nice okay?" my mama responded as Chad nodded his head to let her know he understood.

My mama got to know Chad mama better because of the whole incident and they became good friends. So Chad and Theo was around us all the time. Me and Chad got into all kinds of trouble together. He was a natural-born thief and so was I. We definitely had that in common. First we was stealing lil shit like candy and snacks from all the gas stations and corner stores on the northside whurr we lived. An by the time we got banned from most of the local stores in walking distance, Chad had learned how to hotwire a car watching the other niggas in the neighborhood cuz that's all them niggas used to do.

I never learned how to hotwire a car but I showl knew how to drive one. Everybody knew I had that wheel too. They knew if I was driving and the police tried to pull us over I would get away.

We would fly down every street in the neighborhood just so everybody could see us running from the police in stolen cars. Then go back on the block to brag about how we got away. We made it look easy and fun. It was like a video game to the lil niggas a couple years younger than us who was still stuck on the porch. They mamas would never want them hanging with us because they knew we stayed in trouble. But after a while they would sneak a couple blocks over and hang with us on Gamble anyway.

Gamble was the busiest street in the neighborhood. That's whurr all the killers and the dealers hung out. Everybody had a gun in they possession on Gamble and you could find every drug known to mankind. You either sold it or used it. Anything we stole out the cars we hit was sold on Gamble. And any cars we stole got parked in the alley behind Gamble. When the police pulled up everybody knew to run and not say shit about nothing if they got caught.

It was always bodies getting dropped on Gamble cuz niggas stayed sliding through shooting that muthafucka up. You could be standing around smoking a blunt with a nigga one minute and the next he shot dead. Young niggas from other hoods fresh off the porch would try to come through shooting and get the whole car shot up from every angle. It was definitely a gamble coming on Gamble, but that's still whurr we all wanted to be. That's whurr everybody came when they got old enough to shake the porch.

"Hey yall wanna come to my birthday party?" Lil Rodney asked, after finally getting the balls to sneak over on Gamble himself. Lil Rodney was a few years younger than us but his daddy sold dope so he stayed hella fresh. He never really stole nothing unless he was just tryna fit in cuz his daddy always made sure he had money in his pocket.

"Man you know yo peoples not finna let me an Chad chill over thurr witchu lil nigga," I said pushing him playfully. "Yo mama gone be like, aww hell naw Rodney they gots to go! Soon as she see our ass," Chad added, laughing hysterically.

"Hold on. Who is that?" Lil Rodney asked, noticing the girl across the street getting her baby out the back seat of a red Neon.

"How you doin?" Lil Rodney yelled as he waved to get her attention. "That's Trouble sister Nikki," Chad answered as Nikki rolled her eyes then went in the house and shut the door.

"Man Trouble crazy as fuck, I think that nigga on nat shit asumn cuz he be trippin. Nikki stay cussin nat nigga out. She be embarrassin the fuck out that man," Chad said, curious to know if Lil Rodney was gone hop down on Trouble sister anyway.

"She fuck wit that one nigga from na Skan. I heard he be ova thurr beatin her ass too," I added, putting him up on game about the bitch.

"Man she cute as fuck, why Trouble not tryna fuck dude up tho? I know damn well he aint lettin nat nigga pullup ova hurr knowin dude be puttin his hands on her," Lil Rodney said, shammin Trouble for tolerating the shit in the first place.

"Shid I guess it's cuz they got that baby together but he was just over thurr yesterday," I said hoping he would take the information I was giving him into consideration before making his next move. But Lil Rodney aint give a fuck about none a that.

The next day Lil Rodney pulled up on Gamble in a big ass go cart his dad had gave him for his birthday. We all wanted to ride that muthafucka too cuz it was fast as fuck. He pulled up on Trouble sister while she was standing on the front porch talking on the phone trying not to smile.

"Come take a ride wit me Nikki," Lil Rodney said knowing he had her undivided attention even though she was on the phone.

"How you know my name?" she asked with a smile.

"That don't matter. Just get in," he said patting the empty seat beside him playfully.

"I aint gettin in nothin that can't fit no car seat first of all," she said with a smirk and her hand on her hip.

"What size yo baby wear?" Lil Rodney asked, realizing he might wanna step his game up for this one cuz Nikki was around my age and I'm like 4 years older than him.

"He wear a one in shoes an a two in diapers, wasup?" she answered as she rolled her neck with a sassy attitude.

"Iight, when I come back I'ma have sumn for em, an some money for a babysitter cuz we need to go on a date," he said feeling a lil more confident the longer he talked to her.

"You not takin me on no date in nat," she said still smiling.

"We gone hop in the Neon. I'ma fill the tank up an we outta hurr – wherever you wanna go baby," he replied with a smile before pulling away and heading back towards us. He already knew he had a chance with her regardless of his age. She was tryna play it off like she wasn't really trippin off the lil nigga but they both was on cloud nine all day trippin off each other.

The next day he went to the Kid's Footlocker around the corner from the hood and got two pair of Jordan's in the baby size. Then he asked his dad if he could get a couple hundred dollars so he could take this girl he really liked on a date. "She a couple years older than me Pops. I aint tryna look like no lil young fluky-ass nigga. I'm tryna flex on her ass so she can think I'm bossed up an not trip off my age. That's what's gone make her wanna get a room wit me at the end a the night aint it?" Lil Rodney said playfully but seriously wanting his dad to know how big of a deal this was for him.

"Aw you really wannna impress her huh?" his dad asked, realizing his son's happiness depended on how well the night was gone go.

"Yeah she special Pops, I just wanna get her alone an catch a vibe wit her cuz I been trippin off her ass heavy I aint even gone stunt," Lil Rodney explained, hoping his dad would understand how important it was for him to impress her.

"Hurr son," his dad said handing Lil Rodney the keys to his Bentley for the first time in his young life. "An hurr," he continued as he handed him four hundred dollars to blow for the night. "Just stay away from nem niggas on Gamble. Don't go ova thurr pullin no money out. An if you let one a them niggas talk you up out my keys I'ma fuck you an him up son. You might not wanna put cha boys in nat type a danger. I'll beat chu bloody then kill em right in front a yo ass," he added as his son just sat thurr frozen in disbelief.

"Come on Pops I got that under control. You know that," Lil Rodney said, snapping outa the daze he was in. "I'm finna pullup on her now," he said feeling anxious for everybody to see him pulling up on Gamble in the Bentley. Especially Nikki.

"You heard what I said," his dad said with a stern face as he got out the driver's seat and headed in the house. That's when shit got real, so Lil Rodney got in the driver's seat and eagerly headed a couple streets over to Gamble.

When he pulled up on Gamble everybody was out, even Trouble. Lil Rodney aint really know how Trouble felt about him pushin up on his sister, but it was hard for him to give a fuck after hearing about her baby daddy beating her ass and still being able to pull up over thurr. Lil Rodney got out the car with the Footlocker bag and walked to the porch. "Wasup Lil Rodney? Whatchu doin over hurr on Gamble boy, lookin like a lick in na Bentley?" Trouble said jokingly as he noticed Lil Rodney approaching the porch.

"I'm bringin my stepson some shoes nigga wasup?" Lil Rodney replied with a smile as he held the bag up real quick tryna flex.

"Stepson! Fuck naw bruh. Aint no nigga from na zone finna be bussin my sister down homie. That's out," Trouble said with a serious face feeling offended.

"Hold on nigga. You mean to tell me you rather her fuck wit that bitch ass nigga who be puttin his muthafuckin hands on her over me?" Lil Rodney responded, losing the smile instantly. "You gone trip wit me, but the nigga that be beatin her ass still be pullin up over hurr. What type a bitchass shit is that? What the fuck is you on Trouble?" Lil Rodney said as he pulled his pants up letting Trouble know they could square up and fight about it if he really wanted to take it thurr.

"Man that's on her dumb ass, she shouldnt've got pregnant by the nigga. You aint finna fuck wit her tho," Trouble said in a hostile manner as Nikki walked out the front door after hearing all the commotion.

"Um, Trouble stayda fuck out my bizzness. Don't be tryna tell no muafucka they can't fuck wit me. You aint nobody. Matter fact, get the fuck off my front before I mase yo ass again. You always tryna start some shit!" Nikki yelled as she grabbed Lil Rodney hand an pulled him in the house with her.

"These cute!" she said happily, once she opened the boxes and saw the shoes. "Sorry about Trouble ass tho. He be doin to much all in my fuckin bizzness like I aint grown," she said rolling her eyes ready to change the subject. "But thank you for the shoes," she said with a sexy grin, making Lil Rodney forget all about the bullshit Trouble was just talking. He sat down on the sofa while she put the shoes up. Her son was still in the backroom sleep with the door open so she could hear him if he woke up. "Why you bein so nice to me? Whatchu like me a sumn?" she asked softly before climbing on Lil Rodney's lap. "You like me baby?" she asked again in his ear, encouraging him to whisper back into hers.

"You know I like you," he whispered. "I can't stop thinkin about chu," he added as she slid her tongue in his mouth with a kiss. Nikki had on a white tank top wit no bra, so her nipples was showing clear as day. She had on some lil bitty ass black shorts too. Lil Rodney pulled them muafuckas right off, knowing she wanted the dick right then and thurr. The sex was everything he thought it would be too. He even told Nikki he loved her. "You mine now girl I love yo ass," he whispered while she continued to grind on top of him. She was still going crazy on the dick when her phone rang face up on the table. He looked over only to see her baby daddy programmed DeadBeat in her phone, then start fuckin her harder knowing she wouldn't answer. They reached they climax after her baby daddy called for the third or fourth time in a row. They held each other speechless until a text came through the phone. She looked over at her phone to see the message and it jus said "On my way!" So Nikki hopped up in a panic reaching for her shorts, still trying not to wake up the baby by making too much noise or talking too loud.

"Look Lil Rodney, my baby daddy finna come get my son so you gotta go. Ion't want no drama wit him. We can hookup later tho," she added, hoping that would take the disappointed look off his face as she rushed him out the door.

"You better not be fuckin nat nigga no more Nikki, I aint playin I just nutted in you," Lil Rodney said feeling insecure about the relationship Nikki had with her baby daddy. As far as he was concerned, whatever the two of them had going on before he came along was over.

"I'm not Rodney, but I still don't want no drama wit chall. You gotta promise me you won't ever get into it wit him. Please just let me handle his ass cuz I do not wanna keep him away from his son. An Ion't want yall havin no static if we finna be together either cuz that's too much drama. I just want me an him to have a understandin about bein nothin more than co-parents so it won't be no confusion when he see I finally moved on. You just gotta trust me baby. Now please go" she said in a hushed tone, kissing him one last time before reaching for the door. "Come back later," she said as she gave him a playful push out the door with a smile.

When she shut the door he floated to the car feeling a natural high. The type a high he never felt before. He hit a couple corners in the hood hoping somebody would flag him down tryna get in with him but Gamble had cleared out. All the police had to do was park at the end of the street to make Gamble a ghost town. But after so long they felt like they had to ride around to actually catch us doing shit.

"Damn boy you whippin the Bentley now?" Rambo from the other end of Lil Rodney street said with a smile as he pulled up in a rental with dark tint on every window. Rambo was Lil Rodney age but was already selling dope. He stayed in a rental tinted up dippin through traffic and he was always in something different.

"Yeah, this how you gotta ride bruh," Lil Rodney answered, putting on his dad's Gucci shades with a grin.

"That muafucka is clean as fuck, I just hit a nigga up in nis hot muafucka tho. I need to hop in ner witchu foreal" Rambo said checking his surroundings.

"Get in bruh," Lil Rodney replied as he took the shades off in a more serious manner. "Who you hit bruh?" Lil Rodney asked as Rambo got settled in the car after parking the rental.

"That nigga from na Skan who be wit Trouble sister baby daddy. Them niggas pulled up on Gamble the other day. Ol' boy hopped out an ran in the crib wit ol' babe, what's her name. What's Trouble and Cap sister name? I can't think a her name for shit," Rambo said ready to tell the rest of the story but feeling bothered because he couldn't remember Nikki name.

"Nikki" Lil Rodney answered, trying not to smile.

"Yeah, Nikki. He went in ner wit Nikki an nis nigga on na passenger's side bucked my geek down right in front a me. Looked me dead in my muafuckin face an smiled like I play games asumn bruh," Rambo explained, remembering how furious he was at the time. "I was finna air his ass out right thurr but I aint wanna burn up the set. Plus dude came back out to the car wit the baby. So I just put the situation on the backburner til I jus seen his ass leavin nis one bitch I be fuckin wit crib a minute ago straight lackin. I hit the lights, pulled in na alley, hopped out, kept the car runnin, left the door open, ran up on nat nigga swift like swiper. Put the barrell to his head, smooth criminal-type shit. Bwah, you outta commission nigga, straight like that. Then I got the fuck up outta thurr. That was like a hour ago," Rambo explained, being dead ass serious about the entire incident not leaving out a single detail.

"Damn foreal? Let's go slide thru thurr now an see what's goin on then. You probably aint even drop em," Lil Rodney responded, feeling amused and entertained by the whole situation.

"Bruh, he is outta fuckin commission trust me. But we can slide back thru that muafucka tho," Rambo assured him feeling certain but wanting to set the record straight so Lil Rodney could be just as sure.

"I showl jus got thru bussin Nikki ass down. Her baby daddy gone catch one too if he start trippin wit me once he see she my bitch now. I'll lay that nigga out so quick, you already know," Lil Rodney blurted out, happy to get the situation he had with Nikki off his chest for the first time.

"Damn, you fuckin Nikki nigga? Hell naw, do Trouble know?" Rambo asked as he laughed, clearly amused.

"Fuck Trouble man! That nigga actin like a bitch, I'll smoke his ass too. Howda fuck he let her baby daddy bitchass keep pullin up ova thurr knowin he be beatin her ass but wanna tryda call hisself checkin me when I'm over thurr bringin the baby shoes an shit. What type a bullshit is that?" Lil Rodney vented, getting worked up about the incident with Trouble all over again.

"Hell naw, you gotta lay Trouble ass down that nigga in the way" Rambo said jokingly as he laughed, not knowing Lil Rodney was gone end up killing Trouble for real.

"Fuck that nigga tho, foreal bruh. He probably is smokin nat shit, his bitch showl goin aroun tellin everybody he is. An the nigga do be trippin so Ion't know he might is shid," Rambo said putting his two cents in about Trouble.

"Damn, yellow tape, yep that nigga ova wit," Lil Rodney said as they approached the scene of the crime.

"I told you bruh, Ion't play no games out hurr," Rambo responded as he looked at all the people standing around devastated about what had happened. "I'ma end up fuckin nat bitch. She sexy as fuck," he added, focusing in on this pretty ass bitch out thurr crying hysterically. She was the center of attention cuz she was questioning the girl whose house he was leaving in the mist of all her grieving. There was sure to be more drama and entertainment if they stuck around longer but at that point it was about time for both they asses to get the fuck from over thurr.

"Let's go pull up on Dashon an Chad nem," Lil Rodney suggested, ready to brag about what he knew.

"Man I pulled up on nem niggas when nat shit first happened. They thought I was fakin," Rambo responded, realizing he now had proof cuz Lil Rodney was with him. "Yeah, pullup on nem niggas," he said eagerly ready to talk about the incident altogether.

When they pulled up on Gamble, they approached me waiting for the perfect moment to bring the incident up. "Wasup killa?" I greeted, smiling at

Rambo. "I was wonderin when you was gone get up out that hot ass Maxima," I added, referring to the rental he had tinted up, parked a couple streets over.

"Man I'm so smooth criminal, I coulda slid in nat muafucka all night if I wanid to," Rambo said playfully rubbing his hands together before shaking my hand to greet me.

"That nigga ova wit foreal tho, bitches ova thurr cryin an shit," Lil Rodney added as he laughed.

"Aw yall pulled back up ova thurr?" I asked, impressed they had the balls to do so.

"Damn right, this nigga thought I was fakin too," Rambo said pushing Lil Rodney playfully as they laughed.

"Hell yeah I'ma go validate the shit. We low key as fuck in the Bentley jus passin by. We'ont know what's goin on," Lil Rodney said letting me know how smooth they was pulling back up over thurr.

"Whurr yo crazy-ass lil bother at? I stay hittin Chucky ass. I'm tryna shoot," Rambo asked, ready to take all Chucky money in a dice game like he always did.

Jessica Whitfield

OFF THE PORCH

Chucky and Theo was more influenced by niggas on Gamble than me or Chad ever was. They stayed on the block, either shootin dice or poppin off on all the niggas that was sliding through tryna catch a body. It happened more often the older we got too.

The neighborhood had developed a reputation for having a lota scandalous-ass, cutthroat-ass niggas around twenty-four-seven. Other hoods felt like catching a body on Gamble was a trophy an it got ten times worse once we all start poppin perks an Zanex pills. We would crunch em up, mix em with some Nyquil and juice, shake the bottle up a lil bit, then keep binkin that muafucka til the shit was gone. It was a good high but we felt like we needed that shit so bad we start snaking each other out for it. I mean if a nigga from the hood aint have a certain reputation he could get robbed on the block like a outsider.

Chucky kept a reputation for being real trigger happy so everybody could know he wasn't to be fucked with. He was always on Gamble with at least two guns in his possession, ready for some shit to pop off. Him and Theo always kinda stayed in the house playing video games n shit in they younger days while me and Chad ran the streets hitting cars and hustling. Once Chucky and Theo finally made it off the porch they jumped in headfirst. Just allaway in the streets full throttle, you couldn't tell them niggas shit. They was straight up block monsters, instantly. No rules, now laws, and wasn't worried about no consequences or repercussions.

They hung with some other niggas on the block who was just as hotheaded as them. They used to pull up on us in all types a different hot boxes, tinted up, flashing a gun in every hand whenever they dropped the tint. Basically just letting us know what they was out thurr on. They usually stuck together like me an Chad but if they did branch off on they own mission, Chucky would usually branch off with Savage. Savage was a lot like Chucky. They had the same mind frame when it came to getting money and taking shit. Them niggas was all about guns and money. That's all they knew.

When Theo would branch off on his own he would most likely branch off with Dre, who was just about the hoodest albino nigga you could ever meet. Dre was with the shit but he was still kinda chill compared to Chucky and Savage. Dre was the type to just go with the flow and let whoever else take the lead. But that was a nice change of pace for Theo who was always tryna keep up with Chucky and Savage knowing it was more pressure to get money with them.

Dre had money to get high with though. Ion't know if he used to get a check for being albino or what but he always kept some money in his pocket some kinda way. He was less risky to ride with too cuz the guns he had was registered to his dad. So the police couldn't even take em if they did get pulled over. It was always better to be with somebody with more money than you anyway cuz we was all chasing that same high. And whoever you was with at the time was who you was getting high with even if you aint have no money. Chasing that high kinda divided us in a way cuz the real deal hustlers on the block started to shy away from the niggas on the block that wasn't really on a paper chase like they was supposed to be. We still had all love for each other but supporting our own habit was turning into a full-time job. Plus the less muafuckas you had around you, the less muafuckas you felt obligated to share yo high wit.

Passing around that Nyquil bottle was all the fuck we ever wanted to do. But it was one major rule to the shit an it was crucial – don't take to big of a sip when a muafucka hand you the bottle. Especially if you aint put in on it. Niggas got kilt for doing shit like that I swear. A nigga from na zone would pop yo ass up right thurr on the spot, knowing not a soul gone tell. Ion't give a fuck if it was a alley fulla niggas. Everybody just gone run. Gun shots go off, run and ask questions later unless you the muafucka that's shooting. That's how it's always been in my neighborhood. And aint nobody talking to no police about nothing. Ever. So it was in everybody's best interest to pass the bottle only to the niggas they was rockin with everyday. Muafuckas was clicked up like a muafucka all of asudden. It definitely mattered who you was rockin with cuz once them drugs took over we all was on a mission with whoever was down to ride.

"He back hurr shootin now," I told Rambo, leading him back to Chucky who was gambling in the alley with Theo.

"Man howda fuck you lose the twenty-dollars you owe me twice?" Dre said playfully to Theo as Chucky picked up Theo's money.

"Naw I'm finna take that bruh, pull all that shit back out," Rambo said playfully reaching for the money Chucky had just collected.

"Naw bruh you got me last time I'm done. I racked up off these niggas today. I aint finna let chu fuck my day up fool you missed out on nis," Chucky responded, stuffing the money further down in his pocket with a smile.

"I heard you went ape shit on ol boy from na Skan," Savage butted in with a smile as he shook Rambo hand to greet him.

"Yeah nigga, real deal block monster this shit a fuckin movie," Rambo replied as he laughed.

"Niggas aint fuckin wit the zone when it come to that gun play an nat paperchase for real. They ass gone learn to stayda fuck out the way tho," Lil Rodney added proudly. Everybody knew if you was from na zone you seen a lota shit and you did a lota shit. Especially if you was from Gamble, the hottest street in the neighborhood.

Rambo wasn't from Gamble but he jumped off the porch hella early. So he was exposed to Gamble lifestyle before all the other lil niggas his age including Lil Rodney, who was probably about the closest person to him.

"Whatchu finna do bruh?" Savage asked as Rambo shook Chucky hand to greet him.

"Get in wit us. We finna go on nis mission," Chucky said as he looked at his phone to view the text he had just got.

"I'm showl finna go get on nis mission wit Nikki ass" Lil Rodney interrupted with a smile, knowing it was breaking news to everybody but Rambo.

"Damn, you fuckin Nikki? Do Trouble know?" Chucky blurted out, making everybody out thurr burst out laughing. Especially after Rambo let em know he said the exact same thing when Lil Rodney told him about it. The situation was funny cuz Trouble was hella crazy. He wasn't like they older brother Cap who basically just did his own thing and didn't really give a fuck who his sister fucked with.

"Man fuck Trouble! If you see his ass tell em I got Nikki face down ass up flatout," Lil Rodney said walking towards Nikki house as everybody else kept laughing.

"Ol girl finna pullup at my crib wit her homegirl, we finna get they ass fucked up. I'm tryna fuck both they asses foreal," Dre said smiling after reading the text he had jus got.

"Hell yeah! That bitch from earlier? Im on nat, her lil potna cute as fuck," Theo said before shaking Chucky hand goodbye.

"Yall keep yall faces up. Stay alert," Dre said as he shook Rambo and Savage hands before leaving with Theo.

"This bitch Carmen got a lick for me," Chucky announced as Rambo and Savage hopped in the car with him.

"What kinda lick bruh? You know that type a shit right up my alley," Rambo said feeling like he definitely got in the car with the right niggas.

"She said he got like ten bucks on em and she took all the bullets out the nigga glock cuz he in the shower," Chucky answered, reading another text Carmen had sent to his phone.

"Shid I aint trustin Carmen scandalous ass. I'm layin dude down regardless I'm tellin you that right now bruh," Savage stated, just ready to catch a body like Rambo.

"Ion't give a fuck about dude, just make sure my bitch stay safe nigga or everybody die," Chucky responded with a smile as he sat in the back seat holding up the two guns he had in his hands playfully.

"Carmen gotcho ass straight pussy-whipped, that shit sad bruh," Savage said rolling his eyes as he drove.

"Naw Carmen just gone do whatever I say no matter what, that's why she my bitch. I'll kill a nigga ova that pussy, on na set," Chucky said putting the address Carmen sent him into his GPS.

Carmen was a real petite, high-yellow, curse you out, sassy type. She wore her hair short an blonde, with hazel brown eyes and a cute face. She was stunning but Chucky was the only one that had the balls to make her his bitch. She had a reputation for being a setup artist so she was real street and he loved that about her. He wasn't worried about her setting his ass up cuz she knew that shit was suicide. She always seen him passing by, but he was always either with another bitch or just surrounded by the niggas he kept around him twenty-four seven, like Theo, Savage and Dre. She was always out with a new victim, getting him drunk and putting shit in his drink so her hands was usually pretty much tied anyway. Not this night though.

This one night, Chucky and Savage went to the hookah bar downtown with some bitches they had met earlier that day. Carmen was sitting at the table with some clueless-ass white boy she had just met sitting right across from her. So Chucky made sure he sat at the table right next to theirs, forcing her to make eye contact with him at some point. This was the prettiest he had ever seen her look. She had on a red halter top, barely covering her fairly small breast and a black miniskirt that gripped her small frame. She wore wedges with red straps going up her legs. And her hands and toes was painted silver. Chucky kept looking at her as he walked past, immediately getting her attention. They had never spoke before, but it definitely wasn't they first time seeing each other. He sat down at the table with Savage and the random bitches they had with em, facing Carmen before putting on his shades so he could stare as long as he wanted without making her uncomfortable. After about twenty minutes and a few drinks, the white boy ordered another round before excusing himself to the restroom. This was Chucky's chance to finally talk to her and he wasn't finna let no random bitches or no corny-ass white boy get in the way. So Chucky got up and sat down in the white boy's seat.

"I be seein you aroun," he said, taking off his shades so she could look him in his eyes.

"I know who you is," Carmen replied with a smile. "Don't getcho girl fuckedup cuz she steady muggin like she gone do sumn," she added, noticing the girl he was with behind them rolling her eyes and frowning her face up at her.

"Fuck that bitch, you wanna beat her ass? I'll have to kill her if she hitchu back tho cuz Ion't need nobody puttin ney hands on you. How would that make me look?" Chucky said in a calm voice and serious face.

"I mean I can't really blame her tho, you is bein mad rude," she said still smiling as the waitress sat the drinks on the table.

"Naw that's just my character," he responded as he took the extra shot of Ciroc the white boy had ordered with his drink.

"Now what I'm sposed to tell him an I'm drinkin Henny," she asked still smiling.

"He gone know I aint take the shot cuz I'm drinkin dark," she added, not knowing how to explain the empty shot glass once the man came back.

"How about I leave his ass right hurr leakin if he question you at all," Chucky responded, looking in her eyes still mesmerized by her beauty.

"How about we pick this back up at a later time so you won't fuck up a future lick" she said, feeling intrigued but realizing the white boy would be coming back any second.

"Cool, I'll be at cho crib at six a'clock tomorrow. We can go somewhurr an eat so be hungry," Chucky said as he got up to go take a piss hisself.

"How you know whurr I live?" she asked, feeling flattered he knew so much about her already.

"Girl you been mine you jus aint know," he said as he put his shades on an walked away.

"Hey, did you miss me?" the white boy asked jokingly, after walking back to his seat less than a minute after Chucky left. "Hey what happened to the shot?" the white boy asked, noticing his shot glass was empty.

"Yeah, the waitress dared me to mix dark an white shots," Carmen answered as she took her shot of Henny with a wink.

"Wow! That's badass," the white boy responded, still feeling his first few drinks.

"Get us a couple more shots I gotta pee," Carmen said as she got out her seat and headed toward the bathroom. She didn't really have to pee but she knew Chucky was back thurr. She was relieved that the white boy didn't come back until Chucky walked away but something was still pulling her back to him after he left. She just wanted more of him, so she walked to the back whurr the bathrooms was at.

Chucky was coming out the bathroom looking Carmen up and down full of lust as she approached him seductively with a kiss. Then he basically took it from thurr, picking her up and stepping back into the men's room confident that it was empty cuz he had just walked out. He made his way to the stall a couple steps away and shut the door anxious to get up in that lil pussy real quick. She was light as a feather so he was able to un-buckle his pants an pull out his dick without having to put her down. Her lil black skirt rose exposing her sexy red panties. Then he pinned her up against the wall, before ripping the panties completely off and stuffing them in his pocket. She grinded on his dick as he inserted it inside her, and her petite size made it easy for him to handle her lil ass the way he wanted to. She looked him in the eyes as he maneuvered her body on his dick taking her to ecstasy. This was the best sex she had ever had. It felt like he was taking over her whole body and she loved it. After Carmen snuck out the men's room without being seen, she told the white boy that mixing dark and white shots wasn't a good idea and that she needed to go home cuz she was feeling sick.

Carmen was on Chucky mind all night. He couldn't wait to pull up at six thirty the next day, not wanting to show up exactly at six cuz he aint wanna seem to geeked up about it. He knew if he showed up at six o'clock or earlier, she would already know how crazy he was about her ass and that would make her dangerous.

"She said the back door unlocked an ney got the music turnt up," Chucky announced as he read another text from Carmen.

"Ok so we just finna creep in thru the back while the music playin so he won't hear the door right?" Rambo confirmed, tryna make sure everybody knew the game plan.

"Chucky I'm tellin you right now I'm layin dude ass down. I aint got time for the nigga to be comin all on Gamble tryna drop sumn. Plus he gone smoke Carmen ass if I don't so don't trip like you did last time nigga," Savage said, referring to the last time the two of them went on a mission together and shit went left. The plan was just to take the fuckin man money, but Savage trigger-happy ass ended up shooting the damn man in the head. They argued about the shit the whole way home. Then got so high they forgot about the whole incident by the time they woke up the next day.

"Just let me handle it bruh," Chucky replied as they pulled up to the address, hit the lights, then headed to the back door with caution. They crept up the steps as the music blasted slow jams. When they got to the top of the steps there was Carmen, dancing seductively in her black lace panties and matching bra. The man she was entertaining was about 4 hunnit pounds with a mouth fulla golds. His head was shaved bald and he was wearing some blue basketball shorts with his whole stomach hanging over em.

Carmen's eyes widened as they entered the room, alarming the man whose back was towards them. "Turn na fuck back aroun nigga," Chucky demanded, when the man turned around to see what had caught Carmen's attention. "Baby put cho clothes on," he added as Carmen quickly scrambled for her blue jean shorts, tank top, an flip flops she wore over thurr.

"Whurr the money at nigga? We need everything," Rambo said as he approached, pointing the gun directly at dude face.

"Whurr the fuck the stash at fat boy?" Savage added as he pointed his gun at the other side of the man face.

"Man fuck! It's in na safe in my closet man shit! Take that shit," the man said, fearing for his life but tempted to reach for the empty glock sitting on the end table by the couch he was sitting on.

"What's the code nigga?" Chucky asked, putting the two guns he had to one of the man's temple.

"Fuck! I think its 4432," the man said trembling.

"What the fuck you mean you think nigga?" Rambo asked as he pressed his gun to the man's other temple.

"Man shit! Yall got all these fuckin guns to a nigga head I can't fuckin think," the man responded, suddenly pissin all over his basketball shorts out of fear.

"You really not gone be thinkin if I blow yo fuckin brains out cuz the code wrong now what is it?" Savage said, putting his gun closer to the middle of the man's forehead.

Man it's 6432, 6432. Just don't shoot me man yall can have all that shit," the man said still trembling.

"Baby put that code in nat safe," Chucky directed as he took a couple steps back to keep a eye on Carmen while she tried to open the safe.

"It's open," she announced as Chucky walked in the room to assist her with putting the money in the bag as quickly as possible.

"What else in nis muafucka?" Rambo asked, with his gun still pressed up against the man temple.

"It's some shit in my nightstand, in ner under the bed, an in na dresser. Take all that shit man damn!" the man said, hoping they would leave him alive if he cooperated and gave them everything.

"Go help them I got this," Savage told Rambo, taking a couple steps back with his gun still pointed directly at the man face. "Make sure yall check all them drawers," Savage yelled, directing his attention to Chucky, Carmen, and Rambo, who was back thurr in the bedroom grabbing everything worth value as fast as they could. The man knew Savage was gone end up killing him cuz he saw the blood thirsty look in his eyes when Savage held the gun to his face. So he decided to take a chance and reach for his glock but Savage pulled the trigger in a instant. Put one right in the man head. Chucky, Carmen, and Rambo came out the room with all the money and everything else they collected soon as they heard the gun go off. Savage picked up the empty glock the man was reaching for before heading out the door with the rest of them and just like that they was gone.

Carmen was sure to take the man secret phone, which was the only way he communicated with her so his wife wouldn't find out about his infidelities. They took a lot of jewelry, including a ring worth about six-thousand dollars on its own. Carmen picked out the ring while shopping through all the man's jewelry, unfazed by what had just happened.

"This for you daddy," she said to Chucky, putting the ring on his finger with a smile. "Now you gotta get me one," she said playfully as he smiled back, knowing she was actually the only girl he would ever even consider making his wife.

"Man fuck all that lubby dubby shit. How much paper we got?" Savage butted in, ready to see how much his cut was gone be.

"We got about a pound of some gas, I'm finna rollup," Rambo interrupted, putting the weed he took up to his nose so he could smell how good it was.

"Pull up at Dre crib so we can count this shit up an divide it," Chucky told Savage as he pulled Carmen closer to him, ready to hurry up and split the shit up too so he could go duck off with Carmen alone.

"Yeah call Dre," Rambo suggested as he sat in the front seat rolling the blunt right out the pound of weed they had just stole.

"This nigga not even answerin," Savage said, hanging up his phone after calling Dre.

"Call Theo," Chucky responded as Carmen kissed all on his neck and ear with her leg pulled over him comfortably in the back seat.

"This nigga not pickin up neither, I know damn well they not finna jus keep fuckin them bitches while both they phones steady ringin off the hook like this," Savage said feeling disappointed after calling both phones back to back without getting an answer from either one.

"Jus pullup on nem niggas bruh, I know they ova thurr," Chucky said still holding Carmen's leg so she could stay positioned like she was and keep doing what she was doing. Him an Carmen was in they own lil world back thurr.

"Thurr Dre car go, they ass must be in nat muafucka sleep," Rambo announced as they pulled up to Dre apartment.

"Get the fuck up niggas," Chucky yelled as Savage start banging on the door.

"Wasup bruh?" Dre said, after coming to the door without his glasses. He was blind as a bat without em so he didn't even realize Carmen was thurr too.

"Wasup Dre?" Carmen greeted as she pushed passed, waking him up completely once he caught a whiff of the Juicy Couture perfume she was wearing.

"Aw wasup Carmen?" Dre responded, reaching for his glasses and placing them on his face as Carmen sat down on the couch.

"Whurr the fuck Theo ass at?" he asked looking around noticing Theo was nowhere in sight. "The nigga was just witchu! What the bitches ended up leavin wit him?" Savage asked playfully.

"Maan nem bitches came thru for like thirty minutes, then na bitch Theo was sposed to be fuckin wit bust out talm bout her baby sick an her Mama keep callin so they left. After that, me an Theo got high an I nodded off," Dre explained, confused as to why Theo was nowhere to be found. "Look, hurr the nigga phone right hurr," he added, noticing Theo's phone sitting on the couch next to Carmen.

"Whurr you at nigga?" Chucky shouted, walking through the apartment curiously wondering whurr the hell Theo ass was at.

"That nigga prolly ducked off witcho bitch somewhur Dre!" Rambo said jokingly as him an Dre laughed.

"Man my glock gone too tho," Dre said noticing his dad's registered gun wasn't on the table whurr he left it. "An why would the nigga leave his phone bruh?" Dre asked, feeling a lil concerned about Theo's whereabouts.

"Maan nat nigga somewhere high on a mission," Savage assured him. "Just ready to count the money they got from the lick really."

"Yeah that nigga aint too far witout his phone. Let's count this money up," Rambo added, eagerly ready to count the money and figure out his cut.

"Yeah let's count up, baby empty that bag out on nis table," Chucky said before Carmen dumped the bag of money on the table.

"Dre look thru that jewelry, see if you want sumn homie," Chucky said tryna take the worried look off Dre face from being so concerned about Theo's absence. Then he sat down an counted the money while Dre shopped through the jewelry impressed.

Meanwhile, Theo was somewhere high on a mission for real. Theo's habit had gotten a lil worse than the rest of ours but he never really had enough money to keep up with it. He was always waiting around for one of us to get high with him. Not that night though. Theo felt like he had to get himself high that night. Dre had nodded off after they got high together but Theo wanted more. And he was gone do whatever it took to get it too, so he took Dre gun and snuck off into the night.

Theo was already high as hell when he left Dre apartment. So he thought it would be a good idea to break into the older man's house on the corner. The man was about 45 with a seemingly good job. He always kept his yard clean even though he stayed in a bad neighborhood. He was still content with whurr he lived cuz he minded his business and stayed to himself. Theo felt like he must've had something worth value in his house cuz he drove a nice car and wore nice clothes when he wasn't in his work uniform. One day Theo noticed the man leaving for work and knew that when the time was right he would break in.

The time was now cuz he had just seen the man leave with his uniform on again about a hour ago. He went to the back of the man house an climbed through the window. He walked around with caution, making sure that no one else was in the house. Theo was so damn high that once he knew the house was empty he just got outrageously comfortable. He sat Dre gun down on the man dresser before looking through the man's shoes. Then he pulled a pillowcase off one of the pillows and started putting all the shit worth value in the pillowcase. This nigga was so high he even went in the kitchen and start going thru the refrigerator.

He got about 200 dollars out the nightstand then headed to the bathroom to raid the medicine cabinet. The man had everything Theo was looking for up in that muafucka too. Prescription pills everywhere, Zanex, perks, you name it. Theo felt like he hit the jackpot. Even dry popped a couple perks to celebrate. He was so busy rummaging through all the different pill bottles that he didn't even hear the man coming in the house after getting off work early. Already alarmed by his bedroom light being on and hearing all the ruckus going on in the bathroom as he slowly entered the house. The man crept to the bathroom door bravely but with caution, trying not to make a sound while Theo was putting all the pill bottles in the pillowcase.

Now the man was well over two-hundred pounds at least 250, so it was pretty much impossible to get all the way to the bathroom without being heard. But by the time Theo heard him coming it was too late. He realized he left the gun sitting on the dresser so he darted to the bathroom door in a panic. "Get back!" he said to the man who was slowly approaching the door when Theo finally opened it.

"What are you doin in here?" the man asked bravely standing face to face with Theo, talking to him as if he was just a bad ass lil kid going through all his shit and got caught.

"Get back or I'ma blow yo fuckin brains out old man," Theo responded with his hand in the right pocket of the black hoodie he wore, pointing at the man as if he had a gun while walking backwards towards the real gun. The man was hesitant but still tempted to just tackle Theo to the ground. He was pretty sure Theo didn't really have a gun in his pocket an after he caught a glimpse of the gun Theo was tryna get to dude just went for it.

He charged towards Theo as Theo made a mean dash for the gun but tripped. The man fell on top of Theo and immediately put him in a headlock making it impossible for Theo to get a hold of the gun. "Get the fuck off me!" Theo yelled struggling to break free. But the man still kept him detained while pulling out his phone and calling the police. It was easy for him to detain Theo lil ass cuz he was more than twice Theo's size and age. He referred to Theo as a young punk who was to scared to get out hurr and get a job when he talked to the police on the phone. He urged them to get thurr quickly because he was tempted to handle the situation himself before hanging up the phone. "Just let me go bruh please! I aint even take shit," Theo pleaded as the man had him pinned to the floor showing no mercy.

"Oh now I'm ya brotha, but chu was just goin through all my shit tryna clean me out tho. I guess you aint plan on takin nothin huh? An if I hada let chu get to that gun right thurr you wouldnt've tried to blow my goddamn head off like you said you was either huh?" the man asked sarcastically. "You young punks make me sick! Don't wanna get out hurr an get a job cuz yall think it's cool to just take shit from people that work hard for what the hell they want. What the hell is wrong witchu lil niggas?" the man continued, feeling disgusted with the younger generation's lifestyle choices more than ever.

"Look man, I'm sorry. Just let me go man fuck! I'ma get a job," Theo said, hoping the man would give him one last chance and let him go before the cops got thurr.

"It's too late for that now. The police'll be hurr soon so you can get a job when ney let chu outta jail sucka," the man responded, unconvinced that Theo would actually get a job if he would've let him go free.

"You a dead man when I get up out that muafucka nigga! That's if my niggas don't put a bullet in yo head first for gettin me locked up!" Theo yelled lashing out with anger and frustration.

"Naw, you gotcha self locked up Jack! If you wouldnt've brought cho ass in my house we wouldn't be sittin hurr waitin on na police now would we?" the man asked calmly as the police approached the door letting themselves in like they was told to do on na phone.

"Police. What's going on here?" one of the officers announced with a loud voice that echoed though the house as they walked towards the man who still had Theo pinned down on the floor.

"Get that gun officer," the man said looking at the gun Theo left on the dresser. "This man broke into my home and tried to murder me with this weapon officer" the man explained as he slowly got up with caution. "Now he will tryda get away if I let em go cuz he's been tryna get away the whole time," the man warned as the officers proceeded to place the cuffs on Theo's wrist.

IN THE STREETS

"Man what the fuck was up wit Theo goofy ass last night?" Lil Rodney asked when he saw me on Gamble the next day.

"Watchu mean bruh? I aint seen Theo since last night. I had to creep out on yall ass man, this lil bitch I be fuckin wit pulledup tryna get some dick so I ducked off wit her. Chad worsm ass made the bitch drop him off alla way in na damn county some fuckin whurr. That nigga be in na fuckin way," I answered, already talking his ear off like usual as he shook my hand to greet me.

"Man I heard that nigga straight took Dre gun an broke in dude crib down ner on na corner. The man ended up wrestlin Theo to the ground for the damn gun. Now Theo booked, no bond, they finna slam his ass," he explained as I stood there frozen in disbelief.

"Fuck naw! Is you for real? Who said that?" I asked in denial about the whole incident.

"Nikki told me that shit bruh," he answered, trying not to smile but blushing almost every time he said the damn girl name.

"Damn, who told Nikki that shit?" I asked feeling disappointed.

"She said Trouble bitch-ass said that shit bruh," he answered loud enough for Trouble to hear as he walked towards us with his older brother Cap muggin Lil Rodney down. Cap was just a couple years older than me, and Trouble was Lil Rodney age. So it was kinda unlikely to see both of them together cuz of they age difference. Cap was more in my lane as far as the streets go and Trouble usually ran with the other lil young rowdy niggas on the block. But everybody from na zone made sure they stopped on Gamble at some point on a daily basis, so you was likely to catch any of us rockin out together thurr.

It was bright an early but everybody was already starting to pop out. News travel fast in na zone so everybody in the hood knew about the incident with Theo by then. We call the neighborhood the zone cuz its our own lil world, a land full of zombies like the Walking Dead. Every time somebody get killed or locked up the whole hood knew about the shit almost instantly.

"Watch yo mouth when you say my name fuck boy! Put some respect on my shit," Trouble said as him and Cap approached.

"Will you niggas just give it a fuckin rest. Damn! Yall might as well jus catch a fade wit each other an be boys again" Cap said as he shook my hand to greet me.

"He need to catch a fade wit that nigga who be beatin Nikki ass if he wanna catch a fade wit somebody. Scary ass nigga" Lil Rodney said with his eyebrows raised, throwing shade and talking shit.

"Man fuck all that, Trouble who told you that shit about Theo?" I asked, butting in and changing the subject.

"Dre told me the police called his dad askin if he knew Theo had his gun? He was like naw, said it was stolen," Trouble answered, before walking away to greet the white Ford Mustang that had just pulled up across the street.

"Shid I bet he did say naw. He'll be a damn fool to say he did," Cap said with a chuckle.

"Rodney come help me find what I'm wearin tonight at the mall," Nikki said smiling as she came outside in the skimpy True Religion dress and slides Lil Rodney had just bought her the day before.

"Come on baby," he responded meeting her at the car with a hug and kiss, being sure to grab Nikki ass at a angle whurr Trouble could see. He winked at Trouble who was standing on the sidewalk next to the white Ford Mustang still muggin him down. But Lil Rodney just cracked a smile then drove off with Nikki feeling like he had a million dollars on him.

"Man nat shit crazy, this nigga just got booked for armed robbery. They finna give him hella time," I said to Cap still feeling shocked by the news.

"Yeah that's fucked up, he gone be down for a minute," Cap replied shaking his head with sympathy. "Whatchu finna do tho? My boy Drako finna pullup. You wanna slide out?" he asked, hoping to take my mind off the whole situation.

"Yeah man I'll slide out witchu. The police finna start hittin nis muafucka anyway," I answered, just ready to leave the neighborhood for a lil while really. Gamble was starting to feel like a big ass trap that was gone eventually get all of us. I felt a strong urge to get away for a minute after hearing about that shit for some reason. So I was all for it.

"Drako this Dashon, he from na zone. Dashon this Drako." Cap said as he got in the car, introducing me and Drako for the very first time. Drako hit the blunt he was smoking then passed it to Cap.

"Wasup Dashon, you packin?" Drako asked looking back at me from the driver's seat, flashing the glock forty he had on his lap with a smirk. So I took the glock I had from off my waist, showing him we had the exact same gun damn near without saying a word.

"Enough said homie," he said as he shook my hand in acceptance. Drako from Walnut Park. That's a dangerous ass neighborhood on the northside too. His whole family fulla hitmen and drug lords so everybody knew not to fuck with nobody with they last name cuz they all was some straight up killers. It was a bunch of em too.

I start fuckin with Cap and Drako everyday cuz Chad mama made him move to Mississippi after Theo got locked up. She said if he stayed in St. Louis he was gone end up locked up like his brother or dead. I was so fucking mad though. I couldn't believe that nigga was leaving the hood. I felt like the hood was jus never gone be the same again after that shit. So me and Cap was posted up in Walnut Park most of the time with Drako. We was getting a lil money with him over thurr too shid the zone was getting too hot anyway. We had a safe place to stash our guns and dope cuz Drako crib was the stash spot. And we wasn't burning it up by having a bunch of niggas over thurr. It was just us three rockin out all day unless we was ducked off with a bitch on our own.

One day this lil bitch I was fuckin with dropped me off at Drako crib but when I went to his room whurr I tucked my thumpa the muafucka was gone. "Damn! Wasup Drako? Whurr my glock homie?" I asked feeling annoyed and uncomfortable.

"Shid Cap must've took that muafucka, aint nobody else been up in hurr," Drako answered, eating the bowl of cereal he had just poured. "Call em," he added, urging me to get to the bottom of it real quick so I wouldn't start thinking he took the muafucka.

So I called Cap. "Wasup Cap? Whurr my glock bruh?" I asked, soon as he picked up the phone.

"Chill bruh I got it, I need it right now bad," he answered. With so much going on in the background I could barely even hear what he was saying.

"Bruh you got cho own shit. Whyda fuck do you need mine too?" I asked, raising my voice in anger.

"I had to sell my shit bruh, I'm fucked up cuz I took a loss in nis dice game," he explained barely loud enough for me to hear that.

"Man how you gone take my shit jus cuz you lost yo shit in a dice game. Bring me my shit!" I yelled feeling furious.

"Man I'm on na southside, I'll bring this muafucka back ova thurr later. I need it," he responded before hanging up in my face with no intentions on bringing me my gun back anytime soon.

"Damn nat nigga fallin off," Drako said with a smile clearly amused by the whole situation.

"Fuck you nigga, why he aint take yo shit?" I said cracking a smile myself at that point. Drako always could change a muafucka whole mood just by talking shit and clowning niggas. He was funny as hell when he wanted to be so he was cool to be around with or without Cap.

"He was showl goin back an forth wit some nigga on na phone earlier. Shid he might do need that muafucka. Ion't know what Cap got goin on lately, the nigga been ghost foreal," Drako said hoping to make me feel a lil better about it I guess.

"Man he gone lose my shit too," I said as we laughed. I sat over thurr talking shit and clowning Cap with Drako until my phone rang.

"Whurr the fuck are you at Dashon? Bring yo ass home cuz you goin na fuck back to school tomorrow. They gone let chu in nis alternative school an you better not fuck it up," my mama said soon as I picked up the phone and said hello. Me and Chad stayed suspended from school for staying in trouble and being gang related which was one of the main reasons why Chad mama made him move. We got suspended and high so much we never even remembered when the fuck to go back up in that muafucka. Last time we went back they put both of our asses out permanently though, along with a bunch of other niggas from the zone for starting a huge riot that took place after school on school property.

"Ok Mama I'ma go to school tomorrow I'll be thurr ina minute, Mama whatchu cook tho?" I asked changing the subject with a smile before she hung up in my face annoyed with my lack a interest about school. "My mama be trippin" I said to Drako as I looked at my phone realizing she had hung up without telling me what she cooked. I wasn't really interested in going back to school tho. It was a fuckin joke to me after a certain age. The only reason I even wanted to go is cuz we was hella deep and running the whole school.

The high school had a bunch of different niggas from every hood on the northside damn near in that muafucka but nobody was deeper than us. They might've been with the shit but they still aint want no smoke with nobody from na zone cuz if they had smoke with one of us they had smoke wit all of us and we outnumbered everybody. So niggas usually just stayed the fuck out our way and the bitches was drawn to us like bees to honey for some reason. We had all the bitches on lock. Niggas was scared to even hop down on a bitch if they knew one of us wanted her. We had all respect in that muafucka.

The thought of going to school without Chad bullshittin the day away with me just seemed so lame. Nobody else mama was making them go to the damn alternative school so I wasn't really looking forward to going neither. But I knew my mama wouldn't have it any other way. She was already pissed about having to take me to the hospital a couple days before cuz me an Drako thought we was getting pulled over leaving his probation office. I swallowed the seemingly small bag of crack rocks I had on me at the time cuz Drako said he couldn't high speed his mama car. But the fucking bag was too big and got stuck dead smack in the middle of my throat. That muafucka would not go down or come up for shit and I was tryna get it out for days. I couldn't eat or drink shit cuz the fucking bag was blocking everything I tried to swallow. Once I finally gave in and told my mama what was going on she took me to the hospital and she was furious, I was mad too though. I mean hurr I was probably finna get locked up for some shit I tried to swallow and we never even got pulled over. I felt hella stupid. Then I had to hear my mama mouth about it the whole way thurr making me feel ten times worse. The doctor had to put me to sleep to get the shit out my throat and when I woke up the police was already thurr. The officer wasn't trippin cuz I was still a minor. But he told me if I wasn't he would've took my lil ass to jail and that I was lucky he wasn't taking me to juvenile for the shit. He let me go wit the warning after promising to take me to juvenile or jail if it ever happened again. My mama was still mad as hell though.

She dropped me off at the school the next day and once I got thurr I realized that it wasn't even that bad. Dre was in that muafucka, plus it was all hoes in that bitch. Them city bitches that got put out for fighting was always the easiest bitches to fuck for some reason. It was a couple lil freaks in that muafucka for getting caught suckin dick and fuckin in the bathrooms n shit too. Most of em already knew who I was and they was already on Dre dick just because he was from the zone. We was so heavy they aint even give a fuck about him being albino. Then it was the girls who got put out the county schools for petty shit cuz the county schools was way more strict than the city schools we went to. They aint know who we was but they was showl curious according to they body language. Those was the ones I was most attracted to. And they was just as easy as the bitches that already knew us. The only problem was them city bitches had the county bitches too scared to really give me the time of day cuz they knew them city bitches was gone be tryna fight em if they did.

Crystle was different though. She was short and high yellow with a perfect ass body and a pretty ass smile. She was the cutest bitch in the class and she wasn't scared of them city bitches. She got put out a county school for fighting them hating ass hoes up thurr and felt like them city bitches wasn't no different. She told Dre to tell me she said I was fire, knowing that would give me the greenlight to ask for her number. So I caught up with her after class, walking down the steps. "Why you walkin so close to me?" she asked with a smile as I approached her from behind.

"Cum mer lil girl," I said shoving her in the corner once we got down the steps so she wouldn't keep walking down the hall.

"Why is you playin wit me?" she asked still smiling as she stood thurr with her back against the wall ready for me to make my move.

"I aint playin witchu girl you know I want cho ass," I said getting a good grip of her lil plump ass while pressing my body up against hers for a hug.

"Well what took you so long to talk to me? You be talkin to all them otha bitches tho," she said rolling her eyes with a cute lil attitude while I stood thurr trapping her in the corner so she couldn't walk away.

"Fuck them hoes I want cho ass. Gimme yo number," I said pulling my phone out my pocket so she could lock her number in it. I made sure my dick stayed pressed up against her body the whole time she was locking her number in too.

I was creeped out tripping off her lil ass all day. Her skin was smooth, her feet was small like I like, and she had this natural arch in her back so her ass always looked like it was tooted up even when she was sitting down. That shit drove me crazy. She had on some tan sandals that showed off her pretty feet and polished toes, some all-white shorts, and a lil tan tank top that showed the two lil dents she got on her lower back right above her ass. I wanted to fuck her ass right thurr on the steps.

"You gone come see me?" she asked with a sexy smirk, handing me my phone back.

"Hell yeah! Just let me know wasup when I call you," I answered as I took a step back ready to walk her down the hall and to the bus stop.

"You better come see me," she said seductively pulling my body back closer to her by my belt.

"I'ma fuck you so good," I said softly before she kissed me, slightly caressing my bottom lip with her tongue.

"Let's go, " she said with a smile as we walked down the hall and out the door a full-blown couple.

It wasn't long before them city bitches start hating on her though. They was already muggin when they seen us standing at the bus stop together but I had the situation under control for the most part. Them bitches knew not to fuck with her ass when I was around cuz she was my bitch and I was falling for her fast. She was the only reason I came to school everyday. All the bitches I had calling my phone before I met her got cut off quick. That's how I knew I was falling for her ass.

Crystle mama was a pastor so she was extra sneaky and freaky as hell. She called me up one Sunday morning telling me to come to her house cuz her mama was at church preaching. So Crystle was at home all alone after lying to her mama about being sick. When I got to the house she came to the door in a oversized shirt wearing nothing but her panties underneath. She took me to her mama's room and shut the door, letting me know it was bout to go down. So I pulled her panties off and laid her down on the bed, kissing her softly before grinding my dick in her pussy nice an slow. After I bust a nut, we just laid thurr in her mama bed ready to go again. I waited a couple minutes then pulled her back closer to me as she laid thurr in a daze. I shoved my dick back in her pussy from behind her while she laid on her side, cummin on my dick back to back. After I nutted that time, I just left my dick in her pussy and nodded off. Then when we woke up damn near a hour later I got right back to business, this time I fucked her rough. Laid her flat on her stomach then covered her body with mine fuckin her hard, knowing she couldn't run from it cuz I had her pinned down. She said I had to leave after that round cuz her mama was gone be coming home any minute so I dipped.

The timing was perfect too cuz soon as I walked out the door I got a text from my mama telling me to bring her fucking car back. I was finna pull up on Gamble for a lil minute after I left Crystle house but didn't wanna hear my mama mouth about steady running over thurr every chance I got. Crystle texted my phone telling me I popped her cherry so I was just sitting at home texting her back an forth until I went to sleep. I aint really believe her when she told me I took her virginity for some reason but that pussy was good so I just played like I did. Hell I aint give a fuck no way. All I cared about was fucking her again as soon as possible.

I wasn't really going over Drako crib that often no more cuz I hadn't heard from Cap since he took my damn gun. Cap wasn't really coming on Gamble cuz he was ducking me but little did he know I wasn't even trippin off the damn gun no more. I ended up getting something better from Beezy. Beezy was the youngest out of everybody pretty much. He was playful, and a lot more innocent than he wanted to be, unlike his older brother Murder. Murder just knew murder. That's how he got the name, he was ruthless. All he did was collect guns from different niggas he was snaking out in the streets. But if it wasn't a gun he really wanted he would hand it off to Beezy. So the whole hood knew they had hella burnas cuz Bezzy always showed em off. He always wanted us to buy or trade them out so he could feel like he did business with grown folks I guess. Getting a gun from Beezy was easy, it was like taking candy from a baby.

It wasn't even about the money with him. He really just wanted to fit in. I told him I needed the gun real quick to go do something one day. Then the next time I seen him I told him I was in a high-speed chase with the police and left the gun in the car tryna get away. He aint really believe me but he still played like he did, not wanting me and Murder to go wrong behind the shit. When Murder asked about it Beezy was tempted to lie and say he lost the muafucka but he aint want Murder to find out if he did. So he just went ahead and told him the truth.

"Naw tell Dashon he gotta pay you for that Beezy," Murder said to his brother, feeling some type a way about me taking Beezy shit and not cashing him out for it. "Matter fact, I just seen that nigga on Gamble. I'ma go holla at em myself," he added, ready to go wrong with me if I refused to pay his lil brother for the gun. When he pulled up on Gamble I was standing on the corner with Chucky and Rambo smoking a blunt after passing a Nyquil bottle around.

"Wasup Dashon? Beezy say you aint cashed em out for that thumpa yet homie," Murder said playing it cool until he knew whether I was finna be on some bullshit or not.

"Maaan, how much he want for this muafucka Murk?" I asked with a smile as Rambo and Chucky laughed, knowing I had the damn gun on me right then and thurr.

"Jus give em two for it bruh," he answered, realizing I didn't really lose the gun hisself.

"Iight tell em I'ma pullup on em later on today," I assured him as the car behind him blew they horn, urging him to drive off cuz he was in the middle of the street blocking traffic to talk to me.

"Iight homie," he said putting his middle finger up at the car behind him blowing they horn then pulled off being sure to remind his lil brother to get the money I owed him.

Carmen pulled up in somebody new ball black Escalade so Chucky slid out with her before Rambo rolled up another blunt for us to smoke. "Man these hoes aint shit bruh," Rambo blurted out as he lit up the blunt before taking the first hit.

"Yeah that's why you just gotta get a lil cute-ass freaky bitch wit some good pussy an homebody her ass. In house pussy be on point. Why you say that tho?" I asked out of curiosity as he passed me the blunt looking all stressed out n shit.

"Man one a these hoes straight got me bruh," he said with his head down, ready to get the shit off his chest.

"Watchu mean bruh?" I asked as I hit the blunt, realizing the conversation was finna be a lil more serious than I thought. We sat on the porch of the vacant house we was smoking at in silence for a minute then he just came right out an said it.

"Man one a these bitches straight gave me herpes bruh," he admitted with his head still hanging down in shame.

"Damn foreal? Who did u like that bruh?' I asked feeling appalled and damn near speechless. I aint know too much about herpes but I knew that shit was forever.

"I 'ont even know bruh," he answered sitting thurr kinda zoned out, obviously still in deep thought about the shit. "I think it was one a them bitches at the strip club man. It had to be," he confessed, not knowing exactly who it could've been cuz he was fucking all them hoes, and raw doggin they ass at that.

"Damn man, yo baby mama know?" I asked, remembering how Rambo was going around bragging about his first son a few months back.

"Yeah she know," he answered shamefully. "Luckily her ass aint got it cuz the bitch aint never tryna cum up off no pussy no way. Hell that's why a nigga was steady going up to the damn strip club in na first place. Fuck her," he added feeling the need to blame somebody other than himself I guess.

"Damn fam these hoes dangerous out hurr, you better be glad they aint give you nothin worse than nat," I said just tryna make him feel better about the whole situation but not really sure what to say at the same time.

"Nigga the only thing worse than this shit is AIDS," he responded, cracking a smile as I chuckled.

"Well the bitch aint give you that so count cho blessins homie," I said playfully as we laughed. It was good to know I was able to cheer him up a lil bit though. I mean something that drastic would have had a nigga like me ready to kill every bitch I ever fucked so I kinda respected him for still just living his life like nothing was wrong. I was even touched by the fact that he trusted me enough to tell me that shit. I knew he hadn't told nobody else cuz the whole hood would've known by then if he had.

"Aye yo secret safe wit me homie," I said as Savage approached us cursing out some bitch he had on the phone before hanging up in her face.

SUDDEN DEATH

"Man these hoes just be pointless when yo dick not in ney ass I swear," Savage said shaking me and Rambo's hand to greet us.

"Whurr that nigga Chucky at? I wonder why he was tryna get me to meet em down hurr earlier. What was goin on? What I miss?" he asked as Rambo handed him the blunt he was smoking.

"That nigga slid out wit Carmen crazy ass not too long ago," I said as Savage hit the blunt a couple times before passing it to me.

"She pulledup in nat new ball Escalade. That muafucka was drippin, hella clean bruh on God," Rambo added as I hit the blunt a couple times before handing it back to him.

"Damn man they probably had a lil lick for me knowin ney ass," Savage responded, looking disappointed and feeling like he missed out.

"Naw they woulda told me," Rambo said calmly as he tossed the blunt roach in the grass. "You aint miss shit trust me. I been out hurr all day wit that nigga," he added, making Savage feel a lil more at ease about what all went on in the hood without him.

"Waddup fool?" I said answering my phone as Savage and Rambo start pulling all they money out to shoot dice like they always did.

"Wasup D? Watchu duckin me nigga? I know whurr to find yo ass now," Drako said playfully, turning the music down as he laughed.

"I aint seent cha boy Cap ina minute. That nigga duckin foreal aint he?" I answered, laughing at the way everything played out myself by then. "I took a thumpa from a lil nigga in na hood too tho shid that's jus how it go" I replied, letting him know I wasn't still fuck up about Cap taking my gun.

"Yeah but whurr you at fool? I miss the gang man yall on all bullshit straight trippin," Drako said reminiscing about the good ole days when the three of us would linkup everyday just to get money and chill.

"I'm right hurr on Gamble bruh pullup on me," I said missing the good ole days myself. When Drako pulled up we hit a few corners then stopped at a random store on the north to get some rellos so we could keep smoking.

"Get some juice bruh," I said breaking down the one rello we already had and rolling the first blunt while he went in the store.

"Man wherda fuck yo ass been at nigga?" Drako asked with a smile after seeing Cap for the first time in weeks. Cap just happened to be in the store buying lottery tickets at the time and wasn't expecting to see either one of us at that moment.

"Damn! Wasup fool? You gainin weight on a nigga an shit. You lookin swoll then a muafucka boa, ole I been bench pressin on na yard lookin ass nigga" Cap said jokingly as they laughed greeting each other with a handshake and hug. Cap was happy to see Drako despite them not being around each other on a day-to-day basis like they used to be. And he was unsure about whether or not me and Drako stayed as close as the three of us was before me an Cap fell out over that stupid ass gun. He was tempted to ask about me outta curiosity until Drako beat him to the punch.

"Damn man nis shit crazy. It must jus be meant for you an Dashon to go ahead an talk it out cuz I showl just picked that nigga up. He out thurr in na car right now, yall need to squash that bullshit bruh," Drako suggested, hoping the two of us could finally move on from the whole gun incident so everything could go back to the way it was.

"He out thurr right now?" Cap asked with a smile, knowing I couldnt've still been mad at him about the shit by then. So he was finally ready to clear the air even though he took the gun and never did bring it back. But who cared at that point.

"Yeah he out thurr bruh, go holla at cha boy man nat shit dead. I need the gang back homie, I was just tellin nat nigga that shit," Drako said, before walkin to the back of the store to pick out a juice from the freezer. "That shit petty man foreal squash that shit," he added, encouraging Cap to come outside and talk to me.

"Ion't want no smoke bruh," Cap said with his hands up, walking towards the car with a smile.

"Man you sposed to be armed an dangerous fool, and you had the ups on me shid ion't want no smoke," I said playfully as we laughed before shaking his hand through the window.

"I aint got shit bruh, it's all bad ova hurr on God," Cap responded, raising up his shirt a lil bit so I could see that he aint have a gun on his waist.

"Come on Cap, why you out hurr lackin bruh?" I asked, happy to see him but feeling a lil disappointed at the same time.

"That was the whole point of you takin my shit in the first place so you wouldn't be out hurr lackin. Now look at cha ass, out hurr ass naked. Just green as a highlighter huh," I said jokingly as we laughed.

"Man, look I – pow pow pow pow pow – What the fuck bruh!" I yelled reaching for my gun in a panic after watching Cap get gunned down right in front a me. It was some niggas in a black Ford Fusion and they was still slow-rollin down the street until I start bussin back from the car.

"What the fuck!" Drako yelled running out the store and bussin back at the black Ford Fusion immediately. The car skirted off and out of our sight as we both focused our attention back on Cap, who had just taken his last breath.

"What the fuck man, who was them niggas?" Drako yelled as he dropped to his knees shaking his hand on Cap shoulder in denial. I just stood over him in disbelief looking down at his lifeless body fulla regret. Wondering if he would've still been alive if he hadn't came over to the car to holla at me. I suddenly felt bad about the way I acted when he took my gun, even after he told me he really needed it cuz obviously he did. I was standing thurr wondering how they let off all them shots but only hit Cap when Cap was standing right by the car talking to me at the time. I wanted to know who them niggas was so bad I swear.

"Come on Dashon," Drako said as he got up filled with anger and rage.

"I'ma find them niggas Cap," he said as he stormed back to the driver's side wiping the tear that fell from his face quickly so no one would see.

It had been about three days since Cap got killed and we still hadn't found out shit. Nobody could find that black Ford Fusion and nobody knew shit about the niggas that did it or why. Cap was just so ducked off and secretive in the weeks before he died making it hard to pinpoint who the fuck wanted to kill him. All we knew was it was most likely over some money cuz Cap had developed a real bad gambling habit along with chasing that same high the rest of us was chasing. So he had two monkeys on his back for real.

After watching Cap get killed like that I start focusing on what was most important in my life and that was Crystle. I just loved how she would make me come drop her off some dick every time her mama left. Plus she start actin real freaky at school which was turning me on and making them city bitches hate her even more. Them bitches knew I was fucking her right just by the way she was acting and that made them want me even more.

"Man you need to teach a class on pullin bitches asumn," this boy Cris said as Crystle walked past with a smile brushing her hand across my dick.

"Just let me rock witchu one time shid I need some new hoes. My line dry as fuck," Cris said playfully but serious at the same time. "Tell yo girl to put me on one of her homegirls asumn," he suggested, hoping it would be a sure thing if me an Crystle hooked him up with somebody.

Iight what's yo line bruh? We can pullup on em this weekend," I said realizing Crystle had just told me her cousin was gone be with her all weekend so she probably wouldn't see me until we came back to school on Monday. It was Friday but I wasn't tryna wait til Monday to see her again cuz it was gone feel like forever to me. She called me that night telling me her mama was preaching at one of her old friend's funeral the next day. So she knew her mama would be gone for hellas fucking with that funeral and repass.

"Yo cuzzin over thurr?" I asked hearing another girl giggling in the background.

"Yeah she wit me but it's cool she just gone be downstairs chillin while we up hurr," Crytle answered with a smile encouraging me to still come over anyway.

"I'm sayin, Cris want me to come pick him up first so he can keep yo cuzzin company while I get up in nat pussy," I said letting her know I had the whole visit planned out an all she had to do was tell me it was ok for me to bring Cris.

"Ok I'll tell her now," she replied, loving the ideal of somebody coming over for both a them instead of just her. "My mama leave at nine in na mornin.

The Streets of St. Louis

I'ma call you," she said eagerly ready to get off the phone so she could tell her cousin about Cris wanting to come over too.

"Wasup homie?" I said when I called Cris phone the next morning already fully dressed.

"Wasup bruh? What's poppin?" he replied like he wasn't still half asleep at the time.

"Pussy my nigga!" I said with a laugh. "Let's go get it fool, get dressed an send me yo address. I'm finna get my mama keys so I can come get chu," I said putting on my shoes before heading down the steps to beg my mama for her keys while she was still sleep.

It was never hard to get my mama keys, especially after Cap got killed. She knew my driving reputation so she wasn't worried about me messing up her car. She was more so worried about some niggas pulling up on me while I was standing on a bus stop somewhere. Knowing it would be wide open with no whurr to hide and no way to get away quick enough without me being behind the wheel.

"Mama let me get the keys real quick," I said busting in her room as my dad rolled over and pulled the cover over his head annoyed with me breaking his sleep.

"No son. You aint tryna do nothin but pullup on Gamble an Ion't want chu over thurr so no," she answered still half sleep feeling just as annoyed as my dad.

"No I'm not mama! I'm finna take Crystle on a date, she want me to take her to breakfast," I said with a smile knowing damn well I was just tryna fuck.

"You aint finna take her on no date, you just tryna get in nat lil girl panties I aint stupid," she said before pointing to the keys that was sitting on the dresser, knowing I would've caught the bus if I had to as crazy as I was about Crystle ass. "Do not bring me no grandbabies no time soon sir. I am way to young for that. Thank you!" she yelled as I grabbed the keys off the dresser then headed out the door.

When me and Cris got to the house Crystle introduced Cris to her cousin who was clearly ready to come up off some pussy just so Crystle wouldn't be the only one getting dicked down I guess. So it was definitely a sure thing for Cris. I pulled Crystle in her mama room where I supposedly took her virginity and got right to business. But like ten minutes after we fucked, her cousin busted in the room with Cris right behind her. "Biiiitch, yo mama just pulled up," She blurted out as me and Crystle hopped up out the bed in a panic not even having enough time to think. Crystle ran to the front door hoping her mama hadn't gotten out the car yet but she was already on the porch fixing to turn the key in the door.

"Hide," her cousin whispered as I dashed behind the couch while Cris ran and hid in the kitchen somewhurr.

"What's that smell?" her mama said walking through the door smelling the aroma of sex from the four of us all getting down in her house.

"What smell?" Crystle asked nervously, completely nose blind.

"Well it smell like sex," her mama answered with her eyebrows raised as a fucking mouse ran right across my fingers while I was kneeling on the floor behind the couch.

"AAAAAH!" I yelled as I hopped up off the floor from behind the couch.

"Oh so that's what it is," her mama said as Crystle looked at me with disappointment. "What in God's name is goin on in here Crystle?" her mama asked as Cris came out the kitchen from his hiding spot realizing the jig was up and we was all caught. "Oh, so both of yall in here bein grown. Great, what's your name young man?" she asked directing her attention to me.

"My name Dashon Ma'am, this my friend Cris," I said tryna handle the situation as delicately as possible by acting all polite and pretending to be the good guy, like I wasn't just fucking her daughter in her bed.

"What intentions do you have with my daughter Dashon, well other than sneakin in my home to have sex her of course?" her mama asked boldly, knowing I was fulla shit.

"Ion't know Ma'am, I love her tho," I answered, saying it out loud for the very first time as Crystle stood thurr trying not to smile. Knowing she was in too much trouble to be smiling at the moment.

"Well do you go to church?" she asked, still feeling upset and disappointed but respecting my honesty at the same time.

"I haven't been recently. My mama used to make me go in my younger days tho," I answered, hoping she would continue to respect my honesty since I was being so truthful with her.

"Well maybe it's time you go back Dashon. That is if you wanna continue to see my daughter. Attending church with us on Sunday's is simply the only way. Is that something you're willing to do?" she asked with her bible and purse in one hand while the other hand was placed on her hip as she talked to me.

"Yes Ma'am, I'll be ready," I said looking at Crystle with a smirk on my face wanting her to know she was worth it without actually telling her.

"Ok great, we'll pick you up at ten a.m. every Sunday morning. Oh, and I need you to learn the ten commandments so write em down ten times an have it for me when we get thurr. Are you willing to do that?" she asked, curious to see how far I would go to keep seeing her daughter so she could know how serious I was about her I guess.

"Yes Ma'am. I'll write em down for you, that's no problem at all," I said with a full-blown smile feeling amused with her request.

"Great. Ten times, and yall can excuse yourselves now so I can talk to my girls, thank you," she added as me and Cris made our way to the door in a hurry. Ready to hurry up an get the fuck up outa thurr anyway.

I didn't talk to Crystle until the next morning when they came to pick me up for church. We was happy to see each other but her mama kept me hella busy making me a young deacon immediately. It wasn't so bad though cuz Crystle would still sneak and come around me actin all slutty in the church when her mama wasn't paying attention. I'm just hella attracted to shit like that for some reason so it kinda made me fall for her ass even more the more we went to church. It wasn't long before I got her pregnant but that's when everything started to go downhill.

BLOOD BROTHER

Meanwhile Lil Rodney and Nikki was closer than ever. He was her shoulder to cry on after Cap got killed. He was even willing to put him an Trouble differences aside at that point. But Trouble was grieving and mad at the world so he kept the same energy he had towards Lil Rodney letting him know they friendship was over and it was no turning back.

One night Lil Rodney and Nikki was in the bed laying down watching TV together until Nikki fell asleep. He held her in his arms comfortably imagining how they first child was gone be while softly rubbing her stomach. Nikki had just found out she was pregnant and he wanted her to get all the rest she needed. Of course she was sure to wake up after Trouble showed up banging at the door demanding her to let him in quickly for whatever reason.

"Open na fuckin door Nikki damn hurry up!" Trouble yelled as Lil Rodney rolled his eyes wishing Trouble would just leave so she could sleep peacefully like he wanted her to. "Nikki open na fuckin door foreal I need to come in!" he continued still banging on the door, waking Nikki up out of her slumber. She got out the bed and headed to the door while Lil Rodney laid there pissed off an annoyed but tryna stay calm outa respect for Nikki. "Damn! Whyda fuck it take you so long to open na fuckin door Nikki, Shit! Niggas slidin through this muafucka lookin for a body an you in hurr laid up wit this lame ass nigga takin all day to answer the fuckin door" he yelled as Nikki opened the door and closed it behind him.

"Man get cho bitch ass out I'm sicka this nigga," Lil Rodney said as he got out the bed, grabbing his gun from off the nightstand.

"Trouble I was sleep an baby put that damn gun away yall doin to much," she said standing between them tryna calm them both down.

"Fuck that! This bitch ass nigga heard me bangin on na fuckin door fuck him!" Trouble yelled, clearly intoxicated and most likely high outa his fucking mind.

"Fuck you nigga, Do sumn!" Lil Rodney yelled back stepping closer to Trouble hoping Nikki would just move out the way if Trouble was really tryna take it thurr.

"Nigga you a bitch!" Trouble yelled charging towards Lil Rodney, bumping Nikki out the way to tackle him to the ground. They both hit the floor and – pow. Just like that Trouble was gone.

"Rodney! Rodney what the fuck did you do! Why is this happenin!" Nikki screamed dropping to her knees to hold her brother as he took his last breath in her arms, bleeding out from the gunshot wound to his chest near his heart. "Why would you do this to me Rodney, I thought chu loved me. Why would you do this!" she continued crying hysterically over her brother's dead body.

"Baby I do love you, I aint mean for this to happen. Baby please listen to me," he said pulling her away from her brother's dead body to comfort her.

"How could you do this Rodney? I can't believe you would do this to me," she cried as Lil Rodney held her up so she wouldn't drop back down to her knees again.

"Baby look, I need you to pull it the fuck together ok?" he said grabbing her by her shoulders and looking her in her eyes as the tears fell down her face like a waterfall. "We need to figure out what the fuck we finna do, Trouble is gone an I'm sorry baby I swear. I swear I aint mean to take it this far," he explained as the tears kept flowing down her face uncontrollably.

"Ion't know what to do," she cried, almost dropping to her knees again as Lil Rodney continued to hold her up.

"Baby pull it the fuck together, I'ma tell you what to do," Lil Rodney said as calmly as he could but jerking her shoulders outa frustration. "You gone tell the police he ran up in hurr an some otha nigga ran in hurr behind'm ok?" he continued, wanting her to calm down and get her story straight before he left.

"I can't do this Rodney," she cried, feeling like she just wanted to lay down next to her brother and die too.

"Nikki if you don't I'm goin to fuckin prison. So you can do it unless you wanna raise my son witout me," Lil Rodney said grinding his teeth as he talked trying not to raise his voice at her.

"It's a girl Rodney, I don't want another boy don't say that," she said softly with her head down feeling grateful that the son she did have just happened to be with his grandmama at the time.

"Well baby whatever it is I just wanna be thurr for you an my kid no matter what. I wanna get pass this baby please. You gotta do this for me, for us, so we can be a family. Let me make this right," he pleaded as even his eyes filled with tears realizing how hard this would be for her to actually do and just regretting how much pain he was causing her.

"You can't make this right Rodney you just can't," she said as the tears continued to flow.

"I will make it right baby. I'ma spend the rest of my life tryna make it right for our family, but right now I gotta go. Call the police an remember what I said. Don't forget Nikki, you don't know nothin. All you know is you seen a nigga wit dreads run up outta hurr after the gun went off. Don't say shit else about nothin, youon't know shit else. I gotta go baby. I'ma make this right just trust me. We gone be okay if we stick together you my everything," he said before picking the gun up off the floor and heading out the door.

After he left Nikki went to her room trembling as she grabbed her phone to call the police. "Nine-one-one, what's the emergency?" the operator asked immediately.

"My brother was just shot in my living room after being chased in the house and now he's not breathing" Nikki said, tryna talk as clearly as she could but still crying as she glanced over at her brother's lifeless body.

"What's the address Ma'am?" the operator asked quickly but calm.

"It's 2800 Gamble," Nikki answered, staring at her brother's body with endless tears flowing outa pain and disbelief.

"Somebody will be there shortly Ma'am. Are you safe?" the operator responded, most likely repeating these same responses for the millionth time that day.

"I think so," Nikki answered softly before setting the phone down on her bed then laying on the floor next to her brother's dead body.

"Ma'am are you okay?" the officer asked as they let themselves in the house and helped her off the floor.

"Yeah I just wanid to be wit my brother he hate bein alone," she said with her head down as she stood to her feet feeling weaker than she had ever felt.

"Ma'am, this is detective Whiteford. Are you feeling well enough to go with him to the station and answer a few questions on your brother's behalf?" one of the officers asked with his hand on her shoulder sympathetically.

"Ok," Nikki answered taking one last look at her brother's body before heading out the door with the detective. Meanwhile Lil Rodney was with his dad telling him the whole story from start to finish. Pops sat on the couch listening to every word his son was saying carefully without interrupting him with any questions or feedback. "Ion't know what to do pops, I really fuckedup an Iont know how this finna go," he vented before putting his hands on his head fighting back tears. He would never let a tear drop in front a his dad as tough as he had always raise him to be. He knew his dad had to already be disappointed with him even though he showed no emotion and hadn't said a word since Lil Rodney started talking. So he held his tears back an pulled himself together. "What I'ma do pops?" he asked ready to finally hear what his dad had to say, desperately needing his advice.

"You sit back an do-nothin son. I'ma put chu in a hotel room for a few days while I figure all this out," his dad said calmly as Lil Rodney sat thurr giving him his undivided attention. "Listen don't leave that room for any reason once you get thurr. You get hungry order room service but don't leave that room at all. No company, stay the fuck off the phone or I'ma take it. Don't call nobody, not even Nikki. An you won't be takin any calls either, the only calls you'll be takin is mine. You need to just lay low for a minute son, let me handle everything else. Just do as I say," his dad explained before lighting the blunt he had sitting in the ashtray and passing it to his troubled son.

"You know a muafucka hit Trouble last night," Rambo said when he seen me on Gamble the next day looking for perks and somebody to get high with.

"You bullshittin, swearda God," I answered feeling blown away by the news.

"On na zone bruh," Rambo replied shaking his head with sympathy.

"Damn what happened?" I asked curiously, ready to get the 411 on the whole incident which apparently took place right down the street at Nikki house.

"Man I heard some nigga wit dreads chased em up in Nikki crib, gunned em down right thurr in na front room," Rambo said already sensing that wasn't really what happened but letting me know what the streets was saying.

"Damn, whurr Lil Rodney was at? He always up in nat muafucka?" I asked suspecting that wasn't what really happened my damn self.

"Ion't know man he aint answerin na phone," Rambo answered wit his eyebrows raised, letting me know we was both thinking the same thing.

"Naw," I said in disbelief and denial but knowing deep down we was right about what we was thinking.

"Lemme call this nigga man nis shit crazy," I said pulling out my phone and dialing Lil Rodney number. "Damn, no answer," I said shaking my head, knowing he was tempted to answer my call. "This shit crazy bruh that shit straight went left. I kinda seen nat shit comin tho," I said knowing Lil Rodney would've been called one of us about the news by now if we wasn't right about what we was thinking.

"Aye yall hear what happened to Trouble?" Savage asked, approaching us with Chucky right behind him talking on the phone to Carmen.

"Yeah we was just talkin about that shit man, shit crazy," I said as Savage shook me and Rambo's hand to greet us.

"You talk to Lil Rodney?" Rambo asked curiously, eager to know if anybody had heard from him at all that day.

"Naw, you said you seen em last night didn't you?" Savage asked, turning to Chucky who was still on the phone with Carmen grinning from ear to ear.

"Man get the fuck off the phone, you just left Carmen ass. Yall been together all night damn!" Savage snapped, annoyed with how distracted Chucky was.

"Baby lemme rap wit these niggas real quick. I'ma call you back ina minute," Chucky said, ending the conversation with Carmen before hanging up the phone. "Yeah that nigga was down ner," Chucky said giving us the same look we was just giving each other while shaking me and Rambo's hand to greet us.

"Damn!" Savage blurted out, finally catching on to what actually happened. We all looked down the street at Nikki house in amazement as Lil Rodney's dad pulled up in the Bentley, got out the car, and headed to the front door. We stuck around just long enough to see how long he was gone be in thurr out of curiosity but feeling damn sure we was right about what had happened at that point. Lil Rodney dad sat down on the couch without saying a word after Nikki let him in the house.

"My son made quite a mess hurr last night an I apologize for him but we need to talk about what happened after he left," his dad said breaking the silence.

"I told them what he told me to," she answered honestly with her head down and tears forming in her eyes all over again.

"I need to know if my baby is ok cuz I can't eat or keep anything down," she added, hoping he would offer to take her to the hospital cuz she was genuinely concerned about the well-being of her unborn child despite all the pain and drama she was going through at the moment.

"Well get cha stuff an lock the house up. When you leave the hospital I'ma take you to Rodney, yall need to talk. He gone be in a hotel room until alla this die down so you might wanna pack a bag a clothes," he said calmly as she headed to her room to pack her things.

Jessica Whitfield

MR. ST. LOUIS

Everything was so crazy on Gamble knowing what really happened. My mama was hella worried about us. She told me not to trust nobody in the neighborhood cuz everybody was just getting too ruthless. She told me to be a man and focus on my new family knowing being up under Crystle all the time was probably my best bet. Crystle was pregnant with her granddaughter and my mama was praying that baby would slow me down.

But after Crystle had my daughter she start feeling trapped. She felt like she was missing out on something cuz she had the baby so young I guess. I kept finding other niggas numbers in her phone and catching her in lies about whurr she had just came from when I seen her. She was just playing so many games with me and clearly wasn't taking the relationship serious no more. She knew she had me forever no matter what anyway. I held on to the relationship for as long as I could but lost interest when she got pregnant by a whole nother dude. She tried to say it was mine at first but I knew she had been fuckin other niggas. So I let her know I knew the baby wasn't mine off the bat. She knew I wasn't no fool so she came clean and told me she was pregnant by a whole nother nigga named Dashon ironically. Fucked me up too, I couldn't believe that shit. Our baby wasn't even one yet an hurr Crystle was pregnant by a whole nother nigga named Dashon who was denying the damn baby before she even gave birth. It was kinda hard to accept that shit though cuz I still loved her and I was feeling some type a way about the nigga getting my baby mama pregnant. So I jus kept nutting in her pussy while she was pregnant with dude baby. On top a fuckin whoever else I wanted to fuck cuz I aint respect the relationship no more neither. She was just some in-house pussy at that point.

When she had dude baby she was so determined to prove the lil girl was his that she literally took the nigga on the Maury show to get a blood test and make him pay child support. When Maury revealed that the baby was his she danced full of joy on stage, putting on a show by taunting him about finally having to pay her child support. But shortly after the show he was convicted for killing a well-known football player who had just made it to the NFL. Dude was back in St. Louis visiting his family and celebrating his success when her baby daddy crept up on him while he was at the ATM. He shot that nigga smack dead in front of the camera for the money he had just pulled out. So Crystle looked like a damn fool after doing all that for some child support that she still didn't end up getting. And to make matters worse I start treating her completely different after that. I was so embarrassed about her going on national TV with a nigga the whole city hated. Cuz the football player he killed was actually from St. Louis and had all love in the streets. Dude had hella fans. The whole city knew who he was which was probably why her baby daddy hated on him like he did. I aint want my friends and family knowing I still loved her after seeing her on the show and knowing what they knew so I start doggin Crystle ass out.

	Crystle never had problems with me and other girls up until this point cuz she was the one who had my heart. But her embarrassing me on that level was a free pass to do whatever the fuck I wanted to. Crystle hated the idea of me fucking another bitch the way I fucked her so she always made sure they knew I was gone keep fucking with her no matter what but she was still fucking around on me too at the same time. So when she got pregnant the third time I was almost sure that baby wasn't mine neither. The lil girl aint look nothing like me or the daughter I do have with Crystle so I was pretty fucking sure. She never admitted that the third baby wasn't mine cuz she knew it didn't really matter. She felt like her and the kids was gone be with me regardless since I kept fucking with her ass after she had that other nigga baby.

	Everybody else knew that third baby wasn't mine too but I still kept fucking with her ass cuz she was really all I knew. I knew I couldn't love another bitch the way I loved Crystle so I just kept doing what I was doing. Plus Crystle never let a bitch get comfortable enough with me to stick around noway. She always ran em off. Every last one of em. And it was always hard to take em too serious anyway cuz I was so turned on by how hard Crystle was fighting for me. Our relationship was toxic as fuck but the love was obviously still thurr so we start tryna work on being a real couple again despite all the bullshit. Once we realized how strong our relationship really was we felt like it was worth giving it another shot so that's what we did.

    When Crystle got pregnant the fourth time I was pretty sure that baby was mine cuz me and her was in such a good space at the time. Plus that lil girl looked a lot like me an my first daughter. When she was pregnant with the fourth baby her mama moved to Michigan City for the opportunity to preach at a new church in a better location. It was definitely a safer city to live in so she urged us to move down thurr with her and we did despite me not really wanting to go. I had never really left St. Louis for real. My mama took me to Atlanta one time when I was little and I was literally homesick the whole time. I was throwin up and everything but soon as I got back home I felt fine. I hadn't left St. Louis since then so I was feeling a lil anxious about going. I knew it was dangerous in my city but it was still my comfort zone which kinda tempted me to stay. The only reason I didn't is cuz I wasn't really willing to let her and the kids leave without me, especially with Crystle being pregnant at the time.

    We aint know if the baby was a boy or girl back then but after being in a house fulla females for so long, I was hoping we was finally finna have a son. When we got to Michigan we found out we was having another lil girl making me a lil frustrated with Crystle for some reason. I mean I was already frustrated cuz we had to move in with her mama when we first got thurr. Espeically after being all comfortable living in our own crib before we left St. Louis. It got a lil better when we moved up out her mama crib though cuz Crystle was always up in that muafucka getting drunk and turning up with all her lil cute ass friends and cousins. They was just as sneaky and slutty as she was too, so I was cool.

    I was content with just going to work and coming home even though I didn't know nobody outside the people Crystle knew. She had hella family up thurr though. Shit was gravy until Crystle start peeping how all her lil friends and cousins was always kinda on my dick. I found it hilarious how she blamed me knowing damn well I wasn't provoking em to act like that. Hell I barely even said shit, I used to just be sitting back sizing bitches up, reading they body language. But knowing damn well them hoes was gone let me fuck em if I wanted to made Crystle act a lil more crazy than usual.

I met a dude named Twon at work one day when he was peeping how hard the bitches was on my dick in that muafucka. He was a pretty boy type so all the hoes was usually on his dick, making him notice how hard they was on mine.

"Damn bro! These hoes be on you, you must be from outta town huh?" he said as this lil cute preppy bitch walked past flirting a couple minutes before we was scheduled to clock out.

"Yeah I'm from St. Louis," I said with pride, realizing it was probably hella obvious that I wasn't from around thurr. "Stickin out like a sore thumb in nis muafucka huh?" I added, shaking his hand to greet him with a chuckle.

"Yeah man these hoes on you tho, must be that St. Louis swag brody," he answered playfully, hoping we could just tag team the bitches rather than compete with each other. "My name Twon bro, what's yo name St. Louis?" he asked, knowing I most likely needed a friend who knew his way around and had access to all the hoes.

"My name Dashon homie. I showl don't know nobody up hurr. My baby mama got peoples up hurr but Ion't really know nobody. I be goin straight home when I leave this muafucka then be right back up in nis bitch, that's it," I said as we laughed.

"What's yo line bro? I'll show you around this muafucka. Gotta phone fulla bitches too so we can turn up every weekend I'm tellin you bro," he said pulling out his phone as my face lit up with excitement.

"Yeah bruh I need that, Ion't know shit about this muafucka. That's why I just be at the crib fuckin wit my baby mama an na kids. Ion't be on shit bruh on God," I said happy to have a new wingman in a new city. He wasn't Chad but he was Michigan City's version of Chad I guess so I was with it.

"Oh shit we can step out tonight matter fact, it's Friday and we finna clockout this bitch. The whole city finna be lit in a few hours," he explained, locking my number in his phone so he could call me later. He called a couple hours later asking if I wanted to go to the beach cuz that's where most of the bitches hung out on the weekends and I was all for it.

"Hell yeah bruh, I'm finna text you the address pullup on me," I said eagerly before getting off the phone and heading to the bathroom to get in the shower.

"Why you gettin in na shower so early?" Crystle asked with her face all frowned up as I was fixing to take my clothes off.

"My boy Twon finna come pick me up, he finna show me the beach an shit nothin major," I said with a evil grin, feeling amused with the attitude she had for no apparent reason whatsoever.

"Yo boy Twon? You out hurr makin friends now? What chall goin to the beach to do? You'ont even know what this nigga be on while you call yoself tryna make friends," she said rolling her neck as she talked.

"Um ma'am, don't worry about me hoppin in na car wit a nigga not knowin what he be on. Don't forget I'm from na streets, I size niggas up before I have em pullup at my crib an slide out wit em trust me. Now close the door behind you cuz I'm finna get in na shower," I said with a smile, being a dick like always.

"Get in na shower nigga! I gotta leave the bathroom just so you can get cho dusty ass in na shower now?" she replied, with her hand on her hip being worsum.

"Whatchu want some dick a sumn?" I asked playfully, knowing that's all she really wanted.

"Naw wash yo ass so you can go fuck a bitch on na beach," she said before storming out the bathroom annoyed. Now usually I would've bent her lil ass over and fucked her on the sink right thurr in the bathroom but I wanted to go to that beach hella bad. So I decided to just go ahead and leave her be, made a mental note to fuck her real good later on that night and left it at that. "Don't forget when I wanna go to the beach wit my homegirls it better not be a problem," she said rolling her eyes as I headed to the door.

When me and Twon got to the beach I was blown away by the scenery. It was like an image straight off the TV screen, the shit looked like a straight up movie. I had never seen no shit like that before in my life. The bitches was coming up out the water like Bay Watch. Then this lil mixed bitch walked right up to me with her homegirl wearing this skimpy ass bikini. She threw me off a lil bit though cuz she had just bust out tryna kiss me outta no whurr. "Damn girl! You act like you tryna get fucked," I said playfully, leaning back to avoid the kiss cuz that aint even how I move.

"How much you got?" she asked, putting her hand on her hip like we was bout to negotiate a price for some pussy.

"Aw baby Ion't pay for no pussy. I got inhouse," I replied as me an Twon laughed at the thought of actually having to pay a bitch to come up off some pussy knowing it would never happen.

"What about chu? How much you got?" she said to Twon, smelling like Bath and Bodyworks mixed with pure vodka so she had obviously been drinking.

"Aye pussy just happen to fall right into my lap baby girl," Twon said with confidence, putting his hands up playfully as he laughed.

"Girl they aint talkin about shit come on," her homegirl butted in before pulling her away from us.

"Damn, that's how these bitches be rockin down hurr?" I asked, wondering if it was normal for a bitch that cute to be out on the beach selling pussy and tryna kiss niggas she aint even know.

"Yeah bro. That's exactly what these bitches be on up here, every day all day. I swear to God. But these hoes get so drunk they'll be ready to fuck whether you got some money or not foreal. They be wanting some dick anyway," Twon answered bluntly, unfazed by the whole lil episode like it was nothing out the ordinary.

"Speakin of drunk bitches, it's a bunch a them hoes at the crib right now. These hoes actin up," I said looking at the video Crystle had just sent of her twerking and turning up with a bunch of her homegirls in the background hyping her up.

"This gone be me at the beach this weekend," I said reading the text she sent with the video out loud with a smile. "This bitch jus want some dick," I said arrogantly as me and Twon watched the video.

"Oh shit it look like we need to be at yo spot, fuck the beach nigga yo shit poppin. It's all hoes ova there" Twon said, entertained by how live the video was.

"Yeah we might as well pull back up over thurr," I said giving Twon the opportunity to hop down on one of Crystle homegirls or however many he wanted. They was all on his dick when we got thurr so it was really just up to him to pick and choose. They had two big ass bottles of Goose. One of the bottles was completely empty and the other one was almost gone so them bitches was pretty fucked up, especially Crystle ass. Her cousin Becky was over thurr acting all extra freaky along with the rest of them lil sneaky bitches. Crystle was to fucked up to catch on to all the lil slick shit her cousins and friends was doing behind her back that day though.

"Wasup bitch!" Becky screamed, answering the phone with the music still blasting in the background while she talked. "Bitch we finna have to come pick you up cuz we hella lit ova here, turn up!" she shouted as Crystle and the rest of the bitches hyped her up by yelling "ayyyye" and twerking to the music.

"Whatchu mean I shouldn't be driving! You probably right tho, just get dropped off. I'm finna text you the address," she said holding her finger to her ear so she could hear the girl on the phone more clearly.

When the girl Becky was on the phone with got to the house, me and Twon was surprised to see it was the same damn girl that had just tried to kiss me at the beach earlier. That shit was way too ironic. Me an Twon just looked at each other and bust out laughing at the irony knowing this same fuckin girl had just tried to sell us some pussy earlier that day.

"Michigan City too fuckin small bro," Twon said as we laughed.

"We need some more drink!" Becky yelled, holding up the second empty bottle of Goose before collecting some money from Twon who was definitely entertained enough to help keep the party going by putting in on the drink.

"Baby gimme some money," Crystle said pulling on my pants before snatching all the money I pulled out my pocket. The girl from the beach watched us out the corner of her eyes discreetly but I still caught it cuz I'm just hella observant.

"Let's go yall," Crystle said heading to the door with the money she had just took quickly counting it up then placing it in her bra.

"Well everybody can't go cuz everybody can't fit up in that lil ass car," Becky said bluntly as she headed to the door behind Crystle.

"I'll stay, Ion't gotta go," the girl from the beach said as she took a seat next to Twon with a smile.

"Ok let's go yall," Crystle said to the rest of em, not even thinking twice about leaving this cute ass girl who she had never even met in the house with me and Twon alone. The kids was in the back sleeping and Crystle had been stuck in the house with they asses all day. So she was really just ready to get the fuck up out of thurr. After they left, me, Twon, and the girl from the beach went and sat at the table to play cards giving me the opportunity to reach my hand under the table an start rubbing her pussy through her tights. She let me do it for a couple minutes before getting up to go to the bathroom… I knew what that meant. I looked over at Twon who was encouraging me to follow her by the expression on his face while nodding his head in her direction.

"Look out for me bruh," I said as I got up from the table and followed her to the bathroom knowing he would let me know soon as Crystle nem pulled back up. I went to the bathroom and opened the door as she stood in front of the sink looking in the mirror at me smiling. So I closed the door behind me and got right behind her ass. I pulled her leggings down to her knees then bent her over on the sink like I started to do to Crystle earlier that day when she was acting like she wanted some dick. I stuck my dick in the bitch on some quick shit, then fucked her real good for bout a good five minutes before pulling my dick out her pussy with a smirk knowing she wanted more. I walked back in the kitchen just as Crystle and the girls was pulling back up in the driveway. The girl from the beach stayed in the bathroom probably wiping her pussy down cuz her shit was drippin. That pussy was hella wet.

"Aye yall friend too drunk talm bout she gotta throwup. Twon finna take her home," I said knowing Twon was gone go along with anything I said for sure. "We finna go pullup on his cousin for these perks too so I'll be back," I added, letting her know I was leaving with them without making her suspicious.

"Where Melody go?" Becky came in asking, referring to the girl from the beach who still hadn't come out the bathroom after getting fucked on the sink like a slut.

"She probably in there throwin up. I'ma go check on her cuz she was saying she wasn't feeling good," Twon said heading to the bathroom to put the girl Melody up on game so she could know to play sick when they asked.

"Aw yeah, drop her ass off cuz I aint tryna clean up no throwup on God. Hell naw," Crystle said with her eyebrows raised. She wanted to get Melody ass out the crib as quick as possible so she wouldn't get stuck cleaning up the bitch throw up if she did cuz she knew damn well it wasn't gone be me cleaning the shit up.

"Go to yo crib bruh," I said once the three of us got in Twon car and pulled off with out nobody suspecting nothing. When we got to Twon crib, I took the bitch over to the couch before pulling her panties and leggings down to her ankles. Then I pulled my dick out so she could ride it right thurr on the couch. I held her body nice and close while she grinded on top of it. Twon sat down on the couch right next to us enjoying the show until I lifted her up and sat her ass down on him. He already had his dick out and everything, knowing he was next. So he took right over fucking the bitch and she was just going with the flow. Twon must've been a lil too drunk or something though cuz he ended up laying the bitch down on the couch, then start licking the bitch pussy and all. That shit fucked me up! I couldn't even put my dick in the bitch mouth. She was laid all out wit her mouth open like she wanted me to but I was just too appalled that the nigga was even doing all that. He was acting like she was his straight bitch, knowing she was just a slut. But aye to each its own I guess, I wasn't fucking with it though.

After he licked the bitch pussy he sat back down and pulled her head down on his dick. So since she was conveniently sucking his dick bent over with her ass tooted up all perfect for me, I slid back up in that pussy til I nutted then we took the bitch home for real. Me and Twon was linkin up with bitches every chance we got after that shit, he had hoes on deck like a muafucka too. His cousins had perks and shit on deck so when me and Crystle would have our lil house parties poppin off they was always welcome to come turn up with us, making our shit even more lit.

Twon and all his cousins was pretty well known in the city. So once bitches start hearing about how live we was in that muafucka more and more hoes start coming through. Twon cousin Kevin was the one who had the perks. That nigga was hella friendly with them muafuckas too. I aint even give a fuck about his ass checkin my baby mama out when he thought I wasn't paying no attention. Shit as long as he was coming up off them pills I really aint give a fuck cuz the high was takin me back to whurr I really wanted to be which was back in St. Louis. It made me think about all the memories I shared with my boys in the zone and it made me wonder what all was goin on back home. It kinda made me miss my old life and the day-to-day bullshit Gamble had to offer. I just couldn't stop feeling like I was really meant to be thurr.

"Wasup nigga? I done come back to the hood an yo ass den shook this muafucka too. All that shit you was talkin when I left, fuck outta hurr man," Chad said playfully when I answered the phone thinking it was just my lil brother Chucky callin to say what's up.

"Man what the fuck is you doin back on my set bruh? You aint from aroun ner no mo nigga," I said hopping out the bed smiling ear to ear while Crystle rolled her eyes annoyed.

"This nigga done moved the family to the suburbs whurr it's safe n shit, ol my wife an kids lookin ass nigga now huh, fuck outta hurr bruh," Chad joked as we laughed. "When you comin back to the Lou tho nigga? Muafuckas talm bout how yo scary ass don't even be comin back to visit. They say they ran yo ass up out this muafucka," Chad added still joking around with me like he always did making me want my old life back even more.

"Man I got a job down hurr bruh, I'ma take off Friday tho so I'ma be on my way down ner Thursday soon as I get off. I'll just have to drive back hurr Sunday night. It's only like a four-hour drive so I'll be iight it's all flyway anyway," I answered, eager to go back home to my city. I hadn't been back to St. Louis since I left so I was hella excited to go back even if it was just for a couple days. Of course Crystle had a problem with me leaving for the whole weekend and calling off work but I aint give a fuck cuz I was gone do it whether she wanted me to or not. We argued about the shit all week but Crystle knew damn well my mind was made up and it was nothing she could do or say to change it.

Jessica Whitfield

BACK IN THE TRENCHES

When I got back to St. Louis that Thursday, I stopped at my mama house to see her real quick then called Chad to let him know I was back in town so we could link up. "Waddup nigga? Whurr you at? I'm finna pullup in na zone now," I said when Chad answered the phone with one of them throwback Future Hendricks CDs bumpin in the background slightly turning the music down so I could hear what he was saying.

"I'm in na car wit Hustle pullup on Gamble bruh," Chad said as I made my way back to whurr it all fucking started, ready to jump back in the streets full-throttle. Hustle was a well-known hustler from the zone. That's how he got the name. He had been doing the shit for hellas and never did no serious time cuz he never really got caught up with nothing. That was kinda rare too cuz niggas from the zone tend to crash out real quick once they start serving but not Hustle. He had people calling his phone for the dope left and right. He wasn't scared to pull up on another nigga geek and serve em real quick with his number knowing niggas was killing over that shit. That's how he got his phone thumpin like it was though. He was a few years older than me and Chad so he was always just a lil more advanced. Growing up he kinda stayed distant from certain niggas in the hood cuz it was hard to pinpoint who all would snake him out with everybody being so slimy and snake-like. Hustle never really knew how slimy me and Chad was but he knew our reputation. He wasn't worried about that though cuz we was the type of niggas he wanted to keep around him anyway. He just needed us to establish some trust and show some loyalty to him. Hustle knew he needed a squad with a ruthless reputation so other niggas from different hoods wouldn't be to quick to try and get up on him. He had every reason in the world to worry about that type of shit though cuz his name was ringing all through the city. And a lot of niggas felt like he was in the way cuz he was so well known with the geeks. They only knew who he was cuz everybody geeks had Hustle number too.

On top a that, his bitch had niggas hating on him cuz she was hella pretty, well known, and niggas just wanted to fuck her. She from na zone too so we all grew up knowing they liked each other. She would still flirt with the rest of us whenever he wasn't around though, letting me know she was a slut like I like. But the bitch was in special ed when we was little and that kinda turned me off. So I pretty much ignored her ass when she was on that extra shit with me. Plus I kinda looked up to Hustle and respected his relationship especially once he got her pregnant.

Lotoya was sexy as fuck though. She had caramel brown smooth skin, full lips, and her eyes turned light brown in the sun. Her body was perfect. She was short like I like with a fat ass and small feet, she had some nice size titties on her too.

Hustle thought she was a lil trophy but I would never fuck with a bitch from the zone. Them bitches aint even my type, Ion't give a fuck how cute they is. They just be to hip like a nigga. Most of them hoes ended up strung out tryna chase that high like they seen us doing. The thing is once you can't find them prescription pills you start trying other shit if you got that kinda mind frame. Yo body be hurt without them pills so it's still considered dope and very addictive. Hustle made sure Latoya stood out by keeping her in designer clothes and some fresh ass shoes though. They had a lil girl after she had his son so he made sure she always had enough money to take care of the kids too, while he ran the streets hustling all day.

Hustle pulled up on Gamble with Chad and Cutthroat that night. Cutthroat another nigga from the zone with a ruthless reputation. Everybody knew that nigga would lay a muafucka down quick and wouldn't think twice about the shit. So it was pretty obvious that Hustle was just tryna build a team around him for protection despite the risk. Niggas from the zone was just naturally scandalous and untrustworthy but it had got to a point whurr he had to take that risk with us. He knew it was only a matter of time before niggas got on his ass unless niggas knew it wouldn't be so easy to take him out. He knew if he recruited some niggas that wasn't from the zone they would automatically have him outnumbered and would be more of a threat, so he decided to just take his chances with us.

"Man get cho Michigan City ass from down hurr boy. You in na trenches this aint the suburbs nigga," Chad said playfully as he shook my hand to greet me with a smile.

"This nigga hurr man," I said to Hustle, shaking his hand to greet him too.

"Wasup Dashon? Nigga you been ghost in na streets. Straight missin in action bruh, whurr you go?" Cutthroat said playfully, knowing I was back whurr I truly belonged and loving every minute of it.

"Yeah man I had to come back real quick to see if you niggas was holdin shit down for a nigga like yall sposed to be," I said jokingly shaking Cutthroat's hand as we laughed.

"When you comin back for good tho nigga? I need a driver that's gone shoot. An I know ya background homie, don't think Ion't be keepin tabs on you lil niggas," Hustle said with a smile tryna get me to shake Michigan City for good.

"Man bein back on na block after all this time make a nigga wanna move back for real asap," I said jokingly but actually pretty serious. "This Mississippi-ass nigga hurr left this muafucka before we even hit puberty damn ner. Then wanna talk shit soon as he touch back down, get the fuck outta hurr," I said pushin Chad playfully just happy to see my nigga again after so long. I was never really myself once he upped and left to be honest. So it felt good to be back in my hometown with my right-hand man like neither one of us never even left.

"Well you hurr now nigga wasup wit this mission tonight?" Cutthroat asked basically forcing me to snap back into that St. Louis mode and not give a fuck what all came behind it. But I knew if we went on a lick with Cutthroat somebody would most likely get killed cuz he trigger-happy as fuck. Gamble just had a way of bringing out the worst in all of us. Being on Gamble was like being in the jungle with no rules. And together we was like a pack of lions making any other animal scared to cross our path. I felt that animal instinct we all had rise inside me the longer we stood on Gamble listening to Cutthroat tell us bout the lick he had set up.

"Whurr the nigga from?" I asked curiously, ready to just go ahead and run it up real quick since I was back on my stomping grounds and in my comfort zone.

"The nigga from na Blue," Cutthroat answered, pulling out his phone ready to set the whole thing up right then and thurr. "I was just wit the nigga earlier when his baby mama came to his crib trippin talm bout how he got all that money in nat muafucka but can't even give her five bands for the car she want. The whole time I'm sittin ner knowin he must've hit that lick he was tellin me about but wit somebody else cuz he showl hadn't said shit else about it. An as much as he was gassin me up about the shit I feel like we need to go collect that homie. Gas money nigga, fuck you thought," Cutthroat explained feeling some type a way about dude cutting him out the lick but knowing we could still get the money cuz he knew it was somewhere in dude crib. "The nigga went in na back room an came back out wit the five bands so the bitch would leave like it was nothin. So I know his dumbass got that money just sittin up in nat house somewher, it's most likely in nat back room. We can go up in nat muafucka an take that shit," he continued, stressing how sure he was that the money was there so we could all be down to go get it.

"Let's do it then shid, I wouldn't mind goin back home wit a couple extra racks in my pocket. I need that shit foreal, that silly ass job aint got me racked up," I said giving Cutthroat the green light to go ahead and make the call like he was itching to do anyway. He knew Chad and Hustle was gone be down if I was so he aint waste no time.

"Wasup bruh pullup," dude said on some quick shit before hanging up the phone when Cutthroat called to set the shit up. It wasn't really unusual though, Cutthroat was pulling up on that nigga everyday before that which was why Cutthroat was feeling so salty about dude not including him in the lick like he said he would.

"Ok duck down, I'ma go in first an text yall from na bathroom. Just come in once yall get the text," Cutthroat directed as we pulled up at the dude crib cautiously. "Make sure yall get alla way down low so he won't peep that chall in hurr, we gotta catch em off guard," he explained as me, Hustle, an Chad ducked down in the car so dude wouldn't see us when he came to the door to let Cutthroat in.

"I hope that nigga got some pills I need a pack after this shit," Hustle said nervously breaking a sweat while ducking down in the front seat uncomfortable. Hustle wasn't even the type to be doing shit like this cuz he sold dope and really didn't need to. He was just going with the flow to see exactly how ruthless the three of us was I guess.

"Man I'm takin everything worth value up out that muafucka. If he got some pills in ner I'll find em trust me. Yall just focus on gettin na money so we can get the fuck up outta thurr as soon as possible," Chad said ducked down in the back seat next to me. Then we listened for the door to close so we could sit up in the car a lil more comfortably until it was time for us to go in.

"Open up the door nigga hurryup I gotta shit," Cutthroat said knocking on the door tryna get in the house as fast as possible so dude wouldn't notice us outside in the car. Cutthroat was focused on two things when he first went in. One, he was checking for any other niggas that might've been in thurr with him. And two, he was tryna get a good ideal on whurr dude firearm was located cuz he knew damn well he wasn't just sitting around without one. Not living the life we live anyway.

"He said come on," Hustle said looking at his phone reading the text Cutthroat had just sent to him.

"Come on, leave the doors cracked open when yall get out," I said pulling down the black skull cap I wore while slowly opening the car door without making a sound. Chad and Hustle followed my lead, getting out the car quietly and creeping up to the front door behind me.

"Damn, I left my muthafuckin phone in na car. I aint takin no shit witout my phone bruh," Cutthroat said playfully laughing his way to the front door really just to let us in after texting (come to the door) from the bathroom.

"Nigga don't fuckin move, I'll blast yo ass before you even blink," I said coming in the house with my gun pointed directly at the dude soon as Cutthroat opened the door. "Don't even think about it homie. You make one move you gone regret it trust me," I said noticing the glock 40 he had sitting right thurr on the couch. Knowing he was tempted to try and grab that muafucka until Chad casually walked over thurr and picked it up.

"Damn Cut, you cutthroat for real huh? This how you gone do me?" Dude asked, looking at Cutthroat with tears forming in his eyes out of anger and fear, wondering if he would really go as far as killing him once he got what he wanted.

"Welcome to the zoo nigga," Cutthroat said calmly with a smile picking up the blunt dude had just rolled but dropped on the floor soon as he seen us come in. "You know you gotta feed the gorillas or they'll go ape shit right?" he added, taking a lighter out his pocket and lighting the blunt with one eye closed and the other looking straight into his with no sympathy or remorse whatsoever.

"So whurr the money at nigga? Whurr the dope?" Hustle butted in just ready to get the shit over with so we could get the fuck up out of thurr.

"Kiss my ass man yall gone kill me anyway. Fuck you nigga find it," the dude answered lashing out with anger while looking around at me, Hustle and Cutthroat. Chad was in the back getting the random shit worth value together already by that point.

"You sure that's whatchu want nigga? Cuz I was gone leave yo soft ass breathin an wish the fuck you would do sumn behind nis shit. You aint gone do shit nigga. You really think you coulda got up on me like I got up on you? Fuck naw you aint finna do shit homie you know wasup," Cutthroat said pulling out his gun and pointing it at the dude head close range. He was basically just tryna make him a lil more humble so he would cooperate and make it easier for us.

"Man nat shit in na attic. The attic in na closet at the top," dude answered with his head hanging down feeling defeated. He was hoping Cutthroat was stupid enough to leave him alive after taking everything he had though.

"Chad hit that attic in na closet," I said to Chad, who was in the back probably tryna get up in the attic already anyway by the while Hustle made his way back there to assist him.

"Hold it down Dashon," Cutthroat said lowering his gun from the dude temple before heading to the back room with Chad and Hustle. He really just wanted to make sure they wasn't cuffing no money before we got a chance to split it up evenly though. Dude had like forty bands in a bag with four zips of dope in it.

"Damn!" Hustle blurted out as his eyes lit up like a Christmas tree watching the dope fall out the bag with the money in it.

"Hurr Hustle put the dope in another bag," Cutthroat said fishing the four zips of dope out the bag and handing em to Hustle.

"Gimme that Lacoste bag Chad," Hustle said collecting the four zips as Chad threw him the empty Lacoste bag that was lying on the bed. After that he grabbed the two pillowcases full of random shit he collected then made his way to the door.

"Come on Dashon we out," Chad said as he reached for the door with Hustle right behind him. So I took a couple steps back towards the door with my gun still pointed at dude but once I hit the door I just ran to the car behind Hustle and Chad. Cutthroat was right behind me but he aint run out to the car until after he let off three shots to the dude's chest. I wasn't surprised but I was way more in a rush to get the fuck away from thurr that's for damn sure.

"Cumon nigga we gotta go!" I yelled as Hustle started the car in a panic. But while Cutthroat was running to the car the dude's two cousins just happened to pull up. And they already knew something wasn't right cuz they seen Cutthroat running to the car wit his gun out.

"Aye wasup nigga!" the driver yelled hopping out the driver's seat, barely putting the car in park first. So Cutthroat let off two shots at the nigga with no hesitation at all before hopping in the car and taking off as fast as Hustle could possibly drive that muafucka. Cutthroat had obviously missed his shot cuz the driver got right back in the car an followed us at top speed while the dude on the passenger's side was firing all shots at the car from behind us. Hustle was trying his best to shake they ass but he was nowhurr near the same type of driver as me.

"Fuck! I think one a these tires just went out what the fuck!" Hustle yelled terrified of what would happen if the car gave out on us before he got a chance to lose em. I knew if I didn't stop ducking down and start shooting back they was gone hawk us down making it more likely we get hit. We all had guns but we would've been stuck on foot while they was still rollin making our chances way slimmer than theirs. So I put my gun out the window and start shooting at the driver since I was sitting behind Hustle. I knew it was too risky for Chad or Cutthroat to shoot back cuz the passenger was the one letting off all the shots.

I must've hit the driver though cuz the car started spinning outa control and the passenger stopped shooting right before they crashed into a parked car that was sitting on the side of the road.

"Hit this corner Hustle," Cutthroat directed, pointing to the very next street.

"Ok but we need to get up out this muafucka like now," Hustle said sweating uncontrollably as he hit the corner before putting the car in park. The four of us dashed out the car quickly running in four different directions out of fear and instinct. We knew we had a better chance of getting away on our own. Everybody knew to meet on Gamble just as soon as we could get thurr but we wasn't finna mob thurr altogether. That shit just look too hot especially since we wasn't in a car behind tint. The car we was in was stolen so we wasn't worried about neither one of our names being attached to the incident. We aint leave nothing behind. Cutthroat had the money, Hustle had the dope, and Chad had two pillowcases fulla guns and other shit we could sell. Unfortunately everybody made it back to Gamble but Cutthroat so we all took a loss on that. Cutthroat took the biggest L getting a five-year sentence on top of getting all our money took by the police though. But it was kinda hard to be mad about the money shid we was just happy to still have our freedom at that point, not to mention the four free zips of dope we had along with all them guns and shit.

Hustle had a phone fulla geeks calling for the dope already. So the dope was just like money to him. "What chall wanna do wit this dope cuz I'ma knock my zip off in na couple days then I'ma be tryna buy yalls for the low," Hustle said with a smile as he handed me and Chad our zips.

"What we doin wit Cutthroat shit?" Chad asked, noticing Hustle still had two zips left after giving us ours.

"Shid we gone split that shit. That nigga booked," Hustle answered playfully but a hunnit percent serious.

"Man fuck this dope bruh. You can buy my zip right now and my cut off Cutthroat shit," Chad said handing Hustle back the zip he had just gave him.

"Bet! I'll do that right now," Hustle replied, knowing he was getting a hell of a deal cuz Chad aint even know what the damn zip was worth.

"Whatchu gone gimme for the shit nigga count it up," Chad said playfully as Hustle pulled out all his money ready to negotiate a price.

"I'ma give you twelve hunnit bruh, right now," Hustle said with a smile, hoping Chad would seal the deal right then and thurr.

"Hell yeah cumon wit it," Chad said happily, feeling satisfied with what he made off the shit cuz he showl wasn't tryna put forth the time an effort into selling it hisself.

"Man I'm mad then a muafucka. This nigga done got booked wit all the fuckin money. I'm tryna make everything I can off my shit," I blurted out, feeling frustrated and unsure about how to knock all my dope off before going back to Michigan that Sunday.

"I'll let chu knock yo shit off on my phone after I knock me an Chad shit off. I can't do it by Sunday tho nigga, you straight bullshittin goin back down ner foreal," Hustle said, putting a lil more pressure on me to move back to St. Louis.

"Let me knock my shit off this weekend bruh, I'll come back Friday when I get off so I'll be back Friday night. Do that for me bruh," I replied, hoping I had a reason to come right back to St. Louis like I wanted to do anyway.

"Yeah our shit'll be gone by next weekend fa sho. I'll let chu run it up when you get back homie but for now take this wheel bruh," Hustle answered handing me the keys to his Hemi Charger with fake tags so we could slide through the city without leaving a trace of who we actually was. Like everybody else in the hood Hustle knew my driving skills was more on point than anybody else's. So he felt comfortable and safe every time I took the wheel even when the police did get behind us. If Hustle wasn't in such a rush to get away from dude crib he would've told me to take the wheel then. But we really would've been in trouble if Hustle was sitting whurr I was cuz he wasn't really a shooter, or a killer at all for that matter. He was strictly a dope boy, fresh as hell and quick to make niggas feel like shit if they wasn't out thurr chasing a bag like he was.

BACK TO THE BASICS

"Iight well wasup wit these guns tho? I'm tryna see some type a profit right now after all that man Damn! We got all merch," I said with a smile as the three of us headed to Hustle's charger.

"Looney back in town runnin it up wit Chucky nem. You know them lil niggas aint passin up no guns," Chad said feeling pretty sure we could sell them the guns easily. Looney was a lot like Chucky, they was hella close. My mama never let Looney come back over our house after he shot a big ass hole in the wall playing with my dad's shotgun when we was younger though. He was bad as fuck but so was we. That's Chad first cousin so you had to have known he was trouble from the jump. Looney mama was the one who moved to Mississippi in the first place. So Chad was down thurr all that time wit Looney who was dying to get back to St. Louis too, putting them both in pretty much the same boat.

Looney mama didn't want Looney getting locked up like his older brother Truck who got sentenced twenty years soon as he turned eighteen and been locked up ever since. Truck was the one me an Chad ran with while Looney ran with Chucky and Theo most of the time. I fuck with both of they asses though shid we all grew up on the same shit.

"I'm keepin nis muafucka right hurr," Chad said holding up the gun he wanted to keep for himself so we could know not to try and sell it to nobody.

"Right I'm keepin one too. We can each take one an sell them lil niggas the rest. They got enough guns anyway," I added before calling my lil brother Chucky so we could pull up on him and the gang to make the transaction. I knew for a fact the guns would get sold fucking with they ass.

"Wasup fool, whurr you at?" I asked, once Chucky answered the phone with a million other niggas talking in the background making it kinda hard to hear what he was saying.

"We at Savage lil bitch crib. I'm finna send you the location," Chucky answered, walking away from all the noise so I could hear him a lil more clearly.

"That nigga Looney witchu?" I asked, eager to see his lil ass after so long too cuz it had been hellas.

"Yeah he ova hurr lettin Rambo take all his fuckin money in na dice game wit his silly ass," Chucky answered with a smile watching Rambo stuff even more of Looney money in his pocket after hittin.

"Iight we finna pullup ova thurr," I said before hanging up the phone feeling positive that the guns was as good as sold. I was satisfied with just having a couple extra hunnit dollars in my pocket for the time being after doing all that I guess. I was feeling a lil salty not having the few extra racks I thought I'd have in my pocket by then but a couple extra hunnit did help. Plus I was excited to see everybody that was over thurr. I hadn't seen Savage and Rambo nem in hellas neither.

"Look at these lil niggas, St. Louis aint changed a bit," I said proudly watching all the activity going on as we pulled up to the address Chucky sent. "Aye Rambo don't be takin all my son lunch money an shit nigga," I said playfully as he picked up even more of Looney's money and stuffed it in his pocket.

"Oh shit my nigga back in nis bitch," Rambo yelled, excited to see me back after being away from the hood for so long.

"Nigga I aint seent cho ass in hellas, wasup fool?" Looney added, happy to see me but still kinda tripping off all the money he had just lost fuckin with Rambo ass.

"Yeah man I had to make my way back to the trenches shid, it aint no money out thurr in no muafuckin Michigan City foreal," I said shaking Rambo's hand to greet him as we laughed.

"I'm hip bruh. I was scramblin like a muafucka down ner in Mississippi, me an Chad ass," Looney said shaking my hand to greet me.

"Damn homie! When you touch back down nigga? I aint seent cho ass in a minute," Savage said walking towards us with the lil bitch who's house he had trapped all the way out unapologetically just because she let him.

"Yeah I'm back in na field man, tryna run it up before I get up outta hurr on Sunday. I'll be back next weekend tho," I said shaking his hand as the lil bitch he walked up with gave me a sneaky lil smirk letting me know she was a slut and probably tryna get ran. But that wasn't even the mission cuz I was on a paper chase. The bitch ass wasn't fat enough to distract me from the money no way.

"Yall know Cutthroat ass booked right," Hustle blurted out, knowing nobody knew the whole story behind the shit yet.

"Yeah man his mama told me this mornin, that shit fucked up. They finna hit em wit like five," Savage answered, giving us a update on all Cutthroats charges.

"I heard that nigga had like forty bucks on em too. I know he hella mad," Rambo added, putting his lil two cents of information in not knowing the fucking forty bands Cutthroat had on him was our money too.

"It is what it is man, we got four guns tho wasup? Who want em?" Chad said after explaining how me, him, Cutthroat, and Hustle would've had a extra ten bands each in our pockets by then if Cutthroat hadn't got caught with all the money.

"Lemme see cuz my shit was showl jammin on me earlier, my main gun too. It prolly is time for me to grab sumn else," Rambo said following me, Chad and Hustle back to Hustle's car to shop through the guns we was selling.

"I need one fa sho. Just let me pick first cuz Savage muafuckin ass always happen to want the same damn gun I want for some reason. Don't show that nigga shit hold on," Looney said, counting the little bit of money he had left after losing most of it to Rambo in the dice game.

"Cumon bruh, this nigga prolly aint even got enough for that muafucka. Rambo been tearin his ass up all day," Savage said playfully shaking Rambo's hand to congratulate him as they laughed.

"Chucky come get these guns bruh," Looney said playfully as Chucky headed over to Hustle car after serving some people he had pull up.

"Lemme see, we better get a discount on nem muafuckas cuz we certified killas. We'll take yall shit," Chucky said jokingly, just talking a bunch of bullshit like usual.

"See you playin Chucky, I'm finna grab all four a these muafuckas don't worry bout it. How much yall want for em?" Rambo said smiling at Looney, knowing he was gone end up buying the guns with all the money he won in the dice game.

"Fuck naw nigga, this one me right hurr. Whatchu want for this bruh?" Chucky asked, picking out the gun he wanted before Rambo got a chance to snatch them all up.

"These muafuckas two-fifty a pop, run me that lil bruh," I said before collecting Chucky money for the gun while Savage picked out the one he wanted.

"Hurr bruh this me right hurr," Savage announced before handing his 250 to Chad.

"Lemme get them last two bruh, I got five for you hurr," Rambo said with a evil grin, knowing Looney wanted one too but couldn't really afford it after losing most of his money.

"Nigga you on some bullshit! Chucky grab one a these bangas for me bruh," Looney said pushing Rambo playfully, knowing Rambo was just tryna flex on his ass with the money he had won.

"Nigga shut cho crybaby ass up hurr," Rambo said, handing Looney one of the guns after handing me five hunnit dollar bills.

"You lucky I feel bad for cleanin yo ass out like I did," Rambo added as he laughed.

"Naw you gone be lucky when I'm gettin some niggas off yo ass wit this muafucka," Looney said happily, getting comfortable with his new gun.

"Yeah you know I gotta make sure the squad stay loaded. Plus I can blow a couple hunnit on my nigga after takin everything he made today," Rambo said as he laughed.

"Wasup wit Lil Rodney, whurr that nigga at?" I asked curious as to why he was nowhurr to be found at the moment.

"He been kinda distant since that shit went down wit him an Trouble. He'ont really fuck wit the hood like he used to," Rambo explained, feeling some type a way about it. He was fucked up about Trouble being gone too but he was more fucked about him and Lil Rodney not being as close as they used to be behind the shit. "I mean don't get me wrong I fucked wit Trouble too but Lil Rodney was my right hand. Whyda fuck he not sure if I'm rockin wit his ass regardless, right or wrong shid ion't give a fuck. That's my nigga we sposed to be better than that bruh that's some bullshit," Rambo vented, lighting up the Newport he had in his hand while shaking his head in disappointment.

"Lil Rodney just don't know who all wanna snake em out for killin Trouble shid, I'll be skeptical about steady pullin up in na zone after that shit happened too. Niggas feelin some type a way about that. I aint take it too personal myself but I did fuck wit Cap tuff an Trouble was his lil brother. Plus he was from na zone so even I halfway fuck wit Lil Rodney because a that shit. I wouldn't go as far as tryna snake em out behind it but some a these lil niggas will tho. Most a they ass fresh off the porch on all bullshit," Hustle stated, sharing his thoughts about the topic of discussion.

"Man ion't know, I kinda think that shit was on Trouble ass foreal. Lil Rodney was just chasin some pussy an Trouble was in na way cuz Nikki his sister. But I'll park a bitch brother if he steady comin for me too tho shid I need some type a respect from any muafucka aroun me. A nigga gone either respect me or respect this iron. Straight like that, ion't give a fuck who brother you is. That's just how I am," I said giving them my honest opinion about the situation too.

"But Trouble from na zone tho. I could see if it was a regular nigga in na streets. This a nigga you jumped off the porch wit," Chad said putting his lil two cents in so everybody could know how he felt about the situation.

"Man nat shit don't matter when a nigga got chu fuckedup on na wrong day, flatout. Don't keep provokin no straightup killa witout bein prepared for that shit to go left at some point. Trouble kept on comin for Lil Rodney ass man," Rambo said defending his once close friend even though Lil Rodney had been distant ever since the incident happened.

"All I'm sayin is they could've just caught a fade if it was that serious nigga damn, They could've got past that shit an prolly would've got back cool after a while. That shit was just overboard bruh," Hustle explained, tryna get me and Rambo to see the shit from his point of view so we could understand whurr he was coming from.

"Damn, I remember Cap said that shit when we was all on Gamble that one day too. Trouble an Lil Rodney was out thurr trippin then, the shit jus crazy man foreal," I said wondering how Cap would handle the situation himself if he was still alive an knew what went down. I knew it would've been a war between the two of them but Cap was already gone so Lil Rodney automatically won that battle.

"Man look, at the end a the day Trouble dead an gone. Aint no comin back from nat shit ever. Lil Rodney still hurr an nat's still my lil nigga so when you see em tell em I'ma catch up wit his lil ass this weekend when I get back if ion't bump heads wit em before I leave," I told Rambo as he nodded his head.

"We gotta pullup on nat nigga anyway, cumon Ram," Savage said to Rambo when he came back outside after tucking his new gun away somewhurr in the bitch crib real quick.

"Aye if yall start feelin like that nigga kinda fluky yall can always start compin from my plug. Ion't know what Lil Rodney nem got but my shit got the city on lock so let me know," Hustle said playfully, knowing the shit they was getting from Lil Rodney was just as good as his if not better. Rambo, Savage, and Chucky each had three phones that was always ringing for the dope Lil Rodney was giving em. Plus he was supplying half the city with the shit. Looney ass was already about to get a second phone cuz the one he had was ringing non-stop for Lil Rodney shit and Looney had just got back. The shit had to be good for him to get a phone booming that damn fast. Rambo knew Hustle was just fuckin with him cuz he was taking up for Lil Rodney so he just put his middle finger up at Hustle with a smile as him and Savage made they way to the car.

"Fuck you Hustle, " Rambo said playfully before getting in the car with Savage and pulling off.

"Bout time these niggas pulled up," Chucky said noticing Heavy and Don-Don pulling up in a dark blue LTZ Impala tinted up. Heavy and DonDon was brothers who was around the same age like me and Chucky. They was from the zone too but spent a lot of time in and out of jail so it was kinda rare to catch em both out at the same time. Usually they was both locked up or at least one a they ass was. Heavy was the older brother. He was just as big as Hustle fat ass but nowhurr near as black. They was both fat, fly and fresh as hell though. Heavy was just a lil more humble and less flashy than Hustle. His girl was real average looking, definitely not a head-turner like Latoya. But she was loyal and he respected that. Heavy wasn't really the type to be tryna impress a bunch a random cute bitches like Hustle was. He knew nine times outa ten the bitches only wanted his money and he wasn't having that. He used his money to take care of his family and to stay high like the rest of us. He aint give a fuck about shit else, especially not no begging ass hoes.

DonDon was the type a nigga that wasn't flashy at all but bitches was still drawn to his lil dreads that always hung in his face like Odog's off Menace II Society. He was slugged up too, and having a mouth fulla golds with some dreads be right up these St. Louis bitches alley. So they was on his ass even though he never put forth any effort to impress em. They just always thought he was fun and entertaining cuz he was hella flirty with all the bitches we brought around. He never made em uncomfortable like he was really tryna fuck though. Shid most of the time them bitches was tryna sneak and give DonDon ass some pussy. He was charming the shit out of them hoes on the low and for fun too. Oddly enough, his baby mama was hella big, hella black, hella ugly, hella loud, and hella ghetto. But the bitch was all the fuck he cared about I swear, he loved the shit outa Tyresha ass we just never understood why. It was hella confusing. Outa all the bitches he chose her and wasn't leaving her for nobody. DonDon aint give a fuck, then anytime we asked him about it he would just laugh the shit off cuz he was so playful. Heavy was more of the serious type that was always just willing to sit back and listen while DonDon was the more talkative one to joke around and play with.

"Wasup big boy," Hustle yelled with his hands up looking at Heavy as him and DonDon approached.

"Wasup fat boi," Heavy answered as he shook Hustle's hand to greet him.

"Yall just missed out," Chad said as DonDon shook my hand to greet me.

"What chall had some guns?" DonDon asked with a smile knowing us like the back of his hand.

"You know we gotta keep the lil niggas on na block armed an dangerous," I joked as we laughed.

"We got these tens tho nigga so yall might wanna count all that up an hand it over. How many guns was it?" DonDon asked with a smile rubbing his hands together playfully.

"I got tens nigga! Fuck you mean we? You aint got no parts in these Don. I said I would get high wit cho goofy ass that's it," Heavy said jokingly, pushing his brother's shoulder as they laughed.

"Yeah I'm finna loadup shid that was a quick 800 we jus made I got it. I'll buy Heavy out an dip on yall ass," Chad said playfully, feeling cocky cuz he had some money in his pocket. And it was more than what I had so I was feeling kinda salty.

"Man it wasn't shit quick about that punk ass eight hunnit dollars bruh, you racked up already damn, you might as well let me an Hustle split that. All we got is some fuckin dope an jewelry," I said with a smile not wanting to split the eight hunnit dollars three ways.

"It aint my fault chu aint sell Hustle yo dope nigga! Yall split six then, I'm at least gettin two yall got me fucked up," Chad answered as he laughed.

"Man lemme buy you out Heavy, dollar for dollar. Chad ass aint finna pay no dollar for dollar," Hustle said with a smile once I counted out the three hundred dollars and handed it to him.

"Showl the fuck aint! Shid I might as well just put in on sumn fuck that," Chad replied foolishly, not realizing that Hustle could make his money back plus some if we all gave Hustle some money to put down wit him.

"Yall got some blood?" DonDon asked referring to the Nyquil we used to mix the pills with after we crunched em down.

"I already got some blood, juice too its all good," Hustle said handing Heavy the money for the bag of pills.

"Meet us on Gamble. I got somebody waitin ney been sittin ner for hellas too cumon," Hustle said as we all headed back over to Gamble. Chucky nem had went in the house wit Savage lil bitch so they just missed out.

"Don do not run my shit, " Hustle said before handing DonDon the bottle.

DonDon was real playful with the shit, he never really took shit serious for real. He looked at it more like a game and the only way to win was to stay high. Don was funny as fuck.

"Cumon Hustle why would I run yo pack bruh? You gettin me high nigga, you doin me a favor," DonDon answered with a smile as he put the bottle to his lips watching Hustle watch him like a hawk.

"Man naw I'm not fuckin wit chu Don. You actin real playful an I'll have to beat cho ass," Hustle said reaching for the Nyquil bottle before DonDon could take a sip.

"Naw bruh foreal look," DonDon said before quickly taking a reasonable sip then handing it over to Heavy.

"Wasup wit that nigga Dre?" I asked, curious as to why I hadn't seen him in the mix since I got back to St. Louis. That was pretty unusual for him too cuz Dre ass was always in the mix.

"Man still blind as a fuckin bat witout them silly ass glasses he got. That nigga fought Grip the other day. The shit was so funny bruh on God. Dre aint wanna take them glasses off for shit, then wanna act like Grip crossed the line when he broke them muafuckas right on his face," Heavy explained, clowning Dre like he always did. Dre was Heavy and DonDon first cousin and niggas clown they own family harder than anybody. So Heavy showed no mercy.

"Bruh, I was fuckin dyin that shit was so funny. Dre was hooooooooot," Chad added, happy to have been thurr that day to see the fight himself.

"I was just standin ner tryna figure out howda fuck Grip had enough sense to take off his glasses but Dre slow ass didn't. I mean it aint like Grip just ran up on em bruh. They squared up an was goin back an forth for a minute," Heavy continued, going into more detail about the fight.

"Man what the fuck they was fightin for?" I asked entertained.

"Bruh! Some motha fuckin cigarettes an a pack a tens. I cannot make this shit up," Heavy answered shaking his head in shame trying not to laugh before handing me the bottle.

"That nigga Grip been gettin into it wit everybody lately. He can't keep up wit that habit bruh. That monkey on his back got his ass on all bullshit. He always stealin petty shit like cigarettes an loose pills. Dre just wasn't goin for the shit that day, he knew Grip took his shit so he told Grip ass to square up an it went from ner," Chad explained as I handed him the bottle.

"That's task force yall go!" I shouted, noticing the black SUV turning the corner on Gamble. Me an Chad dashed off running one way. DonDon and Hustle dashed off running the opposite way and Heavy took off in his own direction. They knew they wasn't finna catch me and Chad. Chad lil black ass was fast as fuck and I am too, especially when the police on my ass. They almost caught Hustle fat ass when his pants got stuck on the fence while him and DonDon was jumping the gate though.

"Shit! I'm fuckin stuck bruh what the fuck," Hustle said in a hushed tone squirming around panicking an tryna break free as quick as possible. He was scared as hell cuz the police was right on they ass after choosing to chase them over Heavy fat ass. Me an Chad was long gone I swear, they knew by the way we took off they wasn't catching us.

"Hold on bruh lemme see," DonDon said after turning around to help Hustle unhook his pants from the fence.

"Don't move!" the officer shouted approaching the fence rapidly before Don unhooked Hustle's True Religion jeans.

"Come on bruh!" Don shouted before they dashed off, this time running in two different directions.

HOMESICK

When I got back to Michigan City it just felt so wack after visiting St. Louis. Crystle apparently start fuckin with Twon cousin but I aint even give a fuck. Shid he was the one with the perks n shit so I just played like I aint know nothing hell why not. She wasn't doing shit but giving me the greenlight to fuck all them lil cute ass sneaky bitches she kept around her anyway. Plus Twon had his own crib, no girlfriend, no baby mama, just a straight up bachelor pad and a phone fulla hoes. He used to cook for the bitches and I would bring the bottle it was hella chill. Them bitches loved coming over there, especially them white hoes. They dinky asses would get all drunk and spend the night making me not give a fuck about going home my damn self so I wouldn't.

Crystle knew damn well I knew she was fucking Twon cousin but she still threw a fit when I would spend the night at Twon crib, knowing we had all hoes over thurr. But it was absolutely no respect left in me and it showed. I was a lot more social with the girls Crystle had around her first of all. And them bitches was eating that shit up too, feeding right into my bullshit. They was basically letting Crystle know exactly how easy it would be for me to have them snake her ass out and fuck me behind her back. Them bitches aint give a fuck, they wasn't even tryna be discrete with the shit no more but neither was I.

Her cousin Becky came over to the house one day with these lil bitty ass shorts on. And Becky ass hella fat. She got some nice size titties on her too. This bitch just bust out shaking her ass to this song while she cranking up the volume on the radio. So of course I watched the bitch dance cuz she was right in my fuckin face with the shit. I was sitting on my couch minding my business until then. But Crystle crazy ass came at me like I was making Becky twerk for me or something. The bitch charged in the front room with a fucking fork tryna stab my dick with it.

"Don't be disrespectin me in my muafuckin house lookin at my muafuckin cousin like that bitch!" Crystle yelled as I grabbed the hand she held the fork in smiling and amused by her reaction. "It aint funny bitch! I'll cut cho dick off while you sleep! I am not the one to play wit," she screamed as I laughed still holding her hand with restraint.

"Man fuck that bitch gimme this fork. That shit aint my muafuckin fault," I said snatching the fork out her hand in a more serious manner when I realized how fucked up she had me.

"Fuck you think I'm sposed to go in my room cuz this bitch shakin her ass? This my muafuckin house I pay bills hurr hoe. Yo scary ass need to holla at cho people instead a tryna run up on me. Shid I aint did shit but sat on nis muafuckin couch like I do everyday. I'ma grown ass man so if a bitch shakin her ass in my house I'ma look. Fuck you thought! This my shit ho!" I added before launching the fork across the room with anger.

"Dashon, I don't need yo broke ass to pay shit up in nis muafucka. Bitch you can shake, my real nigga got this ho. Yo dusty ass be in his way sittin aroun nis muafucka anyway!" she screamed as she charged at me again with her fist balled swinging.

"Bitch that nigga aint comin up in my shit! Ion't give a fuck what he payin you ho! Don't have that nigga laid out leakin in nis muafucka. Cuz that's what the fuck gone happen if I catch him in my shit bitch flat the fuck out on Cap. You already know my muafuckin pedigree don't play wit me I'm tellin you. I'll show you better tho bitch I promise. Play wit me if you want to," I yelled pinning her up against the wall by her neck.

"Becky call the fuckin police, this nigga gotta go!" Crystle screamed, still struggling to land a hit. Becky was tempted to call the police like Crystle told her to but felt kinda bad about starting the whole fight in the first place so didn't.

"Yall please stop fightin," Becky pleaded as we all caught a glimpse of some red an blue lights coming from outside. "OMG somebody called the police foreal," Becky said in a panicky hushed tone before the police knocked on the door.

"Girl fuck that, let them in. This nigga gotta go!" Crystle screamed as I tried to muffle her voice by putting my hand over her mouth but couldn't cuz she kept squirming around until Becky opened the door.

"Hey what's going on in here? We received a call about a domestic dispute. Is everyone ok?" the officer asked looking at Crystle and Becky. He was hoping them bitches gave him a reason to lock my black ass up from the jump.

"No sir, this man needs to get the fuck outta my house officer. Please escort him out," Crystle yelled still filled with anger and rage.

"Man like I said this my shit I aint goin nowhurr," I said calmly, still on ten myself but tryna play it cool. I knew the police didn't have a legal reason to take me in or make me leave unless both the girls lied an told them I hit her or something. But hell she was the one tryna stab me.

"Well you're going to jail if you two can't settle down sir. I can tell you that. What is your full name?" the officer asked pulling out a small pad and pin from his pocket.

"That don't even matter sir, I aint did shit an this is my house. So I don't gotta leave. You standin hurr questionin me like I did somethin," I said feeling annoyed, knowing he was tryna lock me up for something or anything really.

"I'm gonna need to detain you sir, please give me your wrist," the officer said calmly pulling out his handcuffs like he had been wanting to do since he got thurr.

"Man nis some bullshit, I aint even did shit. Howda fuck I'm goin to jail," I yelled feeling furious.

"Well I'm not sure if you're going to jail or not sir. But I do have to detain you for not cooperating with an officer. Now I'll ask you again, what's your name sir?" the officer asked calmly for the second time hoping the handcuffs would humble me like they did. After he got my information, he took me to the car and put me in the back while he ran my name. "You have a warrant for possession in St. Louis City sir. You have to go get this taken care of so I do need to take you in," the officer said looking at his computer.

"This some bullshit I aint got no possession warrant," I said denying the allegations but knowing exactly what the warrant was about. I was leaving my apartment one day before we left St. Louis and the police blocked me in when I tried to pull off. They said somebody reported drug activity in my complex and it was procedure to search the vehicle involved. They didn't find much but they still charged me with what they found. I only went to jail for a couple hours before I was released like nothing happened though.

"'That mean they finna send nat shit to the lab to make sure it's what they think it is bruh. After they test that shit they gone put a warrant out on yo ass. So you better make sure you got a lawyer on deck. It be takin hellas for that shit to come back on you too like months nigga. You'll fuck aroun an forget about the shit," Rambo explained when I vented to him and Lil Rodney about the incident back when the shit first happened. I was confused about why the fuck they let me go free after finding all them narcotics in my car. That shit had happened damn near a year ago by then but I guess it just finally caught up with me. When I got to the station they booked me but couldn't find the warrant St. Louis City had for me in the system so I was released. Once they let me go I called my mama immediately.

"Mama why Crystle dusty ass just got me locked up. They talm bout I got a warrant from St. Louis City for that shit that happened at them apartments that day. I was straight finna have to sit thurr til St. Louis City came an picked me up. They only released me cuz they couldn't find na shit in ney system but I know they comin back for me tho that warrant legit," I said giving her a ear full as soon as she answered the phone.

"Slow down son. If you really had a warrant out for your arrest them people would not have let chu up out that place trust me," my mama said tryna calm me down by making me feel like I didn't actually have a warrant even though I knew I did. I had just got lucky because they system was trippin at the time. I kept thinking about what Rambo was saying that day and I knew damn well it wasn't a coincidence that the warrant popped up in my name for possession.

"Mama they gone be tryna come back an get me soon as they figure out they wasn't supposed to let me go. Ion't know what to do I know they comin tho. Crystle ass all at the house trippin talm bout I gotta go. What if she call the police again?" I asked just ranting on and on. "She fuckin wit this bitch ass nigga from down hurr an now I can't even feel safe wit my guns in na house. I know the police finna come back lookin for me an ion't want em to put shit else on me when ney do, that's a warrant mama. That shit aint just pop up for no reason," I continued, hoping she would realize how ugly shit would get for me without her help.

"I'll look into it for you son calm down. I'ma send Lance down ner to pick you up. Til then you an Crystle need to get off that bullshit. She know better than to call the damn police. Yall just out thurr doin too much," my mama said calmly passing my dad the blunt they was smoking ready to get off the phone and go to sleep.

"Mama when he comin? I feel like I need to get from out hurr. Michigan is not my city. If they lock me up out hurr St. Louis City gone take hellas to come get me. I'ma just be sittin ner lockedup, waitin for hellas. They fuck aroun an forget I'm in nat muafucka," I said probably being a lil dramatic but knowing what I was saying was actually true.

"I'ma get up in na mornin an head down ner son. I aint goin nowhurr tonight tho so ya ass better stay the hell out the way til I get thurr. I'ma leave early in na mornin too cuz I aint finna let cha ass tie my whole day up wit this shit neither," my dad said as he hit the blunt a couple times then passed it back to my mama.

"I'm finna call Crystle an see what's goin on cuz you need to go get cho stuff. Ion't want it to be no bullshit when you go get it tho. Let me call this damn girl an make sure she done calmed down," my mama said hitting the blunt a couple more times then passing it back to my dad.

"I'm finna go to my boy Twon crib. He'll take me ova thurr to get my shit. Tell that bitch I'm comin for it an she aint gotta worry bout me no mo. I'm sick a this wack-ass city anyway," I said before hanging up and calling Twon. "Aye bruh, can you come take me to go get my shit. I'ma be leavin in na mornin, my pops drivin down hurr to get me. I need to go get my shit tho, an crash at cho crib if it's cool," I said when Twon answered the phone giving him a ear full too.

"Damn bro, you goin back to St. Louis?" Twon answered, feeling disappointed but still willing to help. "Where you at now?" he asked ready to get right in route to come pick me up.

"Man I'm kinda by the police station, I'm mobin tho cuz I gotta get the fuck away before they realize they wasn't really supposed to let me go. I'm buck ass noid, walkin fast then a muafucka twords this gas station down na street from na police station. Ion't even wanna stop hurr foreal," I answered nervously. Not knowing if they had realized they mistake by then or not.

"Yeah I know where that's at, I'm not even far from you either jus stay there. I'll be pullin up in a couple minutes," Twon replied, heading to the gas station I was walking toward. "What happened bro? How you get locked up?" Twon asked as I got in the car.

"Man nis stupid ass bitch gone runup on me cuz Becky was in na frontroom shakin her ass. Like I was straight makin na bitch dance for me asumn. Becky was bein hella extra bruh, lookin back at me while she was dancin an all. I'm sittin on na couch just watchin like any otha nigga would do, unless the nigga a fag asumn. Becky got all ass, I know this bitch aint think I was finna get up an go to my room. Fuck outta hurr, holla at cho muafuckin cousin ho! Scary-ass bitch, gone run up on me wit a fork tryna stab my dick like it's my fault," I ranted still feeling pissed about the whole situation.

"What the hell bro!!! She tried to stab yo fucking dick with a fork?" Twon responded as he laughed.

"Man for real this some bullshit!" I said finally cracking a smile about the incident myself. I wasn't really in the mood to be laughing and joking about the shit but I had to admit the way she charged at me with the fork was hella funny.

"So why they lock you up instead a her? What chu do?" Twon asked a nxiously ready to hear all about how I ended up getting booked.

"Man ney talm bout St. Louis City got a warrant out for my arrest over some shit that happened damn near a year ago. But when I got down to the station they said it wasn't in na system so they had to let me go. I know that muafuckin warrant really active tho cuz my potna already told me this shit was gone happen. That's why my pops drivin down hurr to get me in na mornin. I know they finna come lookin for me once they find out they fucked up by lettin me go," I explained, letting him know how lucky I was to even be out at that moment. "When I get back to St. Louis I'ma turn myself in wit my bond money an my lawyer on deck so they can book an release my ass. All I gotta do is make sure I go to court but I won't be goin to court from jail tho, that's all that really matter foreal. I'm not finna be up hurr waitin on St. Louis City to come pick me up neither cuz they gone take they time. I'ma just be sittin in jail waitin fuckin wit they ass," I said stressing how much harder it would be for me if I didn't make it back to St. Louis before they got a chance to lock me back up out thurr.

"Damn bro. See that's why Ion't want no serious relationship man these hoes be wild, then they wanna call the police on you and shit. Knowing when the police pullup and see a black male they want a free body. You really a dead man if you got a gun on you. These bitches'll have you on some bullshit," Twon said as we laughed. "But how the hell Crystle gone get mad at you for looking at Becky dance when she was hooking up with my cousin every night when you was in St. Louis bro. She be letting him drive the truck and all," Twon added, reminding me that Crystle wasn't no angel so I wouldn't feel bad about ending our relationship.

I was mad about the truck cuz I had bought that truck with my income tax. But I knew I couldn't take it cuz I couldn't leave Crystle with the kids and no transportation. I felt bad about leaving the girls but there was no way I could've stayed even if I wanted to. I was just too out of place thurr. Me and Crystle wasn't in a good enough space for me to be tryna stay no way. Thankfully she wasn't on no bullshit when me and Twon pulled up at the house though. We didn't say two words to each other. She had all my shit packed in a bag by the door so I just grabbed the bag and left.

When we got to Twon crib he opened the fifth of Hennessy he had sitting on the counter and poured up a couple shots. "Now I know you need a couple shots after all that, here" he said handing me a double shot glass with a naked lady painted on it. "I'm finna call some hoes ova here. It's a fucking goin away party bro. Lets make this shit lit turn up," he said while going through his phone looking for the perfect bitches to call. Now usually I woulda been all for it but this night was a lil different. I was still kinda trippin off what Twon said earlier about Crystle and his cousin. I tried to fuck one of the bitches that came through but my muafuckin dick wouldn't even stay hard steady stressin off that shit. Twon took the other bitch in his room and fucked her til they fell asleep. Then the bitch I was tryna fuck ended up falling asleep too cuz she was hella drunk.

I was up though. I couldn't sleep for shit so I ended up taking Twon keys and pulling up at his cousin's crib to see if my truck was over thurr and it was.

So I put the car in park, turned it off, and just lamped on my shit outa curiosity. I wanted to see if the bitch was really letting dude drive my shit. Plus sitting outside his crib knowing I could catch him off guard and lay his ass down if I really wanted to was satisfying as fuck for some reason.

When they came out dude walked right over to the driver's side and started the car while Crystle went and sat in the passenger's seat. He looked over at his cousin's car, confused about why Twon car was parked across the street from his house in the middle of the night cuz he hadn't talked to Twon since that morning. I'm guessing he was a lil bit nervous about it cuz before he pulled off he tried to start the truck up again when he had already started it up causing the car to make a loud sound. "Probably fuckin up my damn transmission asumn bitch-ass nigga," I said to myself as I watched em drive away. The next morning he called Twon to ask him why his car was parked at his crib so late the night before. Then held the phone in silence when Twon told him that it couldn't have been his car cuz he had been at home all night.

"Damn man you straight about to shake this muafucka, it's been real bro," Twon said sadly as my dad pulled up ready to jump right back on the flyway as soon as possible.

"Yeah man a nigga like me in a city like this a recipe for disaster bruh. They'll book my ass quick. It's time for me to gone back to St. Louis whurr I can move how I move cuz I showl can't hurr. I'm buck ass noid, ready to get the fuck outta hurr," I said as I laughed, still trippin off how easy it would've been to lay his cousin bitch ass down right in front of Crystle like I wanted to. I knew I could've got away with the shit if we was back in my city.

"I feel you bro. Fuck wit me when you come back an visit tho homie. I know you gone wanna come back and see the girls from time to time, just holla at me when you do," he said shaking my hand goodbye.

"You already know bruh, I'ma miss the shit outta this muafucka," I said looking back at his crib with a smile, reminiscing about all the different bitches I fucked thurr before getting in the car and heading back to St. Louis.

HOME SWEET HOME

"Wasup bruh? Yo ass on na fuckin news, whatchu do?" my lil brother Chucky yelled with excitement soon as I answered his call.

"Whatchu mean bruh?" I asked confused and clueless as my dad turned the radio down assuming it was some important news by the way I responded.

"Nigga they lookin for you fool! Yo face all on na damn news big as shit. You wanted like a muafucka nigga, that shit wild as fuck. It aint no body is it?. I know you aint go way out thurr trippin like that did you?" Chucky joked, amused and entertained by the whole situation. "Mama on na phone wit the lawyer right now tho. Niggas blowin my shit up hold on," he added before clicking over to answer Hustle call ready to hype the situation up to him.

"Aye whatchu got goin on lil nigga?" Chad asked soon as I clicked over to answer his call.

"Maan Crystle ass got me locked up an ney accidentally let me go. Now they lookin for me like a nigga escaped asumn this some bullshit. I'm on my way back to St. Louis right now tho," I answered before clicking over to answer Twon call.

"Bro, the police straight looking for you," he blurted out soon as I said hello.

"Yeah I know, I told you bruh. I knew that shit was gone happen, they say they got my damn picture all on na news in St. Louis," I answered, relieved my mama was already on top of the shit.

"Be careful bro, yall talked to the lawyer right?" Twon asked, concerned with all the drama I had following me back to St. Louis.

"Yeah my mama on na phone wit em now. This her right hurr callin on na other end. I'ma hit chu back bruh faces up," I said before clicking over to answer my mama call.

"Look son, you not finna talk my ear off about this shit. I just talked to the lawyer an he said meet em up thurr in na mornin so they can book you real quick an letchu go wit a court date," she said before I was even able to get a word in outside of hello.

"Yo, America's most wanid. What time yall sposed to be pullin up?" Chucky asked playfully in the background as my mama rolled her eyes and just handed him the phone.

"Tell em to get dropped off on Gamble," Chad said as Hustle pulled up at my mama crib to pick him up from over thurr.

Iight I'm finna pullup on Savage real quick, we finna be ova thurr in a minute too. Tell Hustle to keep them perks on deck cuz we gone need em," Chucky answered, tryna make me feel like I was missing out on something cuz I hadn't made it back to St. Louis yet.

When we got back to St. Louis my dad aint have no problem dropping me off on Gamble cuz he was headed over to the neighborhood himself. Pops loved the hood as much as we did, we was all just naturally drawn to it. Him and my mama both from na zone but the zone was a lot less rowdy and a million times safer back in those days. My dad never been locked up still to this day. Not one time, not even for traffic shit his whole life. He did have to shoot at these niggas that kept driving by our crib shooting after Chucky killed they lil brother though.

Before we moved me and Chucky would sit out on our porch all day and night waiting on nem niggas to slide through. And it was a full-blown shootout every time they did. Half the damn neighborhood used to post up on the porch with us most of the time. Just to catch a piece of the action and to have a reason to shoot like they wanted to do more than anything anyway. Everybody from na zone was trigger happy as fuck, especially when niggas called theyselves sliding on Gamble. One night they tried to get out and come up to the house. They was obviously some rookies cuz they had a whole machine gun but didn't even know how to operate that muafucka. Them lil niggas aint have no business with that gun. It sounded like a tech but they aint hit shit with it. They was probably just out there fumbling that muafucka.

"Stay low bruh niggas outside," I said creeping out my room as Chucky crept out his.

"I'm bout tired a this shit!" my dad yelled taking his shotgun out the closet then quickly checking the number of bullets loaded.

"They in na backyard," Chucky said in a hushed tone, kneeling with his two guns ready to shoot anything moving.

"Yeah they is," I agreed, holding the AR Hustle had me strapped with just in case some shit like this was to happen (BOOM).

"Come on in then lil niggas," my dad yelled after blowing a big ass hole through the back door. That shotgun scared the shit out of they lil asses too. We heard one of the lil niggas yell "shit!" before they all took off running. Then me and Chucky let off a round at the door just so them lil niggas could know we was on point in that muafucka. They had no idea how hard it would've been to catch us sleeping up until then anyway. They was already coming over thurr nervous cuz hellas of they peoples had already got killed fucking with us. So when we heard a car skirt off around the corner we knew they wasn't coming back.

"We are leaving this house tonight Lance," my mama said getting up from under the bed ready to let his ass have it if he didn't start helping her pack.

"Get yall shit together. We'll come back tomorrow for this furniture an shit. Just get most of what chall takin an put it in na truck," he said to me and Chucky as he headed back to his room to discuss the game plan with his wife. My dad never been the type to rob, kill, sell dope, gang bang or snake anybody out. The neighborhood was just drastically different for him growing up in his days. He like 12 years older than my mama so he was never exposed to Gamble the way we was as a kid. That whole area just basically got more and more fucked up over the years. The neighborhood slowly transformed into the zone but he still never wanted to leave neither. He fell in love with my mama after watching her grow into a mature woman in the midst of the neighborhood going downhill. He didn't even realize what was going on with his head all in the clouds trippin off my mama.

They had a lot of hurdles in they relationship throughout the years. It probably had a lot to do with the age difference but it was really just typical baby mama and baby daddy shit for real. They had four of us so it was a lot on they plate. My mama named my older brother Lance after my dad cuz he was the first born. Then they had my sister Tasha but by the time he got her pregnant with me he wasn't even sure if I was his. Once he found out I was he got her pregnant with Chucky then they was done. Lance already had two daughters with his ex before him and my mama got together. So any more than that would've probably been more than he could handle. My mama married him knowing he would do whatever it took to keep us taken care of and he did. She was content with who she chose despite him already having two kids with somebody else which made him love her even more.

My mama always spoiled our sister Tasha cuz she was her only girl but Tasha was no whurr near as innocent as my mama thought. Tasha was just hella sneaky. They was in complete denial about her ass til she got pregnant by a nigga from the neighborhood. My mama was pissed cuz Tasha was so young and she wasn't surprised at all when Tasha baby daddy got locked up with a ten-year sentence.

My older brother Lil Lance was a lot like my dad cuz he always stayed out of trouble. He was never in the streets like me and Chucky cuz he was always with his girl. His girlfriend was hella preppy and cute even though she acted like a full blown white girl. He met her when they was like ten and they was completely inseparable every since that moment. They moved in together soon as they got old enough but before they did he was always at her mama house with her. She was to scared to come over our house knowing how bad the neighborhood was. But she was basically the reason Lil Lance never got caught up in the streets like me and Chucky did. When he got her pregnant my mama was actually happy. She even urged him to marry her so his new lil family would be official like her and my dad's. After he got her pregnant he start falling for this city girl type bitch though. She was hella ghetto with a lot of kids already but it was still something about her that made him wanna leave his perfect lil prissy girlfriend/baby mama to be with her. My parents was so disappointed and confused. They didn't even know what to say when his girl came crying to them about the situation asking for advice or clarity. After she finally went to the source and talked to the girl herself which happened to be one of Tasha's best friends by the way, she moved to Texas with his daughter heartbroken. It wasn't until then that he realized he had made a big mistake by letting her go but it was too late at that point. She felt like she aint even know who he was no more and completely moved on. She never even considered giving him chance to have his perfect lil family back.

"Oooh FBI's most wanid in nis bitch," Rambo yelled playfully as me and my dad pulled up on Gamble.

"Aye if they catch ya ass today you'll be thurr til tomorrow so don't call disturbin my sleep Dashon," my dad said as I got out the car to greet Rambo with a smile. I was happy to be back home despite all the bullshit.

"Man ney not catchin no real street nigga pops. I'm back shid I aint lost it. This still my city I got this trust me," I said as me and Rambo laughed while my dad raised his eyebrows and slowly drove away.

"What took you so long nigga," Chad said when he pulled up with Hustle smiling ear to ear knowing I was back for good.

"So wasup nigga? Is you back for good or what? You back back?" Hustle asked smiling too, already knowing the answer and was just as happy as Chad. Me and Chad was his new lil squad so he wanted us around him every day. I was the one who attracted all the bitches so Hustle could flex on em with his money. And chad was the one always tryna rob a bitch blind in the mist of me and Hustle tryna get some pussy. It was a couple bitches we came across that I probably would've took a lil more serious but after Chad got through with they ass I aint stand a chance. I aint really give a fuck for real though shid I wasn't looking for no girlfriend no way. Not after everything I had been through with Crystle ass and I was sure about that.

The next day everybody was out on Gamble. It was showl good to be back. It seemed more peaceful than usual cuz bitches had the kids out, the whole block smelled like barbeque, bitches had on lil bitty ass shorts out thurr twerkin with Latoya ass. Music blasting, blunts in the air, and everybody was sippin on something. It was a warm day with a cool breeze and everything was perfect until some niggas pulled up looking for Chucky and Savage asses. Most of us was at the park that stood on the end of the street. Ironically, Gamble a dead end street (literally), then it's a corner store right across the street from the park. It was chill cuz niggas was scared to come up that dead end shooting. But they could most likely find anybody they was looking for posted at the park on a day like that day.

The chinamen was right next door to the store too. So we had easy access to food without even needing a car cuz you had to walk across to get thurr. "Aye, wasup wit this lil Honda steady slidin thru? This the second time that muafucka den came down Gamble creepin man who is that?" I asked curiously, knowing if it was a nigga from na zone he would've dropped the tint and said something by then. The windows was pitch black, even the windshield so we wouldn'tve known who the fuck was in thurr unless they let the window down.

"Ion't know prolly Lil Rodney. He the only one who be tintin na windshield on everything he drive," Chad answered feeling cautious cuz he was unsure.

"Naw Lil Rodney would've pulled up an said sumn," I said watching the lil black Honda creep down Gamble for the second time obviously looking for somebody.

"An Lil Rodney not finna be in no Honda no way. Who is that?" Heavy added feeling a lil concerned knowing some shit was probably finna pop off.

"That definitely aint Lil Rodney," Rambo said with his eyebrows raised and gun out.

"Jus let me know bruh. I'll light that muafucka up right now wasup?" DonDon said with his gun held low but already cocked ready to shoot.

"It's all kids out hurr tho whoever that is aint on shit. Or why they aint pop off the first time they hit this muafucka," Dre said with a hint of doubt, praying we wasn't finna have to have a full-blown shootout in the midst of everybody having such a good time. Especially with the kids out playing.

"Niggas don't give a fuck about no kids fool," Rambo said clutching his gun ready to pop off.

"I'm hip. That Honda prolly on all bullshit," Chad said getting low with his gun like a sniper.

"That muafucka is creepin," Hustle said with his eyebrows raised, more concerned than anybody cuz Latoya and his kids was on the other end of Gamble clueless while alla this was finna take place.

"Yea they on bullshit," I blurted out as the Honda pulled up to the corner finally letting down the window – pow pow pow pow pow pow pow! They was able to let off a few shots before getting completely trampled by bullets coming from both ends of Gamble. All the kids and females scattered to safety knowing anybody was likely to get hit with all them damn bullets flying.

Murder was already on point after peeping the Honda creep down Gamble the first time. He was posted on one of the vacos by the alley with his lil brother Beezy and the lil click of niggas he kept around him on a daily basis. "Get down Beezy!" Murder yelled with rage, determined to protect his lil brother before anything. Murder hit the driver right in the temple within the first three shots so the rest of them niggas was sitting ducks until everybody stopped shooting. And they showl in the hell wasn't moving after that. The Honda just sat at the corner covered with bullet holes and three lifeless bodies slumped over inside.

"We need to go ova thurr an see who the fuck that was," Heavy said walking towards the shot up Honda with his gun still out just in case.

"Hold on bruh, don't just be walkin up on it fool. You on't know if a nigga in nat muafucka playin possum or not," DonDon said following behind his brother with caution.

"Don aint nobody breathin in nis muafucka trust me," Rambo said walking towards the shot up Honda carelessly.

"Aw it was them niggas," Chad announced as we all crowded around the car curious to find out who came through causing so much commotion on such a perfect day just to end up dead on the corner.

"Chucky used to rock wit the nigga in na driver's seat. They fell out cuz Savage took dude phone an start servin his people," Dre explained, knowing the whole rundown about how the deadly beef first got started.

"Whurr these niggas even from?" Hustle asked curiously, not recognizing the dude in the drivers seat at all.

"They from na Beam, dude used to be wit Chucky alla time," Chad answered feeling somewhat worried cuz the Beam was damn near worse than the zone. They was a lil bit deeper than us too cuz most of our asses was locked up or dead already. So we was all standing thurr feeling the same way. We knew we was gone be at war with them niggas once the streets found out about they clown asses coming over thurr and getting parked on Gamble like they did.

"Man ney ass out hurr doin too much. Chucky just let a muafucka put his ass in all kinda shit," I said feeling frustrated as fuck with my stupid ass lil brother for causing all that commotion by letting Savage take the nigga phone in the first place. He knew he was gone be in the middle of the shit cuz he was the one that had them in the car with each other.

"Aye um I know one thing everybody that got a gun need to break like now. The police finna be pullin up any minute. Last time I checked St. Louis City police department was right aroun na corner an yall know damn well they pullin up ova hurr first," Grip interrupted, walking up to the car reminding all of us to get the fuck away while we still had a chance. Grip was just gone sit outside and wait for the police to pull up so he could give them bullshit descriptions of niggas that wasn't us. Grip wasn't the type to tote no pistol and he wasn't really a killer. All he was focused on was getting high.

"Aye Dashon, that head shot was all me nigga," Beezy said playfully, knowing it was actually his brother Murder doing all the shooting. Beezy was shooting from the ground so the only thing he really did was shot the tires flat.

"Cumon Beezy we out. I just wanid to make sure all these pussy ass niggas was dead let's go," Murder said urging his brother to follow him as the rest of us branched off too.

"Heavy yo fat ass can't drive, put chall shit in hurr before yall get flagged. You might as well jus pull over," I said playfully as him and DonDon handed they guns over to Hustle and Chad.

"That's what's up cuz I know damn well he gone crash our ass out if he tryda take them people," Dre said with a chuckle, handing me his gun before getting in the back seat of Heavy LTZ Impala.

"Them pills too Heavy! Yall gettin booked for that!" Hustle said playfully, hoping Heavy would hand em over so me, him, and Chad could crunch em down and get high.

"Fuck naw nigga! These goin in my ass," Heavy answered as we laughed.

"I'm sayin bruh they good in hurr, Dashon not pullin over," Chad said with a smile, confident that if they did decide to try an pull us over we would definitely still get away.

"Fuck naw nigga I got this. Just worry about the shit I can't tuck like them thumpas fool. I aint finna put a whole glock 40 in my ass now I'll just have to catch a speed wit that muafucka," Heavy answered jokingly as we laughed then pulled off.

"Get the fuck on na highway bruh them sirens close as fuck," DonDon yelled in a panic.

"Thurr they go right thurr," Dre said pointing out the police car making a quick right in my direction. Heavy was following me until he turned left. The police got right behind me and hit the lights though. I took right off.

"Dashon finna take they ass, that nigga gone," DonDon said with a smile, watching the police follow us at top speed.

"Dashon finna loose they ass quick watch, they'll be callin my phone playin an talkin shit ina minute," Heavy said knowing damn well I wasn't finna let them catch my ass with all them fucking guns. He knew I wasn't going out like that.

"Thurr go another one bruh! They probably finna hop down on us," Dre said as the police drove toward them coming from the opposite direction.

"They finna buck a U on our ass watch," DonDon said still feeling nervous even though they didn't have nothing but the pills Heavy kept in the car.

"Damn Don tuck this," Heavy said handing DonDon the bag of pills he kept as the police made a u-turn and got right behind them just like Don said. So DonDon stuffed the bag of pills in between his ass cheeks being sure not to do too much moving around so the officers behind them wouldn't get suspicious. He played it cool though. Don was gone take the case for his brother without even thinking twice about it if they found em. So he made sure they was tucked securely but the police was really only looking for guns that day. Just tryna get a murder charge under they belt pretty much.

"Where are you gentlemen headed this evening?" the officer said with a stern voice as he approached the driver's side window.

"Oh I was just about to take my little brother and cuzin over our grandma's for her surprise birthday party officer, " Heavy said with a fake ass smile lying through his teeth.

"Where does your grandma live?" the other officer asked as he stood at the passenger's side window.

"Well she lives on Salisbury near the highway sir, but we were in the area looking for an old friend of hers so we could take her to the party too. The only problem is we can't seem to find her and I can't really wait around or keep looking because I can't show up late to this party," Heavy answered, making up a reason for them being in the area at the time.

"I'm gonna need everybody to step out the vehicle," the officer on the driver's side announced, sensing Heavy was fulla shit and ready to check the car regardless of what type a bullshit Heavy was feeding them.

"What do you all know about the car full of dead bodies over on Gamble?" the other officer asked boldly, ready to evaluate their responses to determine whether or not they was guilty.

"Not a damn thing!" DonDon blurted out immediately, actually sounding pretty convincing. So the officers was unsure about whether he was lying or telling the truth.

"Oh we heard the shots officer, that's really why we decided to just go ahead and go," Heavy answered tryna sound as proper as possible while the officers patted them down.

"Are there any weapons in the car, any guns?" the second officer asked, patting DonDon down.

"Hell naw! We'ont play wit no guns," Don answered trying his hardest not to cringe up too much so the officer wouldn't suspect he was hiding the pills in his ass when he checked him.

"No sir, we don't have any guns or anything. We was just trying to make our grandma's special day a little more fun by escorting one of her closet friends to the party as part of her surprise," Heavy added as the officer began to search Dre.

"What about you? Can you speak?" the officer asked patting Dre down curious as to why he hadn't said a word.

"Sir yes Sir!" Dre responded in a loud goofy voice tryna make the officers think he was actually retarded.

"My cuzin kinda slow officer. We just need as many people that love her there as possible. Plus he family I gotta look out for em," Heavy said in a hushed tone to the officer who was standing thurr tryna figure out if Dre was for real about being retarded or not.

"Anything in the vehicle?" the first officer asked as his partner checked the car thoroughly.

"Nope, they're clean," the other officer answered shutting the trunk after seeing it was completely empty.

"Stay out of trouble fellas," one of the officers said as they both headed back to they car and drove off.

"Wasup fool? Wher yall at? Pop out wit them pills homie. Ion't want em if you had to put em in yo ass tho bruh flatout," Hustle said playfully as me and Chad laughed in the background.

"Shid DonDon diggin nem muafuckas out his ass right now, they showl jus flagged us" Heavy responded with a smile, putting the phone on speaker so Dre and DonDon could hear us talking shit.

"Cumon bruh, you could've jus put em in hurr wit us! I would've bought them muafuckas foreal man damn!" Hustle said feeling disappointed.

"Yall niggas actin like these muafuckin pills aint wrapped up in na plastic bag tho. Like I was jus dry poppin these bitches up my ass asumn," DonDon said as we all laughed hysterically.

"Cumon Don, you 'ont even wash yo ass like that man shitty as pills, cumon on dude," I said jokingly as we all kept laughing.

"Damn, they on Rambo ass!" Heavy shouted as Rambo flew past the stop sign they was coming up on with two police cars trailing close behind him.

"That nigga trippin, they all on his bumper. He better hop up out that muafucka ASAP!" DonDon added, hoping Rambo could at least get away on foot cuz it looked pretty much impossible to lose em from behind the wheel. He did end up hitting a alley and hopping out though. He said he hid in a vacant building until like four in the morning. They was looking for his ass all day but never found him.

BLOCK MONSTERS

"Nigga you got the hood all hot an shit fuckin wit Savage scandalous ass. I hope you know how much you puttin on na line for that nigga damn. You an Carmen finna have a whole son bruh. You gone wanna be apart a that lil nigga life but chu fuck aroun an be gone before his lil ass even get hurr. Yall niggas just started a straight war bruh," I said to Chucky as he frantically looked around his room tryna find the gun he misplaced the night before.

"Man fuck that shit bruh, Gamble been a fuckin war zone. That aint shit new," Chucky responded carelessly still looking for the gun.

"That shit stupid man. Yall out hurr tryna make a name for yallself but the shit jus pointless cuz muafuckas already know howda zone get down. What's understood don't need to be explained nigga you trippin," I said trying my hardest to talk some sense into his hot-headed ass.

"Wasup bruh," Chucky said answering his phone in the middle of our conversation like I wasn't talking bout shit he wanted to hear or talk about.

"This bitch ass nigga jus bucked a choppa on me an Looney bruh. We ova hurr on 20th, dude still outside wit the choppa an all. He got mad cuz I hit em up in na dice game. Straight upped on our ass, told us we gotta shake cuz we aint from down ner. If we wasn't on foot I swear I'll air these niggas out bruh whurr you at? I'm tryna hop down on nem niggas an slide out this bitch. They must not know who the fuck we is homie," Savage answered giving Chucky a earful soon as he picked up the phone.

Nigga what? Yall on na Dub? I'm on my muafuckin way!" Chucky replied picking up the gun he was looking for after peeping it was lying on the floor beside his dresser.

"Thurr you go again, you aint finna do shit but run off an let the nigga getchu in some mo bullshit," I said as he headed to the front door.

"Man fuck that, niggas just finna respect my gangsta or lay the fuck down flatout," he replied before walking out the door and running to his car.

"Thurr them niggas go. Pull down ner so we can air they ass out real quick," Savage said as they crept back over to 20th once Chucky pulled up to get em.

"Iight look, both of yall get in na back. I'ma pullup on 19th an make a left back on 20th. Soon as I make that left we hoppin out, use the car as a sheild," Chucky instructed as he crept down 19th Street before making that left back on 20th.

"Fuck yo choppa nigga!" Savage yelled after hopping out the back seat with two guns blazing, killing the dude with the choppa instantly. Chucky and Looney hopped right out with a gun in each hand shooting too. And they all had extra clips on em so they was out thurr tripping.

"Fuck I'm hit!" Savage yelled holding his side.

"Shit! Get in bruh," Looney said looking down at Savage who was slowly collapsing to the ground with blood covering his shirt.

"Fuck I'm hit too!" Looney yelled, helping Savage back in the car after getting shot hisself.

"Cumon nigga we hit!" Looney yelled, getting in the car after Savage while Chucky emptied the extra two clips he had at the nigga that hit Looney. Chucky was the only one still shooting by that time but he aint stop til he seen dude hit the ground.

"Cumon nigga let's go," Savage said still holding his side as Chucky got back in the car.

"Yall niggas good? Talk to me," Chucky said as he pulled off driving as fast as he could to the hospital. "Looney wasup!" he yelled tryna stay focused on the road but needing reassurance that Looney and Savage was both still alive and ok.

"Yeah man, I'm losin all blood tho. Savage actin like he goin out on a nigga an shit, nigga getup!" Looney said pushing Savage up off of him with the lil bit of strength he had left.

"Savage, wasup homie? Talk to me," Chucky said trying not to panic but running every red light he came across.

"Man I'm weak bruh," Savage said with barely enough energy to get that out.

"Niggas got us fucked up, yall finna be good tho bruh we almost thurr," Chucky said pulling up to the hospital. "We need a doctor right now they shotup!" Chucky yelled as he pulled up to the emergency room entrance after hopping out the driver's seat to help Looney and Savage out the car. When he got out the car one of the guns he had on his lap fell to the ground. So he picked it up, put it on his waist, then proceeded to help his potnas out the car. But a off duty police that just happened to be standing around at the time peeped Chucky gun in the midst of all the commotion.

"Hey! Freeze! Stop right there!" the officer yelled reaching for the gun he had on his hip as Chucky quickly hopped back in the car – pow. The officer fired his gun hitting Chucky in the shoulder as he pulled off going top speed. After that he blacked out and hit a light pole at the entrance of the hospital.

"So Chucky woke up cuffed at the hospital?" Rambo asked, when I told him everything my mama had told me about Chucky's current status at the time.

"Yeah he made sure they got they ass up off the battle field tho. He could've dropped them niggas off an got away untouched but Chucky a damn slow rack," I added feeling disappointed that he didn't get away.

"Aye I heard them dubhead niggas took all L's tho," Hustle said giving us a update about the incident that led to Chucky, Savage, and Looney all getting benched like they did.

"Yeah most a them niggas aint make it shid Savage an Looney good. An ney aint even hit Chucky the police did," Chad added proudly.

"I heard them dubhead niggas was hella deep too. Muafuckas talm bout they had a whole choppa out thurr but aint nobody get hit wit that muafucka. That shit embarrassin bruh," Rambo said amused as him and Chad shook hands with laughter.

"Them lil niggas straight treacherous bruh on my kids," Hustle added feeling a sense a pride for some reason. We all was kinda geeked up though.

We couldn't wait to pump they lil asses up about that shit. They was lucky to even be able to brag about the shit one day.

"Ooh speakin of treacherous, wasup lil nigga pull ova bruh," I said with a smile, happy to see Lil Rodney again after so long.

"Man you out hurr lackin, you aint even see me creepin up on you," Lil Rodney said playfully as he pulled his SRT8 truck to the curb.

"Man you know I'm peepin everything movin aroun nis bitch," I said as Lil Rodney got up out the car and shook my hand.

Whatchu doin out hurr on na block? You'ont never hit this muafucka foreal," Rambo said shaking Lil Rodney hand to greet him.

"Man nis lil nigga know he can't keep duckin me," I said as we laughed

"Yeah I knew I was gone catch yo ass ova hurr sooner or later. I'm finna go pick up Nikki an na kids ina minute tho, she want me to take em to the mall an shit. What yall niggas out hurr on? I heard about that shit that went down on 20th yesterday," Lil Rodney answered feeling just as proud as the rest of us.

Yeah that nigga Chucky benched. Him, Looney, an Savage all shot up an shit. Them dubhead niggas finished tho bruh. They took all L's fuckin wit them lil niggas," I said hyping the incident up more and more since it was such a trending topic at the time.

"Aw shit, hurr come Tyresha big beggin ass," Hustle announced with his face frowned up as DonDon baby mama came cruising down Gamble with one of her big ugly ass friends.

"Whurr DonDon at yall? I know yall know," Tyresha asked before hitting her Newport cigarette looking high as a kite.

"We aint seen DonDon nem all day," Chad answered knowing they had jus pulled off with some lil block heads from the neighborhood about 30 minutes before she pulled up.

"So yall aint seen Heavy or DonDon all day? Yall ass lyin," Tyresha said as she dumped the ashes to her cigarette out the window with her lip turned up rolling her eyes.

"We aint lyin shid you 'ont see em out hurr do you?" I said playfully as we laughed.

"Shut up Dashon, lemme find out yall tryna cover for they dirty asses. Hustle gimme some pills, I know you got some cuz Heavy already told me he sold em all to yo ass," she replied talking hella slow cuz of the pills she had already crunched up and drank.

"Cumon Tyresha, you know them pills don't last more than a couple hours once I get em," Hustle said with a smile, knowing damn well he wasn't finna come up outa a single pill.

"Mmm lyin ass," she said rolling her eyes and flicking her Newport again.

"Lil Rodney gimme twenty dollars, my birthday was two days ago. I know you got twenty dollars Lil Rodney you can give me that," she pleaded as Lil Rodney reached in his pocket and pulled out a twenty just so the bitch could leave cuz her voice was annoying as hell.

"Man nat bitch annoyin as fuck! Whyda fuck do Don fuck wit that big silly ass bitch? I just don't get it," Hustle said once Tyresha and her friend pulled off satisfied with not leaving empty handed.

"That nigga be pullin some a the baddest bitches too. Ion't know howda fuck he deal wit that shit man foreal," Chad added just as confused about the relationship as everybody else.

"Don said it's that sloppy toppy. He say she be toppin him off all night" Rambo added as he laughed.

"Fuck that, a bitch aint puttin her mouth on my dick unless she bad. Nikki tried to let her ugly ass homegirl get down wit us a couple nights ago my dick wouldn't even get hard for that bitch," Lil Rodney said shivering at the thought of anybody actually letting Tyresha suck they dick.

"Man I need to get high, who got some blood?" Hustle asked referring to the Nyquil we used to mix the pills we crunched down with.

"We might as well mob to the store, I'm tryna get some chinamen anyway. A nigga aint ate shit in bout two days fuckin wit these bops," Rambo said rubbing his stomach before him, Hustle, and Chad headed to the corner store and chinamen at the end of the block.

"Man what cho ass been on bruh? I aint seent chu since that shit happened witchu an Trouble, wasup homie? I thought chu would've came an confided in a nigga by now. Whurr you been fool?" I said to Lil Rodney knowing he felt more comfortable talking about the shit without Chad and Hustle around.

"Ion't know man, you ended up dippin outta town then my pops start trippin wit me. Nikki ass was trippin wit me. Niggas from na zone was talkin shit. I just had to disappear for a minute" Lil Rodney explained looking down still fulla regret. "I ended up fallin out wit my pops for a minute cuz the shit was just to stressful bruh. Aint nobody really understand how fucked up my life was goin after that shit, not even him so I branched off on my own. I start puttin nem Taliban niggas on then took ova they shit. Now them niggas runnin na whole city damn ner. I just had to show pops I was my own man an nat he raised a fuckin boss. But he still come thru for a nigga when I need em tho. Shid my peoples happy I stepped up an took the torch. Now that I done made a lil name for myself I just be wrapped up in na dope game 24-7. Ten toes in na streets an way too busy to keep dwellin off that shit all day that's for damn sure," he continued, relieved that I was thurr to vent to. "Nikki ass always stressin me the fuck out actin like she gone leave a nigga cuz she scared I'ma lay her baby daddy ass down next. That nigga know not to play wit me tho. Dude keep it real respectful like he need to cuz he know damn well his son be fresh as fuck like mines be. Ion't treat em no different, I'll still lay his daddy ass down if it ever came down to it tho," he added giving me a update on him and Nikki relationship status after she watched him murder her own brother.

"So what Nikki be on? Do she be spazzin out on you behind nat shit? or she on't even bring it up?" I asked curiously tryna figure out if they was really able to maintain a romantic relationship after everything that went down.

"Hell yeah she be spazzin. She always throwin nat shit up in my face, bustin out cryin all type a bullshit. She be tryna tear me down about that shit alla time sayin she'll take my son an move outta town so he won't be shit like me when he grow up an all. Nikki be trippin, I make sure her an na kids got everything they want an need an she still make me feel like shit." he answered, realizing the guilty weight on his shoulders was almost too much to bare. "Her family don't really fuck wit her because a that shit. Half my potnas stopped fuckin wit me behind nat shit. We be feelin like we out hurr alone together but she act like we aint even on na same team most a the time. That shit be blowin me," he continued letting me know how hard it was for him and Nikki to maintain a healthy relationship after he killed Trouble.

"Yeah Rambo told me you been a lil distant ever since that shit happened, I understand tho. Hell you sposed to be but chu gotta know who rockin witchu right or wrong bruh foreal. Certain niggas that really fuck witchu gone fuck whichu regardless. Yeah it was fucked up but life goes on. If Trouble was alive I'll tell his ass the same thing. Muafuckas just gotta get past it cuz it aint no turnin back. It's not like you can change it," I responded letting him know I never took sides. "Definitely keep yo guards up tho, especially in na hood cuz it is niggas on na block pumpin Trouble name knowin you the one took him out. They jus not real quick to pop off cuz they know yo name hold weight. But that shit just too close to home for niggas anyway. You still gotta stay on point just in case one a these lil niggas decide to take a chance an try you tho. Niggas be tryna make a lil name for they self out hurr so you gotta stay cautious," I warned, confident that anybody from the hood would at least think twice before coming for him if they did have the balls to but you could never really be to sure.

"I'm hip bruh. Shid you an Rambo bout the only niggas I do trust from down hurr. Rambo don't really fuck wit them Taliban niggas tho. An ney bad blood kinda make me shy away from Rambo a lil bit just to keep the peace. Them niggas a big part a my operation an so is Rambo but Rambo can't serve the whole city on his own," he replied happy to get the issues he was having with Rambo and the Taliban niggas off his chest too.

"Think about it bruh, them Taliban niggas gone respect you cuz you pretty much the head a they operation. They not finna show Rambo that same respect when he aint even a part a they movement tho. An to make matters worse they know this yo right hand man so he definitely gettin na same shit they got for the same price if not lower," I explained breaking the whole situation down so he could get a better understanding on whurr everybody head was really at.

"Niggas stressin me the fuck out worse than my bitch damn ner. All that beefin shit be fuckin up a nigga cashflow. Chucky, Savage, an Looney asses already on na bench for who knows how long. That alone gone make a difference. I'll be damn if I lose everybody else I need out hurr ova some niggas bullshit ass egos bruh, I'm not fuckin wit it," he explained feeling overwhelmed with all the drama.

"Jus keep everybody distant bruh you doin right. Remember you dealin wit different niggas who all be on na same shit. So they typically not finna respect each other cuz the only thing that matter to them is protectin ney muafuckin territory. Shid niggas wit the same dope aint tryna be friends. That's how a nigga back door yo ass," I said with a smile letting him know the drama with Rambo and the Taliban was natural but warning him to keep that distance between em if he wanted to avoid a major conflict.

"Now you know why I been so ducked off nigga. I'm just tryna stay in na bag," he answered happy to know I understood whurr he was coming from.

"I feel you bruh. Don't forget tho Rambo gone be that nigga that rock witchu no matter what trust me. An you know I'm rockin witchu regardless. Ion't give a fuck who caught up on nat shit that happened witchu an Trouble. Chad my right-hand man so he rockin wit whoever I'm rockin wit whether he felt some type a way about the situation or not. Hustle too. Heavy, DonDon, Dre, alla them niggas. Even Drako, an Drako was Cap potna. I know Drako thru Cap but Drako still rockin wit me regardless I know that for a fact. That's the kinda niggas you keep in yo circle. Aint no way in hell a nigga I rock wit finna go against me behind some shit that aint even have nothin to do wit his ass," I preached as he stood thurr takin everything I said into consideration.

"Real nigga shit I feel you," he said as he nodded his head in agreement, knowing I had his best interest at heart.

THE CHASE

"Aye who is them bitches in nat silver drop top? They loud," Chad asked as he walked back up to me and Lil Rodney with Hustle and Rambo eating a order of wings from the chinamen.

"Damn who is that?" I asked noticing a girl with long wavy jet-black hair hopping out the driver's seat looking like a real life Barbie.

"Travis gimme the fuckin picture back, I'm na one that bought it!" she screamed as she stormed to the porch after him. Apparently Travis hopped out the back seat and ran in the house with the picture she was throwing a fit about. Travis grandma lived on Gamble but me and the rest of the niggas from na zone pretty much terrorized his ass just for fun every time we caught him on the block.

"Travis, we literally half naked on na fuckin picture you not finna keep it. You aint even pay for that muafucka!" her home girl who was sitting on the passenger's side yelled. She got out the passenger's seat after realizing they was both putting on a show and every nigga outside was watching. "This nigga straight snatched a club picture like that bitch was a fuckin $1,500 Gucci bag asumn. Who the fuck does this?" her home girl added as the girl who was driving banged on Travis grandma door.

"This some straight bullshit he got me fucked up," she said full of rage while banging on the door with her palm.

"Damn yall good? What's goin on?" Hustle asked with a smile, ready to push up on either one of they asses.

"Okay, who want a hunnit dollars to beat this nigga ass cuz he got me fucked up," The driver said as she continued to bang on the door.

"Hell yeah what that nigga do?" Chad answered somewhat serious but playing it cool like it was a joke until he knew how serious she was about it.

"Me, her, an him took these cute lil pics at the club on Halloween. We kinda like half-dressed wit our lil costumes on an he had on a suite dressed like a pimp. So we flicked it up or whatever but he just snatched the picture then ran in na house wit it," her home girl explained realizing who Hustle was instantly. She was the type that knew who all the major dope boys in the city was. She knew whurr they was from, who they bitch was, niggas side bitches, baby mama's, all that.

"Open up the door bitch!" the girl who was driving yelled after pulling a lil pink and black 380 out of one of her knee-high stiletto boots then start banging on the door with it.

"Damn, you just pulled a thumpa out cho heels? Whurr the fuck you from?" Hustle asked as Rambo and Chad stood there speechless an entertained cuz she was kinda different. It didn't seem like she was from the city for some reason. But she aint really come off like a county girl neither though. Hell I thought the bitch was from outa town asumn. I was mesmerized by her ass though. She was like a bitch I'll see on TV. It damn near felt like I was dreaming. I knew I had to have her. Her waist was hella little and her ass was hella fat. Plus she had this smooth caramel skin with no makeup on her face at all. The only thing she had on her face was some lip gloss that was making her look almost plastic. Her eyelashes flared out full and extended making the money green contacts she wore pop. She was pretty much hypnotizing any nigga tryna have a conversation with her ass I swear. Her ass was looking flawless in them gray tights and black stiletto boots she had on. She had such a small frame but her ass was outrageous so her body was just as hypnotizing as her face. Her nails was bright pink with sparkles and they was just as glossed up as her lips. Thank God it wasn't a ring on her finger cuz Lord knows it wouldn't've stopped me.

"Hold on, hold on, hold on, hold on babygirl. Whurr you think you goin wit all this ass in these heels wit this thumpa out cummer girl," I said pushing past everybody and walking all the way up on her so she could be more focused on me than anybody else. "Call my phone real quick," I said reaching for the phone she held in her hand so I could make sure I locked the number in myself.

"Look I just need you to get my fuckin picture back. Now can you get it or not?" she said before rolling her eyes and walking back to her car without letting me see the phone.

"Baby fuck that picture, I'm tryna getchu in a picture wit me. I'll tell you what, I'ma remember he took the picture you talm bout an handle that situation a lil later on down na line. Trust me, we terrorize this nigga every time he come down hurr. I aint gone forget but for right now I need you to lock this number in yo phone so you can know it's me when I call you," I said, reaching for her phone again so I could just call my phone from it myself.

"Damn you bold! I can do it!" she snapped as the police quickly hit the corner and pulled up on Gamble. "Shit!" she said quickly taking the clip out her pink 380 and throwing it in the center console.

"Everybody freeze, what's goin on? Ma'am is this your vehicle?" One of the officers asked as he approached me and her at the driver's side door. The other officer just went ahead and proceeded to harass Hustle, Rambo, Chad and Dre, who had just walked up tryna be nosey like the rest of us. Lil Rodney had slid out before I even walked over thurr basically tryna avoid the bullshit we was going through once the police pulled up. He was just as curious about em as the rest of us but he knew Gamble was too hot for all that. Shid the jump-out boys pulled up on Gamble alla time but if we aint have shit on us when they checked they aint have no choice but to let us go. We aint even have to break on they ass when they pulled up sometime, we still did outa instinct though.

"Yeah this my car officer. I'm just tryna get my picture back cuz my friend Travis snatched it out my hand then ran in na house an locked the door," the girl who was driving answered in a cute lil pouty voice that was driving me crazy.

"Hey! Deandre, don't move! Whatcha got goin on over there?" the first officer yelled, knowing us all by name at that point. He noticed Dre squirming around with his hands behind his back obviously tryna tuck something before his partner got a chance to search him. "Whatcha got there Dre?" the first officer asked, putting his hand on Dre shoulder while the other hand rested on his hip whurr the gun was.

"It's just a blunt," Dre admitted as the other officer proceeded to check Chad and Hustle.

"Get it, now!" the officer demanded as his partner began to check Rambo after checking Hustle and Chad.

Thurr, it's comin down my pants leg," Dre said with a smile as the small bag of weed fell out his jeans and onto the sidewalk.

"You did all that for a blunt of weed Dre? You must just like puttin shit in your ass huh?" the officer said playfully as they laughed. So what do you got Dashon?" the officer asked checking me but knowing I had to be clean for me not to have took off running when they hit the corner like I usually did.

"Man I jus got all my paper on me right now tryna buy my future wife affection," I answered with a smile, still hypnotized by the girl who was driving despite coming in contact with the police.

"Ma'am would you like to take this with you for your affection," the officer asked jokingly after patting me down and pulling out the big knot of money I had in my pocket.

"Shid I showl will officer. How you doin anyway you kinda cute," her home girl said flirtatiously acting like she was tryna give the officer who was checking me some pussy on some slutty shit.

"Stay away from these guys ladies. They're all assholes, nothin but trouble," the first officer said as him and his partner headed back to they car leaving the small bag of weed Dre had on the sidewalk.

"See we already got harassed by the police together an everything. I'm marryin you girl," I said playfully as the officers got in they car and pulled off.

"Yeah yall den been thru some shit together now yall gotta rock out" Rambo said jokingly, knowing I wasn't finna have it any other way.

"Yeah Dashon woulda been took off on ney ass soon as they hit the corner. This nigga must really like you," Chad added knowing how geeked up I was finna be if I actually got her number and made her my bitch.

"I like yo friend yall need to call us," Hustle said looking at her home girl who was sitting in the passenger's seat smiling from ear to ear.

"Hurr lemme call this number real quick," I said taking the phone out her hand and quickly dialing my number so I could have hers.

"Ok I'ma lock you in," she said snatching her phone back and rolling her eyes annoyed.

"Hold up I gotta make sure my phone start ringin first," I said taking the phone back out her hand swiftly before she got the chance to end the call before it went through. I was so fuckin excited and anxious to actually have her number I couldn't even control my aggression for it. I was just obsessed with everything about her. She had this lil cute ass attitude, then the way she was walking in them heels drove me crazy. Her voice gave me chills, and she had this sweet seductive ass smell that was intoxicating the fuck outa me. It was all any of us could smell in the midst of all the bullshit going on with the police. There was no way in hell I was letting her pull off without making sure I had her number in my phone.

"It's ringin damn, now let me go. I'm tryna get the fuck away from hurr" she said snatching her phone back even more annoyed with how assertive I was about it. She got back in the driver's seat while her home girl sat on the passenger's side with a grin, knowing this was the start of something even though the girl I was so obsessed with didn't seem interested at all.

"What's yo name anyway?" I asked ready to lock her number in my phone under wifey right then and thurr.

"It's Babydoll, I'll call you," she said rolling her eyes while briefly checking the mirror to make sure her hair was still perfect I guess. She put the car in drive and pulled off without even asking what's mine but that was ok cuz I still had her number. I figured she heard the police call me by my name anyway. And I knew she would know who I was when I called her so I was still hella happy.

"Aye you better get her pregnant nigga, we damn ner just got booked fuckin wit they ass," Dre said jokingly picking the small bag of weed up off the sidewalk.

"We definitely gotta link up wit they ass bruh, ol girl was bad then a muafucka. You need to call her tonight foreal. We need to pullup on ney ass asap. I'm tryna see what her home girl on cuz that lil bitch cute as fuck too an she a lil freak. I can tell by the way she was lookin at me," Hustle said filled with excitement and wonder.

"Yeah I know one thing nigga – you better at least get some pussy after all that shit. Man nat damn girl gone have yo nose wide open watch. She already gotchu sleepin on na jump-out boys," Rambo said playfully as I stood thurr staring at her number.

"Man fuck you nigga, whyda fuck you aint see em pullup fool. You sposed to be on point for me but chu let em pop up on a nigga while I'm standin in na street wit my dick in my hands goosin, pants down like a muafucka," I joked pushing him playfully as we laughed.

"Now this nigga finna be smellin na roses wit his head in na clouds. Ol sucka fa love ass nigga hurr," Chad said rolling his eyes as I zoned out waiting for the perfect time to call her.

"Biiiiitch, do you know who the fuck that was? We is callin ney ass tonight! Go to my house so I can change clothes," her home girl said as they cruised through the northside looking for anybody they knew had some weed.

"Ion't know Bre, he kinda pushy. He just seem like too much of a controllin type it's kinda annoyin. Why you crushin on his friend so hard tho?" Babydoll asked curious as to why Bre felt the need to change clothes and get all dressed up just to see Hustle again.

"Girl that's Hustle, that nigga got all money. His baby mama name Latoya, that bitch be laced I'm talm bout fresh as fuck. He keep that bitch in all designer shid I'm tryna be like her. Hoe we can share," Bre said jokingly but actually pretty serious.

"Ion't know Bre, you heard what that cop said. An ney do seem like trouble. I mean na police just busted out an searched alla them for no reason at all. Then you just gotta trip off how the fuckin officers knew alla they ass by name. So they already know what them niggas be on, they got to. Them niggas probably hella cocky, hella arrogant, hella obnoxious. Hell you can already tell they is an we wasn't even aroun em that long. I know them niggas trouble Bre. I'm tellin you be careful wit him," Babydoll warned as Bre sat thurr taking nothing she was saying into consideration. Bre was a couple years younger than Babydoll but they made good friends. Babydoll was kinda chill and laid back usually while Bre was more loud and outspoken so they kinda balanced each other out. Bre was real petite, a lil smaller than Babydoll. She was a lil bit taller than her too but not much. She had a pretty face and a cute lil smile but she was just hella loud though. She kinda had that lil cute ghetto girl swag that Hustle seemed to be so attracted to cuz that's how Latoya acted too.

"Look Babydoll, all you gotta do is call him. We ridin aroun na city lookin for some weed when I know for a fact them niggas'll pull right up wit some right now if we call em. They'll be pullin up in 2.2 minutes bitch," Bre explained trying her hardest to get Babydoll on board to link up with us.

"Ion't like him Bre, he jus kinda get up under my skin a lil bit," Babydoll replied, annoyed that Bre seemed to be so infatuated with some niggas like us.

"Oh my God Babydoll, he will literally give you whatever the fuck you want. That nigga was on you. You can get anything you want outta his ass. If you want that nigga to get cho hair done tell em to get that shit done for you I bet he do it. If you want that nigga to pullup wit some weed I bet he pullup wit some. Why wouldn't you want a nigga on yo side that can help you out wit whatever you need or want. I know you bossin up on yo own an shit, especially after you den cashed out on nis car but at least make the nigga give you some gas money damn. Let em help you out wit lil shit so you can keep savin yo lil money for yo crib. He fuck aroun an furnish that muafucka for you. Just be like baby me an my daughter jus moved out my mama crib an we need this an nat. Yo baby finna have her own lil room too, yall could be laid up in nat muafucka nice an comfortable," Bre explained painting a perfect lil picture for Babydoll and not taking no for an answer about calling us. Bre would've talked my baby ear off all night if she hadn't agreed to linkup with our ass at least just to smoke real quick if nothing else.

"Girl I do not need that nigga gettin shit for my crib. He'll fuck aroun an think that's his shit if he do all that. An aint no muafucka name finna be on nis lease outside a me an my baby name – flatout fuck that. He'll have me alla way fucked up. That's why I waited til I saved up enough for my deposit, plus my first an last month's rent so I can blow my whole income tax check on my furniture. I already got the money for my baby bedroom set an all. Shid I'm waitin on income tax to drop like a muafucka. That's gone cover everything else. I still need to keep stackin if I want big ass flat screens all aroun nat muafucka tho. I need to get pumped up for work tonight so I can go finesse these white boys outta all they fuckin money. I'm tryna have that muafucka plush," Babydoll said as they pulled up in front of Bre house. "Go ask your loser boyfriend if he got some fuckin weed. The northside dry as fuck when you want some weed allasudden cuz alla street niggas wanna sell dope now," Babydoll said playfully making Bre laugh.

Bre boyfriend was another street nigga who stood on the corner of his set with his boys all day looking for trouble. He sold all types a different drugs to support Bre habit and his own cuz all Bre needed was some pills to crunch down on a regular and so did he. They was chasing the same high we was chasing. Corey kept her ass high just so she wouldn't question him about all the other bitches she knew he was fucking. She really wasn't questioning him cuz she was sneaking around fucking whoever she wanted to fuck too though. "Girl that nigga aint got no weed he probably not even hurr. I'm tellin you call Hustle nem they pullin right up," Bre insisted, knowing them needing weed was the perfect excuse to call us.

"Bre they can't pull up over hurr! What if Corey come home?" Babydoll said worried about what Corey would do to Bre if she let some niggas like us pull up at his crib and he found out. Corey used to beat Bre ass an Babydoll knew it. She would always encourage Bre to leave him, urging her to do better but Corey just had Bre heart some type a way so she never took Babydoll's advice.

"Girl fuck Corey! He havent' even been comin home foreal. His ass don't even sleep hurr half the time. He fuckin wit this rachet ass bitch from his hood an shit. Ion't know why he think I'm stupid an don't know. The bitch always out thurr when I pullup to get some money an I know damn well she aint muggin nat hard for nothin," Bre confessed letting Babydoll know how much worse things had gotten between the two of them and ready to get high so she wouldn't even have to think about it.

"Oh my God, girl why this him callin right now" Babydoll announced when I called.

"Biiiitch! Answer the phone tell em to pullup wit some weed," Bre said happily smiling from ear to ear.

"This the type a shit I'm talkin bout Bre, I specifically said I was gone call him. Now hurr he go callin anyway like I was just takin too long to call," Babydoll said hesitating to answer the phone but wanting to cheer Bre up a lil bit cuz she did feel kinda sorry for her. She knew Bre was trippin off Corey and the bitch from his hood more than she made it seem. And despite how much of a dick he was Bre feelings was still hurt cuz she loved him. Babydoll felt like maybe Bre needed Hustle in order to finally get over Corey so she just went ahead and answered. "You is so hard-headed, I said I was gone call you," Babydoll said when she picked up the phone making my heart drop to my stomach the moment I heard her voice.

"I jus gotta see you again an I can't wait," I replied with a smile, hoping to loosen her up a lil bit so I could put a smile on her face too.

"Whatever do yall got some weed? I need to smoke before I go to work tonight an my girl Bre said wasup whicho homeboy," Babydoll responded rolling her eyes at Bre who was sitting in the passenger's seat lit up with excitement. She keep quiet and played it cool until we got off the phone though.

"Hell yeah we got weed on deck baby, rapper weed, best in the city. Whurr yall at? We finna pullup," I answered lit up with excitement myself knowing I was finna see her sexy ass again.

"I'ma text you," she said before hanging up in my face without letting me say another word. "You sure you wanna do this Bre? Cuz this could get messy," Babydoll warned, giving Bre another chance to think about whether she really wanted us to pull up at her crib after just meeting us earlier that day.

"Bitch I am sendin them this muafuckin address you crazy. Them niggas finna pull right up like I said they would," Bre answered with a smile, taking the phone from Babydoll and texting her address to mine. "Cumon, I probably don't even got no time to change. I know they finna pull right up," Bre added encouraging Babydoll to come in the house to help her find a cuter outfit before quickly hopping out the car.

"What the fuck Bre? I thought chu said Corey was gone," Babydoll said in a hushed tone after hearing Corey and his friend talking in the back room when they got in the house.

"Wasup Babydoll, when you gone stop playin an let a real nigga hit," Corey friend Trigger said as he walked towards the front door with a book bag hanging off his shoulder looking like he was up to no good.

"Boy please. You jus tryna check my name off yo hit list gone Trigger," Babydoll said playfully rolling her eyes with a smile. She was always polite to Corey and his friends when she saw em even though she couldn't stand they asses. But out of respect for Bre she still played it cool and kept it cute with em so nobody would feel uncomfortable.

"Naw you the main name on na fuckin list. I'm circlin nat muafucka, fuck around an highlight that bitch," he said jokingly before walking out the front door and across the street to his car.

"I'ma be back later Bre, I gotta go take care a some business" Corey said as he headed out the door behind Trigger.

"See he jus act so weird an distant like wasup? I can't stand his ass sometimes man he aint leave me no money for food or nothin, knowin it aint no food in nis muafucka. I bet he got a pocket fulla money tho, niggas aint shit I swear," Bre said once Corey walked out the door and pulled off with Trigger.

"Bitch you cannot be textin yo address to niggas talm bout pullup an you on't even know if Corey hurr or not. What if them niggas woulda pulled up while Trigger nem was walkin to the car. That don't look right Bre, niggas like them'll get sketched out then start thinkin you tryna set they ass up asumn," Babydoll explained stressing how messy it could get if we ever ran into Corey nem at Bre house.

"Girl fuck Corey cheatin ass this my shit anyway, his name aint on no muafuckin lease an he don't pay rent hurr. I paid my rent up for two years when I turned eighteen an got my settlement check for this accident I was in when I was little cuz you cannot depend on a nigga to pay yo rent. Niggas'll be ghost on yo ass every time na first a the month roll aroun trust me. Corey don't do shit but pay these lil cheap ass lil bills aroun nis muafucka. Hell I can get Hustle to do that shit!" Bre vented, still feeling some type a way about how Corey had been acting and treating her lately. She was pretty much unbothered by it since me and Hustle was on our way over thurr though.

"Speakin of Hustle, I'm pretty sure this them that just pulled up in nis Charger," Babydoll announced watching us pull up in the same parking spot Trigger and Corey had just pulled out of. Hustle was on the passenger's side with the window cracked, dumping the tobacco out the cigarello he broke down.

"Fuck, I aint even get to change! Corey dirty ass threw me off," Bre said putting out the cigarette she had just lit up and running to the bathroom to fix her hair.

"Bre we need to go out to they car, ion't think you should let em come in. What if Corey pull back up?" Babydoll said nervously, not wanting to be in the middle of the situation if it did end up going down like that. She felt like she would've looked like the ringleader having some niggas that called her phone pull up even though Bre was the one who sent the address.

"Cumon Babydoll, why would he come right back an he just left," Bre said smiling as she played with her hair in the mirror.

"What if he forgot sumn Bre? If he walk in while they in hurr neither one a them niggas gone trust us. They all gone think we some fuckin setup artist an take us out. That's how bitches get kilt," Babydoll said smiling but serious. She knew the situation could get outta control if Corey caught us in that house. And the last thing she wanted was for her and Bre to get caught up in a incident whurr niggas like us was invading another nigga territory cuz you just never know how that shit'll go until it happen.

"We comin outside now," Babydoll said before hanging up in my face again when I called her phone to tell her we was outside.

"You so damn scary cumon," Bre said playfully as they headed out the door.

"Cum sit back hurr wit me Bre," Hustle said getting out the passenger's seat and getting in the back.

"Oh what a gentleman," Babydoll said sarcastically rolling her eyes with a smile before getting in the passenger's seat.

"Yeah we some gentlemen. We gone cater to yall every need jus get in an lay back baby. You need help whicho seatbelt? Hurr lemme help you," I said jokingly before reaching my hand all over her body playing like I was tryna help her buckle her seatbelt. I was obviously just tryna touch her hips and ass though. She was so fucking soft and way too close for me not to touch and grab on her ass like I wanted to.

"No I don't need help wit my seatbelt!" Babydoll said pushing my hand away from her ass trying not to smile.

"Aw my bad wifey, I was jus tryna help you out cuz ion't want chu liftin a finger when you wit me baby that's all," I said with a evil grin realizing how pretty her smile was. Hustle had just passed her the blunt making her ass a lot more smiley alla sudden.

"Damn whurr we goin? You just pulled off like yall kidnappin a bitch asumn," Bre said playfully with her legs crossed and propped up on Hustle while he lit up another rolled blunt and passed it to her.

"Jus lay back Bre we in traffic. Yall need to sit back an chill, lemme operate the vehicle. I'ma make sure yall get back home safe trust me," I said looking over at Babydoll while she sat in the passenger's seat comfortably. She had one leg folded up under the other with her back leaning up against the passenger's side door.

"Don't look at me, drive!" she said with this sexy ass smirk on her face moving the leg that wasn't folded side to side tryna be funny.

"Girl you gone make me straight get at cho lil sexy ass quit playin wit me," I said reaching over and grabbing her pussy through her tights like she was acting like she wanted me to do.

"Boy you is not no gentleman," she said pushing my hand away playfully.

"Lemme show you sumn," I said grabbing her hand and placing it on my dick so she could see how big and hard it was for her.

"You play too much, why is yo whole dick out?" Babydoll shouted as the song we was blasting ended. So Hustle and Bre Just happened to catch exactly what she was saying loud and clear.

"Wait what? Nigga you sposed to be drivin bruh. What type a freaky shit is you on up thurr man. Maybe I need to drive so yall can get back hurr if yall got all that goin on straight up," Hustle said jokingly as everybody laughed.

"Seriously tho, yall need to stop saggin so much. I can literally see yo whole boxers damn ner. Do you own a belt?" Babydoll asked noticing how my entire dick was exposed. It was clearly showing through my boxers since my Robin jeans was damn near saggin to my knees.

"We street niggas Babydoll we let our pants sag. That's just how we is," Hustle said with a smile holding Bre legs on top of his comfortably in the back.

"Whatever, that aint cute jus so yall know," Babydoll said playfully.

"Aye who is that in nis Impala bruh? That aint Heavy nem in ner. Heavy shit is not that tinted up," I said noticing the all black Impala behind me hitting every corner I hit.

"Aye yall gotta sit back for a minute, he finna have to lose this car real quick," Hustle said placing Bre legs gently in the space beside him.

"Whatchu mean sit back?" Bre asked sitting up and looking through the back windshield.

Whatchu mean he gotta lose this car? who is that?" Babydoll asked feeling like the night had definitely just took a turn for the worse fuckin with our asses.

"When I hit this next corner I'm takin off. So sit back, buckle up, or brace yall self foreal," I said ready to take off right then and thurr. I was determined to get the girls back home safely like I said I would knowing I could out drive whoever was behind me.

CAUGHT UP

"You sure that aint task force bruh? Them windows hella tinted," Hustle said tryna get a better view of who was following us but it was too dark and the windows was blacked out.

"Ion't know but I'm gone bruh," I said taking off at top speed itching to shake they ass real quick whoever the fuck it was.

"Fuck! They straight followin us, they on our ass too. What the fuck man nis some bullshit," Bre said in a panic after looking out the back windshield again.

"Run nis light bruh," Hustle said pointing to the red stop light straight ahead.

"I know nigga! I got this bruh," I answered fully focused on the road ahead and dodging every accident I came across by literally half a second out of pure instinct. I had pretty much lost the Impala at the light. But I kept driving like it was still following behind me cuz it's kinda hard to snap back out of that getaway mode once I get started. Hell I aint snap up out that shit til we pulled back up on Bre street.

"Man nis Rambo ass I wonder what the fuck he want. It's too much goin on right now homie," I said before picking up the flip phone that was sitting in the cup holder ringing.

"Man you a fool behind nat wheel bruh! On na set," Rambo said soon as I answered the phone while Chad was in the background hyping the shit up to DonDon on his phone.

"Nigga that was yall? Why you playin Rambo. You know you not finna getup on me fool. I damn ner made yo ass wrap that muafucka up while yall in nat muafucka playin," I said as we laughed. I put the phone on speaker so

Hustle and the girls could hear the conversation and get a good laugh outa the shit too.

"Man when I say you had this nigga so spent after you hit that light bruh. That shit was epic. I wish I coulda took a picture a this nigga face the shit was so funny," Chad said still laughing his ass off about the look on Rambo's face when I shook his ass. "This nigga aint know what to do," Chad added while everybody laughed.

"Yall play too much, like why would yall do that?" Babydoll said in a cute lil pouty voice relieved that we aint really have nobody tryna chase us down and kill us.

"Yall straight do the most, I damn near pissed on myself cuz yall wanna play games. I can't stand yall ass," Bre whined as we all continued to laugh.

"Aye you know I wasn't worried bout shit while he drivin. Now if it was me behind na wheel you prolly woulda made me wrap my shit up playin like that nigga. I'd a had to come see ya lil midget ass behind nat shit," Hustle joked teasing Rambo about his height. Rambo wasn't really that short but he was the shortest outa all of us so we always made jokes about his height.

"Naw fuck that bruh, I gotta keep yall niggas on point out hurr. If ya fuck ya shit up that's on yo ass. You'll jus have to come see me homie wasup?" Rambo said jokingly, laughing so hard he could barely even drive.

"Man we got all pussy an ass in nis muafucka while yall in ner playin. You niggas still can't catch me lackin, it's just not gone happen bruh," I said with a smile, reaching over and grabbing Babydoll pussy through her tights again.

"Gone Dashon, yall play too much foreal," she said pushing my hand away playfully.

"Babydoll ass was sittin up thurr tryna play it all cool an shit knowin damn well she was scared, heart beatin like a muafucka huh Babydoll?" Hustle teased as we all kept laughing.

"I was quiet cuz I was prayin you stupid fuck! I thought we was finna fuckin die," Babydoll answered playfully not realizing how geeked up I was that she actually said my name cuz she never did ask me what it was.

"Yall I was literally back hurr finna piss on myself I need to go pee. Come put a pack down wit me before you leave Hustle. I know you got some pills an na Nyquil right thurr on na floor. This half a bottle too," Bre said picking the

Nyquil bottle up from under the driver's seat. "It's some juice in ner cumon," Bre added opening the back door encouraging the rest of us to follow her in the house.

"We finna pullup on yall niggas in a minute bruh," I said before hanging up the phone and getting out the car.

"Who all live hurr?" Hustle asked as Babydoll gave Bre a dirty look hoping Bre wouldn't lie about it.

"This my shit, I can have whoever I want come over ok. An why would we keep sittin in na car when I got a whole crib," Bre answered, taking the key outa her purse then opening the door with it.

"I'm finna leave in a minute tho I gotta go to work" Babydoll announced as Hustle handed her another blunt to roll.

"Whurr you work at?" I asked curiously as I watched her break down the rello before dumping the tobacco in the trash.

"I work at the strip club, it's a white strip club tho. I'm like a waitress but ion't bring drinks. I just go aroun na club an give the dudes massages for ten dollars a song while they drink an watch the dancers," she explained while me and Hustle stood thurr tryna process what the hell she was saying. We was unsure about if she was really telling us what she did thurr or just playing on our intelligence.

"Ten dollars a song? What kinda massages they be gettin for ten dollars a song?" Hustle asked with a smile assuming she was just fuckin with our heads or joking around.

"I sit on na back of they chair an rub they shoulders while they watch the dancers. Then when na song go off I ask em if they want me to stay for another song. If they like me they buy more songs. If not they give me my ten dollars an tell me to fuckoff," she said shrugging her shoulders with a smile.

"So they just give you ten dollars to sit on ney chair an rub they shoulders?" I asked, wanting just a lil bit more clarity about what she was saying her job description was at this strip club I had never even heard of before.

"Yeah, they sign my clipboard agreein to pay for at least the first song. Then they just tell me how many songs they want as I go," she answered, seeming pretty serious so it was kinda hard to tell if she was bull shittin or not.

"So Babydoll, you tellin me you'ont dance? Now if we popup in nat muafucka you sayin we aint gone find out you really just a stripper right?" Hustle asked playfully tryna see if she was bluffing so he could call her ass out if we ended up catching her on stage ass naked.

"She is not a stripper honey, Babydoll don't even like nobody touchin her foreal. She still be finessin all them white boys outta all they fuckin money tho. My bitch bad fuck yall thought," Bre said flipping her hair before giving Babydoll a high five to encourage her.

"So what if I came up thurr to see you," I asked curious to see how she would respond.

"You better have at least ten dollars nigga! Matter fact you need to buy like ten songs so you can sit between my legs an chill for a minute. Bring $100 so I can get comfortable an not have to keep askin if you want another song everytime one go off," she answered making me feel like maybe she wasn't bull shitting after all.

"We comin up thurr Babydoll, don't be lookin all crazy when we find out you a stripper," Hustle said playfully as Babydoll put her middle finger up with a smile.

"Whatever, yall need to jus lemme take this blunt tho. I need to keep sparkin nis muafucka up in na dressin room throughout the night. This all I really need foreal. I hit the blunt a couple times an be juiced up, if Iont got no weed in my system I aint gone wanna be bothered tho," Babydoll answered as she finished rolling the blunt Hustle handed her.

"You can gone head take it then, weed grow on trees aroun hurr Babydoll," Hustle answered winking his eye at her with a smile as Babydoll rolled her eyes and headed to the door.

"Call me ho!" Bre yelled as I followed Babydoll out to her car.

"I need to see you again like asap," I said disappointed that she had to leave so soon but determined to see her again as soon as possible.

"I thought chu was comin up to my job to see me," she said tryna see if I was for real about going up thurr later on that night.

"You really want me to come up thurr an see you?" I asked hoping I wouldn't find out nothing outside of what she told me if I did.

"If you want to, I mean it'll be fun for me cuz it'll make my shift go by faster," she answered pulling me closer so I could give her a hug goodbye.

"Iight I'ma see you later then," I said getting a good grip of her ass when I hugged her. I was ready to just pick her lil ass up and fuck her right thurr on the hood of the car.

"Cumon bruh yall in nis muafucka cakin an shit. My lil piece then burnt out on me, I'm ready to shake too shid I'm mad then a muafucka," I said after walking back in the house tryna rush Hustle out the door just cuz Babydoll shook on my ass.

"Shutup Dashon just sit down an get high wit us damn! Babydoll ass aint goin nowher chill, you'll see her tomorrow," Bre said before taking a sip from the bottle of Nyquil mixed with hella perks and blue Kool-aid.

"Naw we gone endup goin up thurr tonight. I wanna see if she a stripper or not," Hustle said playfully but serious.

"I'm tellin yall she not no stripper, if she was we would just say that. Shid we'ont knock no strippers Hustle. If I had the nerve I'll get up on nat stage too an so would Babydoll," Bre responded as she handed me the Nyquil after taking another sip.

"Who the fuck is that Bre?" Hustle asked in a panic as Corey walked right through the front door after turning the key to get in. He had a confused look on his face but I noticed a whole mack ten on the nigga waist that he wasn't even clutching or reaching for surprisingly.

"Wasup homie?" Corey said as he nodded his head at Hustle oddly showing no emotion at all for some reason.

"Shit, we was just leavin bro," Hustle replied quickly getting up out the chair he was sitting in by the kitchen table. "Cumon Dashon," Hustle said as we headed to the front door with caution.

"Iight Bre," I said before closing the door behind me and running to the car behind Hustle.

"Man what the fuck Bre on bruh? That nigga straight turnt the key on our ass," Hustle blurted out as we pulled off headed towards Gamble.

"He showl the fuck did, I know damn well I locked the door behind me when I came in. Ion't know what that bitch was on bruh," I said feeling relieved that we got up outa thurr without catching a body. I fuck around would've had to park Bre ass too not knowing if she was gone rat us out or not.

"Man whyda fuck wouldn't she tell me a nigga wit a key stay thurr. I specifically asked her who all live thurr. She shoulda just kept it ahunnit wit me that's that bullshit man a bitch'll getchu fucked up quick, on Cap. She dead ass wrong for that shit man," Hustle said feeling a lil disappointed cuz he actually did really like Bre.

"Yeah that bitch on all bullshit, the nigga had a whole mack on his hip bruh. It kinda seem like he already knew who you was tho didn't it?" I asked realizing the nigga wasn't too quick to go wrong with our ass even though we was basically in his crib with his bitch chilling like it was our shit.

"It did seem like the nigga knew sumn you showl right. I thought it was finna be all bullshit when he walked in. I know if I walk in my crib an Latoya got two niggas Ion't know in my shit I'm goin in niggas pockets, strippin niggas down to they draws all type a bullshit. Niggas'll be leavin my shit ass naked an barefoot fuckin wit me," Hustle said shaking up the bottle of Nyquil, perks, and koolaid before taking another sip.

"Niggas be knowin bruh, especially if they out hurr ten toes in na street like we is. You know who all out hurr chasin nat bag if that's whatchu out hurr on fa sho," I said as Hustle handed me the bottle after taking a big gulp.

"Man fuck that shit, that nigga aint won't no smoke. Wasup wit chu an Babydoll tho? We pullin up at the gig or what? I think the bitch a stripper an I showl wouldn't mind watchin her get naked an shake her ass on stage for a nigga," Hustle said jokingly but tryna make sure we was really going up thurr before the night was over.

"Yeah we finna pullup on na gang then we all jus gone mob up thurr real quick," I said pulling up on Gamble whurr Rambo, Chad, DonDon, Heavy and Dre was all standing around passing a couple blunts in a circle.

"Whaddup fool, I heard you stumbled up on some new pussy today whurr she at? I wanna meet her," Heavy said playfully as he shook my hand to greet me.

"Yeah I hurr she look like a lil video vixen too, set that out bruh," DonDon said smiling as I shook his hand to greet him.

"Fuck naw nigga that's wifey, we is finna pullup at her job tho," I said feeling a lil nervous about the whole squad finding out if she was really a stripper or not cuz I was hella unsure myself.

"Whurr she work at?" DonDon asked curiously.

"Man she say she work at the strip club but she'ont strip," Hustle said indicating she was lying by the expression on his face.

"What she sposed to be a bartender? or one a them bottle girls that be bringin niggas drinks an shit, like a waitress?" Heavy asked, eager to know more about Babydoll cuz he had been hearing about her ass all day. The whole hood was talking about how Babydoll and Bre just popped up on Gamble outa nowhurr. Then they damn near got everybody booked cuz we was all so distracted by em when the police pulled up which was kind of a red flag.

"She said she do massages bruh, she sit on na back a niggas chairs an rub they shoulders," I answered finding it kinda hard to explain what she did.

"Wait a minute what? She do massages at the strip club? What strip club she work at?" DonDon asked entertained by the whole conversation.

"What she jackin niggas dicks in nat muafucka asumn?" Chad asked amused as him and Rambo had a good laugh making Dre, DonDon, and Heavy bust out laughing too.

"Ion't know man she work at this white strip club, I aint never even heard a that muafucka. So Ion't know what they got goin on in ner I'm showl finna see tho," I said ready to finally get to the bottom of the shit so I could know what she was really doing at work.

"Man nat bitch lyin bruh, she a stripper! All that ass she got aint no way she workin at the strip club an aint hittin na stage," Rambo blurted out feeling certain that Babydoll was fulla shit for telling us she didn't dance.

"She prolly is fulla shit tho cuz her homegirl showl is," Hustle announced as Dre passed him one of the blunts that was in rotation.

"Wasup wit her homegirl?" Heavy asked curiously, ready for Hustle to spill the tea on Bre ass too.

"Man we was just at this bitch crib an a nigga walked right thru the front door wit a whole mack on em bruh. Turnt the key an everything," Hustle explained after hitting the blunt a couple times then passing it to Chad.

"Whoa, whoa, whoa,!" everybody blurted out at once.

"Whatchu mean he walked in wit a mack on em what happened?" Rambo asked ready to talk a boat load of shit to us for lacking on a count of these same bitches again.

"Shit! Dude said wasup an we burnt out," Hustle answered shrugging his shoulders like it was nothing.

"Man I told yall don't be lackin wit them bitches bruh. You niggas be too distracted fuckin wit them hoes yall better be careful," Rambo preached, feeling concerned about the way Babydoll and Bre seemed to just have us so unfocused.

"Yeah ion't know about them bruh, they prolly got too much goin on," Chad added voicing his concern.

"That's that problematic pussy nigga it's gone be a problem bruh," Don-Don said with a smile even though he was just as concerned as everybody else.

"I jus really wanna know if this bitch a stripper or not. Howda hell she doin massages at the strip club? That on't even make sense bruh," Heavy blurted out feeling confused as DonDon passed him the blunt.

"Man me too I aint even gone lie, I jus never heard a no shit like this before," Dre added putting his lil two cents in curious to see how all this shit was finna play out.

"We goin up thurr bruh foreal fuck that, we need to find out a lil more about these hoes," Chad said ready to find out everything he could about both a they asses at that point.

"Hell yeah, we hittin nat muafucka fa sho," Rambo added after hitting the blunt a few times then passing it to me.

"Come on yall we finna slide," Hustle said hitting the blunt Dre passed to him one last time before throwing it on the ground.

"Iight we finna follow yall, come on let's go," DonDon said eagerly walking to the car with Dre and his brother.

"We jus finna hop in wit chall," Chad said as him and Rambo followed me and Hustle to the car. "What the fuck they be playin in nis muafucka country music?" Chad asked as we pulled up to the strip club Babydoll worked at with Heavy, Dre, and DonDon trailing behind us.

"Damn it's all cowboys an shit up hurr. I wonder what they be on shid we can get some new geeks up out this muafucka matter a fact, big dog geeks too. Look at ol boy I know he get down," Rambo said sizing up the white boy walking to his BMW with this lil pretty blonde stripper bitch.

"Naw bruh, we'ont know how hot this muafucka is or nothin. We already stickin out like a sore thumb cuz it's all corny-ass white boys in nis bitch. Now hurr we go comin up in na mix kinda deep lookin all thugged out like we finna take sumn," I said with a smile but feeling a lil nervous for some reason. "We jus need to play it cool, go in ner for bout a hour, get a couple drinks an jus scope it out a lil bit so I can see what she really be doin in hurr. Ion't wanna draw no unnecessary attention tho bruh I'm already uncomfortable," I said as Rambo rolled his eyes knowing I was right so choosing not to even argue with me about the shit.

"Man Babydoll got cho ass buggin whatchu mean you uncomfortable? Nigga if you 'ont get cho uncomfortable ass out this car! Fuck these goofy-ass white boys nigga we in nis bitch," Hustle said playfully as he opened the passenger's side door and got out.

"Man she probably not even in hurr. What if she got us on a whole mission for nothin? He gone fuck aroun an still be tryna fuck wit the bitch watch. She finna take yo ass on a ride bruh I'm tellin you" Chad said making me even more nervous and anxious to find out what was really going on.

"What's this some country-ass rock n roll-ass shit bruh? It's all weird-ass white boys up in nis muafucka," Heavy said as him, DonDon, and Dre approached us in the parking lot.

"Man nis shit finna be hella entertainin, waitress bring me a drink! Lemme sip on me sumn while I watch this shit unfold," DonDon said playfully as we walked to the door altogether.

"Whurr she at bruh?" Heavy asked ready to finally see who we drove all the way to the eastside to basically spy on.

"Ion't see her," I answered looking around the club feeling like I wanted to just turn around and leave so I wouldn't get let down.

"Thurr she go," Dre said pointing her out as she was walking out of the dressing room with a clipboard in her hand.

"Yeah that's her," Hustle said just as mesmerized as the rest of us.

"Damn bruh she is bad as fuck shid I can see why you trippin off her lil ass so hard," DonDon said as I zoned out feelin like everybody else in the building just disappeared for a minute. I couldn't see nobody but her.

"Wow you actually came. Hi yall," she said approaching us with a smile as I quickly snapped out the daze I was in.

"I told you I was comin girl, I gotta make sure you safe in hurr" Ireplied falling for her more and more every second she was in my presence.

"Yeah right, you came up hurr to see if I was a fuckin stripper!" she said pushing Hustle playfully.

"Look sis, we had to come see for ourselves. I mean you do kinda look like a stripper, howda hell was we sposed to know you wasn't lyin," Hustle explained with a smile as Babydoll playfully rolled her eyes.

"Gee thanks Hustle" Babydoll said sarcastically nodding her head like she understood.

"You is so beautiful baby girl, I can see why my brother like you so much," Heavy said charmingly as he shook Babydoll's handd tryna act like a gentleman.

"Awww thank you, you so sweet," she said blushing with that pretty ass smile she had on her face.

"Aye if he fuckup call me, you probably gone like me better than him anyway. It's ok tho he understand," DonDon said jokingly as Babydoll giggled, already knowing he was probably the most playful.

"Hey Barbie, Lala, Star! Come over here an entertain my friends," Babydoll said inviting the three strippers who had just walked out the dressing room together over to whurr we was at.

"Oh shit lemme see what this lil snow bunny talm bout," DonDon said sizing up Barbie as she walked up to him flirtatiously.

"Yeah I want lil miss Asian persuasion over hurr tho," Hustle said with a grin as Lala walked over directing him to sit down in the chair behind him before sitting on his lap.

"Shiiid, don't nothin beat dark meat," Heavy said with a smile as Star walked over to him with confidence. Star was the only black stripper thurr but she was definitely the most beautiful. She had dark brown smooth skin and long dreads with hazel eyes. She had a slim figure but just slightly more curvy than the white girl and the asian bitch. Standing next to Babydoll her body looked more like a stick figure though. It did seem like Babydoll was supposed to be the one on stage dancing and walking around in them skimpy lil outfits the dancers had on. But she had on some fishnet stockings with some lil black and red boy shorts on and a black lace shirt that exposed her red bra. Her heels was red too and they had her ass sitting up perfectly.

"Do you want a massage? It's soothing an it's only ten dollars," Babydoll looked at me and asked with a smile, talking like a lil preppy cheerleader or something but it was cute.

"Yeah cumon," I said pulling her close to me and grabbing her ass at a angle whurr Rambo, Chad and Dre could see how fat that muafucka was.

"Ok sign my clipboard," she said happily as we went to a seat a couple tables over and sat down.

"Aye Babydoll, wasup wit the drinks?" Dre asked wit his hands up realizing a waitress hadn't came to they table and asked them what they wanted yet.

"Hey Roxy, get them," Babydoll said to the cute lil waitress walking by with red hair and freckles.

"Hi boys, whatcha drinkin?" the waitress asked approaching Chad, Dre, and Rambo's table.

"So they sit hurr between yo legs while you do this shit?" I asked as she climbed on the back of the chair I was sitting in. "An why I had to sign nat stupid-ass clipboard?" I asked curiously as she started rubbing all on my chest and shoulders. "It's just so they can get they cut at the end of the night"

"An yeah they sit in between my legs, I jus stay up hurr til they on't want no more songs shid now do you want another song or not?" she said playfully as we laughed

"Why it's so warm? My back warm as fuck like I'm sittin in front of a heater or sumn," I said with a smile getting more and more aroused the longer I sat between her legs.

"I gotta keep you warm baby so you can keep gettin songs. When I getup you gone be cold," she said seductively, talking closely into my ear so I could hear her over all the stupid-ass music they was playing. Her bottom lip rubbed sensually on my earlobe while she talked making me zone out all over again.

"I wantchu so bad girl you'ont even know," I said feeling like we was the only two people in the club again.

"She finna have this nigga nose wide open I swear," Rambo said shaking his head as him, Chad, and Dre watched us from the table they was sitting at.

"Nigga finna be smellin all roses aroun nis bitch," Chad added as he took a sip of his Hennessy and coke knowing I was falling for her ass too fast.

"Yeah she got his ass goin, he better be careful wit that one," Dre agreed, sipping on his Ciroc and cranberry just enjoying the view. Babydoll ass was propped up perfectly on my seat at a angle whurr all three of them could see. Hustle, Heavy, and DonDon was already being entertained by her lil stripper friends so they wasn't really paying no attention. But Rambo, Chad and Dre showl was.

"You know ol boy walked in on us while we was ova thurr at Bre house earlier," I said tryna see if she was already gone know who I was talking about when I said ol boy.

"Are you fuckin serious! Corey walked in! What happened?" she asked with her eyes wide open ready to hear what happened next.

"Dude jus walked in, said wasup, an we shook that muafucka. Dude had a whole mack on em tho. I thought he was finna buck that muafucka out on us at first but he was cool about it so we just left," I explained as she sat on the chair behind me puzzled.

"Damn I'm sorry yall foreal. I told her not to invite yall in, Ion't know what Bre an Corey be on but I know I need to check on her ass. He probably mad as fuck about this shit man wow I feel so bad for her. I hope she okay," Babydoll said feeling sympathy for Bre even though she didn't take Babydoll's advice about not letting us come in. She was definitely right to worry too cuz Corey was furious, and he showed it bigtime after we left.

RUFF LOVE

"So you got these niggas all in my shit bitch!?!" Corey yelled as he grabbed Bre neck and pushed her against the wall.

"Corey stop! We wasn't even doin nothin!" Bre replied fearfully tryna pry his fingers away from her neck.

"Naw hold on cuz bitch you think I'ma lame asumn," he said walking back to the front door and locking it.

"Please calm down baby we wasn't even doin nothin," she said running to the bathroom and locking the door behind her.

"Naw bitch! You smilin in these niggas face an entertainin ney ass all in my shit bitch cummer," he said walking to the bathroom behind her and kicking the bathroom door open soon as she locked it.

"Baby please don't hit me, we wasn't even doin nothin," she repeated as she held her arms out in front of her feeling terrified.

"Fuck you mean yall wasn't doin shit? Whyda fuck was them niggas in hurr bitch. Is you stupid!?!" he shouted before punching her as hard as he could in her jaw, throwing her to the ground by her hair, then punching her in her head repeatedly.

"Corey stop, baby please let my hair go!" Bre screamed as he proceeded to drag her out the bathroom by her extensions.

"Naw fuck that, bitch you think this shit a game? You entertainin these niggas all in my shit!" he said taking the mack 10 off his waist and putting it to her head.

"Baby please let me go! I swearda God it wasn't even like that," she cried not knowing if he was actually mad enough to shoot her ass or not.

"Matter fact bitch open up yo mouth ho! I'ma show yo ass howda entertain a nigga," he demanded unbuckling his pants and pulling out his dick. "If you bite down on my shit I'm knockin you the fuck out. You hear me bitch? So if you'ont wanna wakeup without no mutha fuckin teeth in yo mouth you better open up wide ho flatout," Corey said ready to make a example outa her ass for bringing some other niggas in whurr he laid his head.

"Baby my jaw swoll, please just let me go," she pleaded feeling unsure if she could even hold her mouth open long enough to suck his dick until he nutted while her jaw was damn near broken.

"On my soul you wakin up without no muafuckin teeth in yo mouth if you bite down on my shit. You wanna entertain these niggas in my shit? Put this dick in yo mouth ho!" he said wit the mack 10 in one hand and his dick in the other. "Bitch suck this dick," he demanded shoving his dick in her mouth recklessly. "Open up bitch," he said as she gagged with tears running down her face outa fear and discomfort. "Yeah bitch swallow that shit," he said jamming his dick down her throat as he nutted while holding her head in a uncomfortable position with the gun still in his hand. "Drink that shit bitch!" He demanded as she gasped for air still trying her hardest not to bite down in any way. "Yeah choke off that nut ho!" he said as she threw up all on the floor soon as he pulled his dick out her mouth. "Now clean nis shit up bitch!" he yelled taking the Gucci belt off his pants and hitting her as hard as he could with it.

"Baby! Stop! Please! I can't breathe!" she screamed still tryna catch her breath.

Ion't give a fuck bitch take all that shit off," he said stepping back and pointing the mack 10 directly at her.

"Baby I did not do anything," she stated trembling in fear as she hesitated to take her clothes off.

"Take that shit off before I leave yo ass in hurr leakin ho!" he yelled with the gun still pointed directly at her knowing she was scared enough to do anything he was telling her ass to do.

"Baby please just let me lay down, I didn't do anything," she pleaded as she took off everything but her bra, panties and socks.

"Take all that shit off ho, them socks too bitch. Come up out that shit," he demanded as she cried taking off her socks, panties, and bra then covering her bare chest with her hands. "Now sleep on na porch bitch," he said, opening the door and pushing her out the house ass-naked in the cold.

"Baby please don't do me like this, it's too cold out hurr," she begged trying not to talk as loud so the neighbors wouldn't look outside and see what was going on. She actually did need somebody to help her ass but she was way too embarrassed to explain why, especially without no clothes on.

"Fuck you bitch freeze Ion't give a fuck," he said heartlessly before slamming the door in her face and locking it. She could've start banging on the door begging him to let her back in but she aint wanna draw no attention to herself. So she decided to just sit at the door hoping he would calm down enough to let her back in without beating her down again. She sat there curled up in a fetal position crying quietly until the sun came up, unable to get any kinda sleep at all.

"Hey what the fuck happened? I was callin yo phone all night. Dashon told me Corey ass came home Bre, I fuckin told you that shit was gone happen. Are you okay?" Babydoll said immediately when she answered her phone once Bre finally called her back the next day.

"I know, we got into it an he took my phone. Shid I'm surprised he aint take it wit em when he left this mornin," Bre replied looking in the mirror at her swollen jaw. "I just need to get out this house for a minute Babydoll. Ion't really wanna be hurr if he finna come back anytime soon foreal," Bre explained with tears running down her face thinking about how coldhearted Corey was being the night before. She put a few ice cubes in a wet rag and placed it on her jaw to make the swelling go down cuz it looked hella bad.

"Okay I'm finna get up an hop in na shower. I'ma call you when I'm on my way so answer the phone," Babydoll said before getting off the phone and rolling out of bed despite the couple hours of sleep she had gotten. "I'm on my way ho, is you dressed?" Babydoll asked letting Bre know she was up, moving around, and headed her way to pick her up.

"Yeah I'm ready, I think I need to call Hustle an apologize to him tho. That shit was fucked up. But I swearda God I aint think Corey was comin back home yesterday. I wasn't expectin that shit at all. I mean he been actin so weird like he jus really don't wanna fuck wit me no more. He stay gone for days at a time an dog me out so bad when he finally do come home. Like what I'm sposed to do? We been together three whole years an he be actin like that shit don't even matter. I swear he aint used to treat me like this. Ion't know what to do," Bre vented as she cried while holding the rag fulla ice to her cheek.

"Don't cry Bre, it'll be fine. Dashon an Hustle just wanid me to make sure you was okay cuz I told em how Corey be trippin witchu like he do. We was all hella worried about you," Babydoll explained letting Bre know it wasn't no bad blood with us behind the shit.

"Hustle wanid you to make sure I was okay?" Bre asked moved by Hustle's concern and surprised he wasn't upset with her like she thought he'd be.

"Girl yeah, Dashon said Hustle not trippin off Corey ass cuz Hustle got a bitch too so it is what it is. He was just caught off guard cuz he aint know about Corey an he showl aint expect nobody to come up in nat house while they was in ner. So of course he was a lil sketched out but I think you should just break the whole situation down for em so he can understand. Hell you know about his bitch," Babydoll said encouraging Bre to call Hustle and straighten everything out so it wouldn't be as awkward when they saw us again.

"I do wanna see him again hella bad but bitch my face swoll. I hope this shit don't turn his ass off cuz my shit fat," Bre said still looking in the mirror trying not to smile knowing Babydoll was bout to freak out about her admitting her face was swollen due to what happened.

"Bre! what the fuck! Whatchu mean yo face swoll? What the hell did he do? Like oh my God, he is literally a fuckin psychopath," Babydoll yelled in a panic feeling even more sympathy for her friend.

"Yeah bitch damn it's cool tho I got some ice on it now," Bre answered with a smile avoiding the main question cuz the last thing she wanted to do was explain exactly what he did to her.

"Bre!" Babydoll yelled still in shock about the news.

"Babydoll you is so dramatic, just come pick me up so we can go see Hustle nem again. I like him foreal, I hope I aint fuck it up," Bre said down playing the shit outa the situation with Corey beating her ass the way he did.

"You aint fuck it up, I talked to Hustle about the shit myself after Dashon told me what had happened. I apologized for you an he said it's all good but yall do need to have a conversation about it yallself tho. I'm finna text Dashon yo number so he can give it to Hustle. An I'm only like 15 minutes away so just come outside when I pullup," Babydoll said before hanging up the phone and texting me Bre number with a message saying give it to Hustle.

"Damn wasup baby? You good?" Hustle said once Bre picked up the phone when he called her.

"I'm sorry Hustle, I been wit him for like three years an we been kinda on an off lately. But I aint know he still had my house key an was gone popup like he did," she lied not wanting to tell the whole truth about that part.

"It's all good baby I'll be yo boyfriend numba two," Hustle answered playfully making her laugh. "I wanna see you tho foreal, call me when you link up wit Babydoll so we can bump heads. I'm finna pullup on nis nigga Dashon right now," Hustle said turning on my street fixing to pull up at my crib.

"Okay, she just told me she was on her way ova hurr to pick me up so I'll jus see you in a minute," Bre said before hanging up the phone.

"Naw lemme see bitch, is yo eye black too?" Babydoll said as Bre came to the car with some big ass knockoff Gucci shades on obviously tryna hide something.

"No Babydoll, my jaw just haven't went down allaway yet an na shades kinda make it look better," Bre answered with a smile still down playing the whole incident like it really wasn't that big of a deal.

"Bre if you pullup wit them shades on ney gone think you got a black eye for sure," Babydoll stated tryna convince Bre to take the big stupid ass shades off before Hustle got a chance to see her with em on her face.

"Fuck all that bitch what's up witchu an Dashon? Yall hella cute," Bre said changing the subject.

"I mean he cool, I guess he kinda growin on me a lil bit. They is fun shid I aint expect to enjoy they company that much," Babydoll admitte, realizing how much fun she had when we came up to her job the night before. "They came up thurr wit them same dudes that was outside wit em when na police pulled up yesterday. They had a couple otha niggas wit em too. One a them niggas was cute as fuck, yo ass gone fuck aroun an endup likin him," Babydoll said jokingly referring to DonDon. "They stood out like a muafucka in ner tho plus they is hella cool," she added finally convincing herself that we wasn't so bad after all.

"Awww this so cute, he really like you too I can tell," Bre said with a smile. "You should test it out an see if he'll get cho hair done for you I bet he do it," Bre suggested anxious to see how fast me and Babydoll's relationship would escalate.

"Ima ask em. I need my shit done so I can get some dick I aint had none in hellas," Babydoll said rolling her eyes.

"Why you aint jus gotchu some dick yet then? It aint like you aint got niggas lined up tryna give it to you," Bre said as she laughed.

"Ion't like gettin no dick when my hair all raggedy. It's just less fun an I'm showl not finna get no new dick wit this old ass sew-in," Babydoll said with her face all frowned up fixing her bangs in the mirror at the red light.

"Yo hair don't even look that bad Babydoll an you had yo shit up fa hellas! I know you wanna get it redone tho. Shid you better let em get that shit done for you, that's what he supposed to do," Bre said tryna put Babydoll up on game about how easy it would be to get me to take care of that type of shit for her.

"Yeah he the one I'ma be tryna give some pussy to once I get it done anyway, he might as well pay for the shit," Babydoll answered thinking about when and how she should ask me to do it.

"Dashon finna make you happy I can tell," Bre said encouraging Babydoll to give me a chance, basically pushing her in my arms.

"They is kinda lit, I mean it's a big ass difference from bein aroun Curtis for sure," Babydoll replied referring to the nigga she called herself fucking with before I came along. "It's jus never a dull moment aroun nem niggas, I think that's why I'm startin to like em they kinda fun," Babydoll admitted hoping everything went right when it came time for her to ask me about getting her hair done. She was just ready to come up off some pussy like she wanted to do anyway.

"Whurr yall at baby?" I asked once she picked up the phone when I called.

"I'm finna turn on Gamble," she answered with a smile realizing how excited she was feeling to see me again.

"Yeah bring yo sexy ass down na street I see you," I said walking out to the middle of the street so she knew exactly whurr to pull over.

"Hi boo," she said getting out the car with a smile as I approached her with a hug.

"Why yall got the top down baby, yall wasn't cold?" I asked, noticing they had the top let back like they did the day before but it was a lot colder than it was that day for some reason.

"Hell naw we wasn't cold, you see we got the windows rolled up. We just had the heat blastin cuz the air an na heat mixed together feel good. Plus I like the way the car look when na top down an windows rolled up. It look kinda exclusive right?" Babydoll answered admiring how the car looked the way it was.

"So yall got the top back an na heat blastin? Yall Hollywood then a muafucka I hope yall got gas tho," Hustle said playfully after walking over to the car and giving Bre a hug to greet her.

"This muafucka showl on Freddy too," I said looking at her gas tank meter as I opened the driver's side door to turn her car off. "How you let this muafucka back up tho? Yall finna get in wit us" I said searching for the switch that let the top back up so I could lock the car before we left.

"Just push that button," Babydoll said pointing to the switch before following us to Hustle car.

"Iight come on" I said leading the way after taking her keys out the ignition, lockin the doors, then putting the keys in my pocket with a smile.

"Um okay, gimme my keys. Whyda hell they all in yo pocket like they yours," she said playfully reaching for the pocket I put her keys in.

"Naw I'll let chu know when you can leave for a minute, long as you let me know when you comin back," I replied arrogantly blocking her hand from going in my pocket to take her keys back.

"You is so rude, you can't jus take somebody keys an tell them they can leave only when you ready for them to go Dashon," she explained amused with the audacity and the nerve of me.

"I'll never be ready for you to leave girl, jus hope I'm nice enough to letchu leave when you get ready to," I said jokingly as she laughed. "Whurr we goin bruh?" I asked Hustle as him and Bre got settled in the back seat.

"Pullup on Heavy nem bruh, I need to grab some pills so my baby can hit that pain reliever. This bitchass nigga got her jaw all swoll up an shit," Hustle answered noticing Bre jaw was still a lil puffy but wanting Heavy and DonDon to see her for the first time anyway.

"That's fucked up sis, I straight feel for you. You can't let shit like that happen tho cuz it get dangerous when certain niggas run across eachother. Then you'll be caught up in na middle a some bullshit if it ever went down like it usually do you feel me?" I explained, stressing how important it was to keep any other niggas she was fucking with far way from us.

"You right brother, that was stupid. It won't happen again I promise," Bre said humbly reassuring me that she would never put us in such a awkward situation ever again.

"Wasup slimes," DonDon said coming to the door to greet us once we pulled up to him and Tyresha crib. "Wasup wifey, remember what I said if he fuck up I'm hurr for you. Don't forget about me now," he said playfully as Babydoll laughed while giving him a friendly hug to greet him.

"Tyresha this Dashon new girlfriend Babydoll. Babydoll this my babymama Tyresha," DonDon said proudly as we entered the front room after walking up the steps.

"Hey boo you look cute that outfit fire," Tyresha said complimenting Babydoll's peanut butter-colored leather jacket with the matching stiletto boots.

"Hey girlie thanks, this my friend Bre by the way," Babydoll replied politely introducing Bre so she wouldn't feel awkward or left out.

"Aw okay, how you doin?" Tyresha responded with a smile. "So you talk to Hustle?" she asked boldly hoping Bre would spill the tea on her and Hustle's status so she could run and tell Latoya just as soon as she got a chance.

"Cumon Tyresha, yo nosey ass just love bein messy don't chu," Hustle blurted out quickly before Bre was even able to answer.

"Right baby damn you always on some messy shit," DonDon added with a smile.

"Ahhhh, don't nobody go in na bathroom for bout 35 45 minutes" Heavy said playfully quoting a line from Friday after flushing the toilet and walking out the bathroom relieved.

"Cumon Heavy, big shitty-ass nigga whurr the pills at fool?" Hustle said ready to hurry up and get the pills so we could get the girls the fuck away from Tyresha big hating ass.

"Hold on nigga lemme wash my hands, the bathroom sink broke," Heavy answered walking over to the kitchen sink and washing his hands thurr.

"How yall ladies doin today? It's good to see you again Miss Babydoll how yo day goin?" he said rubbing the soap around his hands as the water rinsed it off.

"It's goin pretty good nice to see you again too. Did you have fun wit Star?" Babydoll replied with a smile really just making conversation since Heavy was so nice and polite to her.

"Who is Star? Heavy lemme find out you steppin out on my sista," Tyresha said being just as nosey as ever while Babydoll stood thurr wondering if she said too much. She was hoping she didn't cause problems for him by mentioning Star cuz that obviously wasn't her intentions.

"Baby stop bein messy damn that's why my potnas don't like comin ova hurr," DonDon interrupted playfully as Tyresha shook her head still staring at Heavy.

"Tyresha can kiss my ass, I actually enjoyed myself wit Star at the stripclub last night," Heavy answered purposely letting Tyresha know that's whurr we was the night before knowing she was unaware.

"So yo dusty ass was at the stripclub last night? While you lyin talm bout chu was in na studio wit Que ass boy bye," Tyresha said feeling embarrassed and angry that Don lied to her about whurr he was at the night before. Que was DonDon right hand man so he did spend a lot of time in the studio with him. Que sat in that muafucka all day creating music for the street niggas that was out thurr tryna make it in the rap game. Most of the time they still ended up getting locked up or killed like the rest of our ass though. My squad was mostly hustlers, thieves, an shooters. The only one of us who had some real talent when it came to that rap shit was Looney. But even he was more caught up in the dope game. DonDon was more of a hype man bouncing around shaking his dreads while Que would perform the songs he wrote. Don wasn't never the type to try an rap or perform a song hisself though.

"It's cool tho nigga, see if Ion't popup at that muafuckin studio next time you talm bout chu in na booth wit cho lyin ass. I shoulda known you was fulla shit anyway nigga you'ont even rap. Dirty-ass all at the muafuckin strip club some muafuckin whurr lookin dusty," Tyresha said rolling her eyes as DonDon smiled.

"Baby Heavy bullshittin, we wasn't at no strip club last night was we Babydoll?" DonDon asked playfully tryna get Babydoll to help him out the hot water Heavy had put him in.

"Naw don't put me in na middle of it. Hell I wish I wouldn'tve even said nothin about it now," Babydoll answered as she laughed.

"Naw you need to know whurr yo man was at last night while you worried about everybody elses. Shid Don needed some male bondin time wit his boys so we went to the strip club cuz that's what niggas do" Heavy said bluntly as he dried his hands off with a paper towel.

"Boy bye, howda fuck yall doin male bondin shit surrounded by naked hoes," Tyresha replied still pissed off and embarrassed about not knowing what Don ass was really up to.

Ion't know why the nigga aint tell you. Maybe it's cuz you be too busy worried about everybody else nigga Ion't know," Heavy said shrugging his shoulders unsympathetically, definitely not willing to spare her feelings since she was being so messy and annoying.

"I really enjoyed myself tho Babydoll. Star was the baddest stripper in ner shid and she got goals. She goin to school to be a lawyer an all," Heavy added purposely rubbing the whole experience in Tyresha face outa spite making her feel even worse. "What that lil snow bunny was talm bout Don? What was her name again? Barbie right?" Heavy continued with a evil grin as DonDon eyes got big, indicating Heavy was given her way too much information.

"Snow bunny! Who the fuck is a muafuckin Barbie Don? A skinny-ass white bitch Ion't know shit about?" Tyresha said rolling her eyes more pissed off than ever.

"Cumon baby you know Heavy jus talkin shit, quit playin bruh," DonDon lied hoping his brother was just about done getting back at Tyresha for being so nosey and messy at that point.

"Cumon Heavy wasup wit the pills bruh," Hustle interrupted changing the subject as Tyresha scrolled down Facebook with her face all frowned up annoyed.

"Damn you aint gone get high wit me nigga wasup?" Heavy asked handing Hustle the bag of pills as Hustle handed him the money.

"Fuck naw, we finna duck off on you niggas. Tyresha in nis muafucka trippin," Hustle said playfully making everybody laugh but her.

"Ok well maybe you should go home to yo so called wifey who you got two kids wit," Tyresha said bitterly as she rolled her eyes still scrolling down Facebook on her phone.

"Ion't even blame you bruh, just gone head go she on all bullshit," Don-Don said as he laughed.

"I'm hip bruh, we jus gone have to get high witchu niggas later shid Tyresha ass got all bad vibes floatin aroun nis muafucka," I said joining in on the fun they was having by pissing Tyresha off more and more.

"We just gone linkup on na block a lil later tho bruh," Don said still smiling as he shook my hand goodbye.

"Yeah yall can linkup wit his ass on na block cuz that's whurr he gone be livin once I change the locks on his dirty-ass watch," Tyresha said not finding a damn thing funny but knowing damn well DonDon wasn't taking the shit serious.

"Damn Tyresha! You gone put em out on na street?" Hustle blurted out playfully as everybody bust out laughing again.

HIGH SPEED

"Who you tryna pullup on now bruh?" I asked as we all got back settled in the car.

"Pullup on Rambo nem so I can bus they head for half these pills," Hustle answered giving Bre a pill to dry pop before dry popping a couple hisself. He knew if he overcharged Rambo nem for the pills he could basically get high with us for free.

"Them tens?" I asked curiously as he handed me a perk to dry pop before we crunched another pack of pills down with the Nyquil.

"Man ney ass talm bout they back on G code I aint fuckin wit it," Hustle answered referring to Gamble whurr he wasn't really tryna pull back up cuz the police was so hot over thurr at the time.

"How you know they back on G code? Chad just told me they was at Dre crib," I replied confused as to why they left Dre crib just to go post up over thurr on hot ass Gamble anyway.

"He jus texted my phone talm bout they back in na zone. Ion't know what them niggas on shid the police been hittin nat muafucka all day. I aint got time to be gettin harassed by the police right now. My ass got too much dope on me. Plus these muafuckin guns gone take a nigga straight to the feds on some bullshit," Hustle stated skeptical about pulling back up over thurr knowing the police already knew his car and was for sure gone to flag that muafucka on sight.

"Feds my ass shid you know damn well I aint pullin ova wit these thumpas in nis muafucka. Now that dope you can tuck, it's a whole female back thurr whichu. All she gota do is put that shit in her pussy but them guns gone get a nigga booked fa sho. I'm not goin bruh, they ass gone have to catch me fuck that!" I stated with my eyebrows raised as I headed back towards Gamble despite the risk.

"We just need to be quick bruh, we gone pullup real quick, drop these pills off an slide out asap," Hustle said handing Babydoll a perk too.

"Um Ion't want a pill unless it's a ex pill. Ion't know nothin about no perks," she said looking down at the perk Hustle was tryna give her uninterested.

"I'll take that muafucka," Bre blurted out anxiously waiting for the pill she already took to kick in so her jaw could stop hurting.

"It's gone calm you down an put chu on chill mode Babydoll. So you can jus sit back catch a vibe an enjoy yo high," Hustle explained with a smile amused by the fact that she wouldn't take it.

"Ion't need a pill that's gone make me laid back an chill I'm already like that. If I'ma take a pill that muafucka gone have to turn me up like a ex pill do. I just wanna smoke an drink a lil more than my toddler-ass tolerance gone allow me to foreal," Babydoll explained as she laughed.

"She not bullshittin either. This bitch can't hit the blunt more than a few times an can't drink more than a few drinks unless she on a ex pill," Bre said hoping Hustle would just give her the fucking pill instead cuz she knew for a fact Babydoll was not gone take that muafucka.

"Yeah I would say about three or four shots is probably my limit, two if I'm smokin. I gotta stay leveled when I'm doin both or I'll pass the fuck out," Babydoll admitted as Hustle handed Bre the pill he was offering entertained by how oddly different Babydoll was from the bitches we was used to having around.

"Well we gone have to find you a ex pill then Babydoll cuz my boy Chad finna sell me this big ass bottle of Patron for the low and I'm finna rollup. But Ion't need you passin out on our ass tho. Dashon probably wanna getchu all sloppy like that so he can tamper witchu while you out cold, I'ma make sure you straight tho. Who got some ex pills in na hood bruh? Don't savage be havin nem muafuckas on deck?" Hustle asked playfully as I turned on Gamble noticing the police that had just turned off Gamble turning right back around to flag our ass. "Fuck," I said zooming right past Rambo, Chad and Dre as the police turned they lights on like that was really finna stop me from taking off on they asses.

"Go down Glascow an hit Natural Bridge," Hustle said in a panic but still tryna play it cool so the girls wouldn't get too scared and start freakin out.

"I got this bruh jus sit back we good," I said making a quick right then smashing down on the gas as hard as I could. "Wasup bruh," I said answering Lil Rodney call in the midst of the high speed chase. I hadn't lost the police yet and they was still close behind probably calling for backup at that point.

"That's yall flyin down North Florissant bruh?" Lil Rodney asked curiously but feeling pretty sure it was us before I even answered.

"Yeah I'm finna loose em now," I said still focused on the road ahunnit percent even though I had the phone up to my ear letting Lil Rodney know what was going on.

"Whyda fuck are you answerin na phone? He not even that far behind you," Babydoll yelled looking back at the police car that was coming up behind us at top speed. So I hit the speaker button on my phone before letting it drop to my lap then start using both hands to drive again.

"Jus sit back baby lemme handle this," I said making a quick left and after that a quick right.

"Once you shake they ass jus pull up at Nikki homegirl crib. I'm finna have her pull her car out so you can pullup in na garage cuz they gone be looking for that muafucka all day."

"They on ya bumper boy! Don't let em box you in playin," Lil Rodney said jokingly knowing I was gone lose em one way or another at some point for sure.

"You talm bout ol babe wit the fade?" I asked knowing exactly whurr to go cuz I had just pulled up on Lil Rodney over thurr the day before.

"Yeah nigga, you was just ova hurr yesterday talkin my ear off about the new bitch. Don't tell me you den forgot howda get back ova hurr. She aint got cho head all fucked up like that do she?" Lil Rodney answered playfully talking shit like I wasn't in the middle of a whole high speed chase.

"That's hella clutch bruh I'm right aroun na corner from nat muafucka. And I just lost they ass," I said looking in my rearview realizing the police wasn't behind me no more but still hitting every corner I could think of out of instinct until I got thurr.

"I cannot believe you jus did that shit," Babydoll said looking back to make sure the police wasn't still on our ass, surprised we got away and secretly a lil impressed. "You know the police finna be lookin for this car now right?" Babydoll asked still feeling somewhat concerned about how we would make it back to her car without the police tryna flag us again.

"You worry to much baby, I told you I got this. I aint gone let nothin happen to this pussy girl," I said playfully reaching over and grabbing her pussy with a smile like I did the night before.

"Naw don't touch me cuz you play too much" she said as she smiled, rolling her eyes at my arrogance.

"This her right hurr?" Lil Rodney asked after walking up to the car and getting a closer look at Babydoll for the first time when I pulled up in the garage. He had seen her the day before when we first noticed them on Gamble but didn't get a closer look before pulling off to avoid the police. He knew damn well all that yelling, screaming, and arguing they was doing was definitely gone attract em especially on hot-ass Gamble. After we had that lil run-in with the police I pulled up on him to let'm know how on point he was for dippin out like he did. Plus I had to talk his ear off about Babydoll ass cuz she was really all the fuck I could think about after that. I called myself trying not to call her right away but after a while I aint give a fuck how thirsty it was gone make me look.

"Yeah this Babydoll, that's Bre," I answered introducing them both so he could know who was who.

"Yeah I heard her little scary ass all in na background talm bout (why you answerin na phone)," Lil Rodney said playfully imitating Babydoll's voice with a smile. He was seemingly unfazed by her appearance after taking just a quick glance at her face. But he was actually pretty impressed by how flawless she looked. "Come on in yall," he said encouraging the four of us to get out the car ready to catch a glimpse of they bodies. "Babydoll this my babymama Nikki. Nikki this Dashon new lil joint Babydoll an her friend Bre," Lil Rodney announced introducing the girls after leading us in the house.

"Hi ladies," Nikki said softly with a smile making Babydoll and Bre feel welcome and comfortable before her friend interrupted in a more playful manner.

"Hold on Dashon damn I thought chu liked me. Hell I'm sposed to be the new joint," she said jokingly making me, Hustle, and the girls laugh. She was cute an all but I jus couldn't get with the fade. It kinda made her look like a boy to me a lil bit. Plus she was a lil too skinny to be rocking a fade in my opinion. I mean if her ass was real fat on some Amber Rose type shit it would've been cool. But her body was more solid looking by her being so fit and that shit jus wasn't sparking my interest especially after meeting Babydoll.

"My bad sis, I had to hurry up an wife Babydoll ass before anotha nigga came along an snatched her up," I said playfully as everybody but Lil Rodney laughed.

"I mean you aint stand a chance sis. This nigga been pussy whipped since he met the damn girl an aint even smelt the pussy yet," Hustle joked but throwing a lil shade at the same time since Babydoll didn't link up with me once she got off work the night before.

"Trust me I know. Shid the nigga came ova hurr all geeked up talm bout a lil video vixen chick til he left. I'm like um hello nigga, you on't see all this sexy right hurr in yo face negro damn. I'm glad you cute tho boo, I mean I would've been offended if you wasn't cuz this nigga aint look twice okay," she explained as we laughed entertained.

"Yeah yall do make a cute lil couple tho foreal," Nikki said softly. That's when I noticed how soft her voice and tone had gotten. Her demeanor was completely different than it was when we was growing up but it wasn't really hard to understand why after everything she had been through.

"Thanks boo," Babydoll replied with a smile sensing Nikki's troubled past without even knowing her story cuz Nikki jus seemed so fragile and humbled.

"So wasup wit yall? Aint chu Latoya babydaddy?" Nikki friend asked Hustle grinning, ready to let the whole hood know what was going on with him and Bre so Latoya could find out and bring on the drama.

"Yep, that's our que fellas. We finna gone head an slide out cuz bitches gettin a lil to nosey for me," Lil Rodney said getting up from the kitchen table without even cracking a smile.

"Mmm whateva nigga," Nikki friend said rolling her eyes but knowing it wouldn't be wise to say anything more than that.

"Pullup on Rambo nem bruh," I said getting in the passenger's seat of Lil Rodney SRT8 truck while Babydoll, Bre, and Hustle hopped in the back.

"Iight, I was sposed to pullup on nat nigga anyway," Lil Rodney said getting in the driver's seat before pulling off.

"Wasup killa? Whurr yall finna go? Who all yall got up in nis muafucka?" Murder lil brother Beezy asked curiously after walking up to the truck when he saw us at the stop sign about to turn on Gamble. "Damn who is she? Yall got some lil joints up in nis bitch," He said once Lil Rodney let down Babydoll's window so Beezy could get a good look at her and Bre.

"That's Dashon new lil joint lil bruh," Lil Rodney explained as Beezy stared at Babydoll amazed.

"Yeah that's all me lil nigga, you'll be pullin these types a broads when you get a lil older son," I said playfully as he shook my hand through the window.

"Got my nigga Hustle in nis muafucka, wasup bruh? Gang-gang in nis bitch. Yall might as well let me slide on in between her and babygirl ova thurr," Beezy joked knowing he didn't stand a chance with either one of em.

"Hi my name Babydoll, this my friend Bre. Nice to meet chu boo," Babydoll said charmingly just trying not to come off like they was all stuck up and arrogant cuz they really wasn't.

"Nice to meet chu too Babydoll, you beautiful," Beezy replied smiling back at her as Hustle rolled his eyes.

"Nigga ion't care how beautiful she is, yo lil smooth ass aint gettin up in nis muafucka unless you a female. Now gone runoff an play witcha lil guns asumn lil nigga," Hustle said jokingly as me and Lil Rodney laughed.

"Lil guns? I got shit bigger than you nigga come shop wit me," Beezy replied, wanting the opportunity to show off what all he had collected from his brother.

"Naw foreal I'll shop whichu bruh, whatchu got?" Hustle asked knowing he would get a hell of a deal if he bought a gun from Beezy.

"Pull up on me later bruh, I got chu," Beezy answered eager to do business with Hustle just because of who he was.

"Yeah me too lil bruh, we gone pullup on you," I added as we pulled off going down Gamble towards Babydoll's car.

"Iight yall, ina minute!" He yelled proudly as the other lil young niggas from the neighborhood approached him. All the other lil niggas his age from down ner flocked to Beezy cuz they knew his brother had him tied in and untouchable. Plus he was tied in with us too which helped his reputation even more. They knew he was well connected even though he was nowhurr near as ruthless as any of us was. He still had the potential to run the entire neighborhood once he got a lil older though. He definitely would've been the ringleader of his generation if he wouldn't've got caught up in all the bullshit Gamble had to offer. But I'll get to that a lil later.

"Damn yall hopped in wit this nigga? Don't tell me you crashed out bruh," Rambo said with a smile as we all got outa Lil Rodney truck.

"Fuck naw he aint crash out nigga my shit parked," Hustle interrupted as Lil Rodney gave Rambo a blunt look indicating that I couldn't've possibly crashed.

"Man Rambo always playin like heont know I got that wheel. You know wasup nigga," I said pushing Rambo playfully before Babydoll pulled me to the side.

"I need you to take me to the beauty supply store so I can get some new hair," she said cutting right to the chase without beating around the bush about it.

"Iight how much you need?" I asked willing to spend whatever on the shit just to show her she was mine.

"I need like three-hundred dollars, maybe four cuz I gota get some stuff to straighten my real hair too. Can you do that? I'll pay for the sew-in myself," She added hoping I wasn't uncomfortable with given her the money even though we had just met. It felt like we had been fucking with each other for years at that point though.

"That's cool, long as youon't go sit up in anotha nigga face soon as you getcho hair all done an shit," I answered knowin damn well she wouldn't've cuz we just had too much chemistry with each other.

"Well if I wanid to be aroun anotha nigga once I got my hair done, I would've just asked him to buy the hair Duh," She said rolling her eyes before walking to her car.

"Why you jus automatically walk to the passenger's side like you know I'm drivin?" I asked squinting my eyes with a smile.

"Cuz first of all you still have my keys in yo pocket. An second of all you obviously a better driver than me right?" "She answered with a wink before opening the passenger's side door and getting in the car.

"That type a shit straight make my dick hard girl you'ont even know," I said playfully walking to the driver's side hella turned on by the way she was moving.

"Unt unn brother that was too much information!" Bre yelled loudly as everybody laughed.

"This nigga been creeped out fa two days straight, I hope she finna go give that nigga some pussy asumn cuz his ass tweakin," Chad joked as everybody else continued to laugh.

"He jus need to hurry up an get her ass pregnant foreal. He'll be back to normal once he know he got her for good," Rambo added with a smile.

"I'm hip, once he put that baby in her ass he'll calm down. Soon as he know she aint goin nowhurr he gone get on all bullshit watch. It's all fun an games right now tho," Dre said reminding everybody what type a nigga I really was while they was steady clowning me.

"Niggas aint shit, whurr you goin sis?" Bre yelled from across the street before we pulled off.

"She comin right back sis. I aint finna kidnap her lil ass, not yet, ina minute tho," I answered jokingly as Babydoll cracked a smile.

"Girl Hustle jus got me a nice ass hotel room for a few days. We finna duck off an go chill. Whatchu finna do?" Bre asked curiously once me and Babydoll pulled back up after getting what she needed from the beauty supply store.

"Bitch I'm finna take my ass home an take this old ass hair out my head so I can give myself a perm. My shit been braided up for hellas," Babydoll answere dreading the whole process of getting the shit done.

"Ok well call me tomorrow once you get it done so we can pop out ho," Bre said before getting in the stolen car Hustle had paid Chad for and pulling off into the sunset headed to the Lumière Hotel.

"Damn so I gotta wait allaway til tomorrow to see you again?" I asked pulling her body closer to mine while leaning up against the driver's side door. Iont know I might want chu to smoke wit me after I take my hair down an do my perm cuz I can't go get the sew-in til tomorrow," She answered putting her hands under my shirt and gently scratching my back, side, and stomach with her pink pointy nails.

"So you gone call me when you ready to pull back up on me tonight?" I asked grabbing and squeezing all on her ass with my dick pressed up against her.

"Yeah I'ma call you soon as my hair dry. It wont take that long," she answered looking down at my dick instead of my face and that shit was driving me crazy. I kissed her forehead before letting her in the car then floated across the street to the vaco where Chad, Dre, Rambo, DonDon, Heavy, and Lil Rodney was all standing around still talking shit about how pussy whipped I was without even getting no pussy yet. I knew for a fact I was gone have her how I wanted her once I got up in that pussy though.

HIT THE GAS

    She pulled up at my mama crib around ten o'clock that night, so I came out to the car and got in the passenger's seat with the already rolled blunt I had ready for us to smoke. She was sitting in the driver's seat smiling from ear to ear looking just as beautiful as ever with her real hair parted on the side like she had her sew-in. Her hair came past her shoulders and her bangs hung in her face making her real hair look like weave. I couldn't help but to keep smiling cuz I straight had butterflies in my stomach. I was just happy to finally be alone with her ass. We was in our own lil world together that night.

    "Gimme the blunt ugly," she said playfully snatching the blunt outa my hand with a smile.

    "Look at chu, straight tweakin. That's that rapper weed girl it'll have you strung out I'm tellin you," I said jokingly as she lit up the blunt and start smoking.

    "You 'ont understand, doin my hair a straight buzzkill. It jus be braided up for hellas so when I finally take it down it be real hard to comb thru. I'm just hella fuckin tendaheaded so iont be likin that, I feel exhausted," she vented before passin me the blunt.

    "You the type that still look the same whether you got cho hair done or not tho," I said after hitting the blunt a few times then passing it back to her.

    "It's crazy how when I first met chu I jus thought chu was so obnoxious an we would never endup talkin in a million years," she admitted before hitting the blunt a couple more times then passing it back to me. "But now that I actually got to know you a lil bit I think you pretty cool, I like bein aroun you," she continued as I hit the blunt again analyzing everything she was saying in my head. "I mean at first I thought cho eyes was way to buggy cuz they poke out so much. But now I think I like em tho, they cute, like frog eyes," she added playfully making me laugh.

"Well my looks really don't matter, I mean yeah I know a nigga handsome an all," I said rubbing my chin with a smile. "But I aint got nothin to prove wit a girl like you on my arm. You straight came outta nonowhurr wit this perfect ass face an nis perfect ass body an nis perfect ass lil attitude I love. It's like you jus stepped right outta a nigga dreams asumn. I feel a lil bit caught off guard cuz this shit do be feelin like a dream but its straight real life. Every time I'm aroun you ion't know the shit jus crazy," I explained tryna break down how I really felt about her the best way I could before she climbed over to my seat and kissed me for the very first time.

I damn near forgot whurr the fuck I was at. I knew she was gone be mine forever though without a doubt. She made me feel like my life was finally starting to change for the better. I felt like my whole lil world was perfect as long as I had her.

"Why you make me wanna do it to you so bad?" she said softly in my ear sending chills up my spine as she kissed my earlobe seductively.

"Lemme put this dick inside you then, matter fact cummer real quick," I said reaching for her keys so I could turn the car off and take her in the house with me.

"No baby," she said climbing back over to the driver's seat stopping me in my tracks. "I can't do it to you tonight cuz I aint got my hair done yet so I'ma be to uncomfortable," she said foolishly but looking dead ass serious so I knew she wasn't joking about it. "I'ma fuck you better if we wait jus trust me," She added before giving me a quick kiss on my lips but this time from the driver's seat while I sat thurr speechless and confused.

"I'ma nut all in nat pussy when I get it, I hope you know that," I blurted out just saying the very first thing that came to my mind as I tried to gather my thoughts. "Who you be fuckin wit? When na last time you got some dick?" I asked curiously as she rolled her eyes then start squirming around and rubbing her body in a cute lil playful way. She was making it seem like not fucking me was just driving her crazy but avoiding the conversation at the same time. "That shit ova wit Babydoll foreal. Let that nigga know the shit dead straight-up whoever the nigga is, on everything," I said letting her know how serious I was about making me her exclusive and cutting everybody else completely off. "Who you be fuckin wit Babydoll?" I asked again hoping she wouldn't hold nothing back.

"I got my heart broke a couple years ago so I just been kinda stayin to myself for the most part. I been knowin nis dude Curtis since I was like 16 an we was always just friends til we decided to start messin aroun. We was definitely better off friends tho cuz I'm not really attracted to him," she explained being 100% honest about the whole situation like I wanted. "He jus don't do this to me," she added grabbing my hand and putting it in her panties so I could feel how wet her pussy was. It was soaking wet too. So I stuck my fingers in that muafucka hoping I could make her ass just go ahead and let me fuck her right thurr. "Baby stop," she moaned as her pussy got wetter by the second.

"Why you playin wit me Babydoll? Look whatchu doin," I said taking her hand and placing it on my dick so she could see how hard she was making it.

"Lemme see," she whispered taking my dick out my boxers and kissing it softly on the tip. My shit was so hard and she was grippin it like she was finna straight go down on that muafucka. My lil hormones was going crazy.

"Why it keep jumpin?" she asked softly before putting it allaway in her mouth then going up and down on it nice and slow. I felt like I was bout to lose control and nut all in her mouth at any minute but I aint really wanna do all that cuz I wasn't sure how nasty she was with the shit yet. Plus I wanted to bust a nut in that pussy more than anything.

"Lemme show you sumn baby please jus cum in lemme show you," I pleaded as she went even further down on it making me feel like I was about to explode. She grabbed my hand and placed it on the top of her head while she continued to suck my dick like a pro making it impossible for me to resist. "Baby getup somebody comin," I blurted out as I looked up an out the window tryna avoid the nut that was rapidly approaching. Some nigga with a black hoodie on was walking down the street towards the car just tryna get to whurrever the fuck he was going I guess. It still had me a lil sketched out though cuz he was really just a reminder that I could easily get caught lackin with my head down focused on Babydoll sucking my dick like I aint know no better.

"Okay I'm finna go, I'll see you tomorrow. My pussy too wet anyway," she said with a sexy smirk on her face as the dude with the black hoodie on walked right past the car without even looking in our direction.

"Baby jus come in don't leave me like this," I begged, hoping she would finally give in and let me have my way with her.

"No Dashon, its gone be better tomorrow when I have my hair done so don't jackoff neither just let it go down," she said pulling my boxers back over my dick with a smile.

"You dead-ass wrong for this shit Babydoll," I said amused by her crazy ass sense of humor cuz she was obviously getting a kick out the shit.

"Gone, lemme go on home. An I'm keepin na rest of this blunt too," she said reaching for the blunt that had eventually just went out after she start kissing me.

Maaan you aint shit but a fuckin tease, just a big ass fuckin tease I swear," I said jokingly as she laughed.

"Dream about me," she said playfully with a wink before blowing me a kiss goodbye.

"Call me when you make it home lil crazy-ass girl," I said with a smile before closing the passenger's side door and going back in the house alone.

"So you still aint fucked the damn girl yet? How? Rambo nem said yall was all ova each other before she left. You mean to tell me she pulled back up on you late night an still aint give yo silly ass no pussy," Hustle said clowning me the next day when I told him everything that had happened when Babydoll pulled back up to smoke.

"Yeah man it was weird. She jus sucked my dick hella good an left. Said she aint wanna fuck me til she put her weave in. I wanid to fuck her ass, while her hair was like it was tho foreal. I mean she aint ball-headed an when she was suckin my dick she put my hand on her head so I was grabbin all on her shit witout feelin a bunch a tracks n shit. Hell that was a lil better if you ask me," I said telling Hustle all about Babydoll's whole lil stupid ass theory on her not wanting to fuck me without hella inches of fake ass hair in her head. Ion't give a damn how expensive the shit was it was still stupid as hell.

"That is kinda weird. Maybe the bitch was on her period a sumn an she jus aint wanna tell you," Hustle said feeling just as confused about the whole situation as me.

"Naw bruh, that wasn't it cuz she put my hand in her panties an lemme feel how wet her pussy was. I put my fingers all up in nat muafucka an everything," I said getting goosebumps just thinking about how wet and slippery it was when I did.

"Well I showl hope you smelt them muafuckas after you did nigga. That'll let chu know fa sho," Hustle replied, laughing uncontrollably.

"Smelt like water bruh. Ion't know why she aint just come up off that pussy last night. I was trippin off that shit til I fell the fuck to sleep, she jus crazy," I explained as I zoned out again thinking about how good it felt when she was sucking my dick. When she pulled up the next night I came right out to the car, took the keys out the ignition, then put em in my pocket like I did when she pulled up on Gamble with Bre.

"Whatchu doin? I thought we was finna smoke again," she said playfully looking all dolled up and cute for a nigga.

"Yeah we finna smoke come in tho. I left the blunt in na house," I replied encouraging her to get out the car an come in without taking no for a answer this time.

"Dashon you can't jus lure me in yo house wit weed you think you slick," she said rolling her eyes with a smile while getting out the car and following me in the house.

"Shshsh, everybody sleep don't talk too loud," I said in a hushed tone as we crept up in my mama house trying not to make too much noise.

"Who is everybody? Who all live hurr?" she whispered curiously wanting to know who all she would have to worry about walking in on our asses if we did start fucking.

"My mom an pops upstairs an my lil brother baby mama an his son up thurr too. My lil brother ass got locked up so my mama jus gave her an my nephew his room," I explained softly, closin off the entrance to the front room so if somebody did happen to come down the stairs I would have enough time to hop up.

"Oh my God, this dog look jus like you. His eyes pop out just like yours. That's hella cute you straight got a twin dog," she said noticing my mama dog Vegas walking up to her after waking up from his lil nap.

"Gone Vegas, Ion't got time for Vegas worsm ass. He finna get the fuck up outta hurr," I said opening the two doors that closed off the front room so he could get the hell out my way cuz I was on a mission. After I closed the doors behind him I sat down next to Babydoll on the couch then picked up the blunt I had rolled for us to smoke. I was getting ready to light that muafucka up but never even lit it. I jus wanted to fuck her hella bad and couldn't wait another minute. So I put the blunt and the lighter back down on the table in front of us then pulled her body closer to mine. I started kissing her while pulling her pants and panties off. Then anxiously layed in between her legs as she wrapped her arms around my body and pulled me inside her. My dick went in her pussy nice and slow "I fuckin knew it baby, I knew this pussy was gone make me crazy, whurr you goin girl?" I whispered in her ear as her eyes got bigger every second I went deeper "Why you runnin? Why this pussy so wet an tight, cummer girl," I continued pulling her body back to whurr it was before she started scooting back, not knowing if she could handle my whole dick goin in right away.

"Baby this dick so big you drivin me crazy," she whispered trying her hardest to remain as quiet as possible.

"Who pussy this is girl? I'll kill yo ass if you give away my pussy you hear me?" I said gently putting my hand around her neck as I went in deeper trying not to lose control.

"Baby I love this dick, I want this shit forever I swearda God I'm finna nut on it," she whispered as her pussy contracted on my dick almost making me slip up and lose it.

"Mmm hold up," I said pulling my dick out her pussy quickly to stop myself from busin a nut too soon. I lifted her legs up and held em close together then slid my dick back inside as I kissed all on her feet obsessed with every inch of her. After that, I spreaded her legs back open forcing her pussy to grip the dick even more. I start feeling this warm sensation dripping down my dick making her pussy even more slippery and irresistible. She pulled me deeper inside her whispering softly in my ear.

"I fuckin love you daddy this dick so fuckin good," she moaned as she wrapped her legs around me making damn sure I nutted in that pussy like I said I would. I nodded off right thurr on top of her and she nodded off right thurr too. But when I heard somebody walking around upstairs I immediately hopped up causing her to wake up too.

"Baby put cho pants on real quick we finna smoke this blunt," I said tryna play it off like that was the reason I hopped up so suddenly. I went to the kitchen and poured a cup of juice then headed back to the front room whurr she was pulling her pants up in a hurry after hearing somebody walking around upstairs herself. "Baby you do not have to get right up that thirsty," I said with a smile watching her grab my cup of juice and drink it with two hands like a lil kid.

"Shut up an smoke the damn blunt so I can get high an go. I wasn't even supposed to end up doin all that cuz we was sposed to wait a couple more days. Now I feel like a ho," she said jokingly after putting the empty cup of juice back down on the table and licking her tongue out at me.

"Naw you not a ho, you a slut. My lil slut that's why I'll kill you," I said with a smile before lighting up the blunt.

"I'm not a slut, I just act hella slutty an do slutty shit cuz that's how I am," she said playfully shrugging her shoulders as I passed her the blunt amused.

"Awww naw, you tryna shut the doors so I won't smell the gas but I smell it nigga pass that shit," my worsm-ass dad said coming in the front room after Babydoll passed the blunt back to me. "Aw you got company, hey how ya doin? Whatchu Dashon new lil girlfriend?" my dad asked noticing Babydoll sitting thurr looking all innocent as I handed him the blunt.

"Well I guess so. I'm not really sure but it's nice to meet chu tho. Everybody calls me Babydoll," she answered politely as she shook his hand to greet him with a smile.

"Whatchu mean you not really sure? Don't embarrass me darlin, we a couple now. I'm pretty sure I explained that to you already," I said putting my arm around her playfully as she laughed. When she left that night I called her phone soon as she pulled off. "Turn yo lights on before you get pulled over or hit sumn," I said before laying back down on the couch in a cloud.

"Thank you officer. I'll talk to you tomorrow," she said sarcastically while turning off my street with a smile that just wouldn't go away.

"You can either call me when you get home or stay on na phone til you get thurr, pick one," I said arrogantly laying on the couch with confidence.

"Um neither one cuz I don't like you," She replied amused with my nerve and arrogance.

"Well why was you sayin all that when nis dick was inside you then? You know that make me crazy right?" I asked as she held the phone just thinking about the way I was fucking her and ready to tell Bre all about it when she woke up the next day.

"Wasup bitch, I finally got some dick last night," Babydoll said with a smile fresh out the shower and fulla energy as soon as Bre called her phone the next morning.

"Wow you sound like you got you some dick, me too tho bitch. Come up hurr so we can talk about it. Hustle left earlier but he left me some money so I'm finna order us a pizza. And I still got the rest of this patron, it's hellas in hurr too. Stop an get some margarita mix so we can do happy hour in nis bitch. Girl the Lumiere hella nice! I love it hurr," Bre said feeling relaxed an enjoying the shit out the room Hustle had got her for the next five days. After her and Babydoll ate they pizza and traded sex stories over patron and margaritas they called us all buzzed up and tipsy ready to link up.

"We on our way baby hurr we come," I said before hanging up the phone with Babydoll.

"Man I need to kinda lay low wit Bre ass a lil bit cuz Latoya on all bullshit. She been hearin about us ridin aroun wit her an Babydoll now she steady textin my phone talm bout we not hard to find. I'm gettin sick a this shit, it's gettin too stressful," Hustle confessed knowing I was finna try and get him to go pull up on Babydoll and Bre with me again.

"Yeah man nat shit aint gone keep flyin bruh. His babymama stay outta town so he can get away wit that type a shit you can't, you know Latoya aint goin fa that fool" Rambo added putting his two cents in as he laughed.

"Latoya not bullshitin neither bruh, she gone end up pullin up on yall ass when yall least expect it too watch," Chad added feeling just about fed up with the four of us always hanging out together anyway.

"An nis nigga act like he can't go more than a couple hours witout seein or talkin to Babydoll ass. Yall gone get sicka each other quick," Hustle blurted out annoyed with how much time I wanted to spend with Babydoll especially after we had already fucked.

"Shid Dashon aint gettin sicka Babydoll ass til she get pregnant," DonDon said playfully knowing I was still slime forever no matter what.

"Dashon tryna wife Babydoll ass up so weather Hustle an Bre keep fuckin aroun or not Babydoll aint goin nowhurr. An Bre still gone be aroun too cuz that's Babydoll rollie," Heavy explained letting Hustle know that he wouldn't be able to get rid of Bre so easily.

"Shid yall jus gone have to keep duckin yo babymama then. You aint the only one, niggas do that shit everyday all day," Dre said jokingly, eager to see how it would all play out once Latoya finally caught us all together.

"Man is you gone pullup on em wit me or not," I asked Hustle, not wanting to keep Babydoll waiting too long.

"Hell if you won't I will shid my babymama sit in na house all day. I aint gotta worry about mines popin out on bullshit," Heavy said playfully just having a lil fun with Hustle since he seemed to be so conflicted with the situation at hand.

"You know she like fat boys bruh. You might as well let Heavy take her off ya hands for you," DonDon added with a smile joining in on the fun Heavy was having with Hustle.

"Fuck naw man! That's my lil side piece, this nigga jus actin like I'm sposed to keep her wit me like she my main bitch asumn tho," Hustle explained putting all the blame on me.

"Naw yall jus gotta let Bre know she can't ride allatime cuz you got a bitch. Babydoll can ride aroun nis muafucka all day. But if she keep her homegirl who Latoya already know about wit her Latoya most likely gone have a problem wit Babydoll too so be prepared for that," Rambo said warning us about what was gone happen eventually.

"Man cumon, let's just go get em bruh fuck it," Hustle blurted out realizing I was gone go pick Babydoll up either way. "We can take em to the Mulah asumn," he suggested knowing a dark movie theater with comfortable couches all around the room was definitely the perfect place to hide from Latoya ass.

He figured he could at least get on some freaky shit in thurr and make it worth the risk.

"Yeah do shit like that cuz if yall out hurr lackin she popin up on yall ass fa sho. Fuck aroun an don't even be in her car neither. Latoya ass likely to pullup wit anybody. You know how messy these hoes be, jus ready for some drama to pop off. They gone be tryna track ya down harder than Latoya ass damn ner to catch a piece a that action," Chad said making Hustle even more paranoid about Latoya catching his cheating ass red handed with Bre.

HEAD ON COLLISION

After we picked the girls up we ended up getting in another high speed when the police tried to flag us again. So we parked Hustle car then hopped in Babydoll lil drop top Spider.

"Man nis back seat hella small, who the fuck sposed to fit back hurr some kids?" Hustle complained as him and Bre sat uncomfortably in the back seat of the small two door Mitzubishi.

"Well Hustle, that's what happens when you put fake tags on yo car okay. They flag cars wit fake temp tags on em dummy," Babydoll said rolling her eyes while sitting comfortably in the passenger's seat.

"Man Ion't even wanna highspeed in nis lil muafucka. Pullup at cho crib so you can put this thumpa up bruh," Hustle said with his face frowned up looking mad and uncomfortable.

When we pulled up at my mama crib I ran upstairs and put the gun up in my room but when I came back out Hustle was standing outside the car on the phone.

"Baby we jus finna go cuz Hustle ass got too much goin on an I aint got time for the shit," Babydoll announced, getting out the passenger's seat and walking to the driver's side annoyed.

"Right, cuz I'm not finna jus be quiet an stop talkin everytime yo fuckin phone ring nigga. I wasn't even talkin to you or listenin to yo conversation while you gettin all out the car wit a attitude like I did sumn wrong. I asked Babydoll a question that aint have shit to do whichu or nothin you was talkin bout. Boy you got me fucked up," Bre said offended by the way Hustle start actin soon as Latoya called his phone from a different number and he answered.

"Hold on baby jus get in na car for a second. Lemme talk to him real quick cuz we still goin," I said standing at the hood of the car as she got in the driver's seat anyway. I was really just focused on fuckin Babydoll ass again so I aint really give a fuck whurr Hustle and Bre went. Me an Babydoll was still going to the Mulah regardless. Shid I couldn't wait to fuck her lil ass from the side on one of them nice ass couches in thurr. We had stopped at Walmart so the girls could pick out them some lil blankets and all. "Wasup bruh, whatchu wanna do? If you wanna shake Bre we can shake her ass but I still gotta take Babydoll to see this movie cuz I already told her I was finna take her," I said to Hustle as he stood thurr frozen watching Latoya pull up and park behind Babydoll car. Then she got out and walked up to the driver's side door.

"Which one a yall talk to Hustle?" Latoya asked aggressively after opening up Babydoll's door.

"Bitch if you'ont back the fuck up off me wit that shit. Don't be touchin my muafuckin door ho!" Babydoll replied clutching the pink and black 380 she had as she talked.

"I'm just tryna see who talkin to my babydaddy cuz we got two kids together an I just wanna know," Latoya explained suddenly a lil less hostile not knowing how trigger happy Babydoll was.

"Well back the fuck up bitch cuz it aint me flat the fuck out," Babydoll said getting out the driver's seat as Latoya took a few steps back.

"Holdup, holdup, Dashon go get my thumpa bruh cuz you straight doin too much Babydoll," Hustle blurted out offended by the way Babydoll seemed to be backing Latoya up in a corner with the gun in her hand.

"Ion't give a fuck about cho gun Hustle! I bet chu he won't make it to that muafucka. Ion't give a fuck if its in his back pocket, I bet chu won't get it! Keep this bitch away from my muafuckin car flat the fuck out!" Babydoll yelled after cocking the gun back so everybody could know that one was in the chamber and she was ready to shoot.

"Look I'm sorry boo, we 'ont want no problems," Latoya said to Babydoll taking a few more steps back and pulling Hustle back with her. "Baby just get in na car wit me cumon," she said to Hustle encouraging him to leave with her.

"Naw fuck that go get my shit bruh," Hustle repeated making me take offense at that point.

"Fuck you mean nigga? You aint finna buck a burner on my bitch cuz you can't control yo ho nigga. Latoya ass shouldnt've walked up on na muafuckin car doin all that shid that's on her, yall jus gotta chunck that shit up!" I replied ready to go wrong with Hustle ass right then and thurr.

"Ion't give a fuck nigga that's my shit go get it!" Hustle yelled fulla anger and rage.

"Iight if I go get that muafucka right now it'll be a problem fa sho, an you can take it however the fuck you want cuz the shit jus not makin sense to me flatout," I said with my eyebrows raised letting him know I'll hurt sumn over Babydoll just like he would over Latoya ass.

"Okay Dashon, you met a bitch five minutes ago an now you ready to fall out wit us who you known yo whole life. Hustle yo best friend, howda hell is you takin her side when she jus pulled a whole gun out on us," Latoya interrupted pissing me off even more.

"Iton't fuckin matter. Ion't give a fuck about none a that shit cuz like I said you shouldn't've walked up to the car an opened her door Latoya. You can't control how a muafucka react when yo ass come questionin nem about a nigga they aint even fuckin an don't give a fuck about! Yall can miss me wit that shit foreal. An like I said muafuckas can take it however the fuck they want to. I'm jus not goin for the shit bruh flat the fuck out," I replied focusing back on Hustle and redirecting the conversation back to him. I wasn't really tryna go in on Latoya outa respect for his ass cuz that was really his job. He should've set his baby mama straight from the jump instead of tryna go wrong with Babydoll anyway.

"Iight Dashon it's all good fuck it. Latoya cumon," Hustle said before getting in the driver's seat and pulling off with her.

"Girl what the fuck! That bitch popped up outta nowhurr, I aint know what the fuck was finna happen," Bre blurted out with a smile, relieved that the situation didn't escalate outa control. "Hell yall can just take me back to the room Ion't wanna be no third wheel. But I showl aint fucked up about noddin off in nat big nice ass comfortable bed her babydaddy already paid for shid. Ion't give a fuck if his ass laid up in nat muafucka wit me or not," Bre said feeling like she still ended up coming out on top even though Hustle left with Latoya.

After we dropped Bre off I took Babydoll to the Mulah and fucked her from the side under the lil soft fluffy blanket we got from Walmart. It was so fucking good too, I jus remember us tryna stay real quiet and make as little movement as possible. I was trying hella hard not to nut but once her leg start shaking while I had my dick just marinating in her pussy trying not to move I finally slipped up and lost it. Soon as I felt that extra warm sensation dripping down my dick I shot all nut in her pussy. We nodded off until they cut the lights on then hopped up as everybody else was walking out the door.

Now I aint even gone lie I was kinda stressin out about the whole Hustle and Latoya beef when I got home. I knew the shit was gone be hella awkward when I saw them again and I wasn't really looking forward to the drama that awaited. But I was still standing on what the fuck I said no matter what. The whole hood knew about the shit the next day, it was the talk of the fucking neighborhood by then. I aint know who all felt like I was in the wrong or who all felt like I was right but honestly I aint give a fuck. Shid I said what I said and I meant that shit flat-out.

So I pulled up on Gamble with my bitch on the passenger's side while everybody was out at the park chillin. "Aye bruh, you gotta get her from ova hurr. Latoya say Babydoll not allowed on Gamble straight up," Hustle fat ass yells out making a big ass scene that everybody outside was all eyes and ears for.

"Fuck that, Babydoll I wanna fight. Wasup? I wanna fight," Latoya said walking over to the passenger's side door whurr Babydoll was sitting.

"Bitch you think I'm…" Babydoll mumbled as she took her gun out her purse, cocked it back then -pow- the gun went off as she pointed it directly at Latoya but missed. "Now get me the fuck away from hurr!" Babydoll screamed after coming to her senses and realizing she almost killed the damn girl in front of a park fulla people.

"Damn bruh wasup?" Hustle said looking at me while everybody else stood thurr puzzled.

"Get me the fuck from ova hurr!" Babydoll repeated, this time pointing the loaded gun at me when she talked. I aint even gone lie I was a lil turned on by the shit but I was still just as shocked as everybody else about what she did. I pulled off after shrugging my shoulders at Hustle basically letting him know I was just as surprised as he was about it. But Babydoll was pissed so I knew to just leave. I seen a fire in her eyes that was even worse than the night before and I didn't really know what to expect from her ass.

"Yall got me fucked up! Im not finna keep puttin myself in these dustyass situations fuckin withchu! I'ma end up blowin nat bitch head off on my soul cuz the bitch keep comin for me like I'm really the bitch to be fuckin wit! I aint got time to be out hurr wrestlin an tusslin aroun wit no bitch, breakin nails an shit! I'm grown as fuck! Fuck yall thought? I aint wit all that back in na day ass shit. That shit aint even my muafuckin style, bitch I get money! Fuck I look like out hurr fightin, gettin tracks pulled an scratches all on my shit. My muafickin face make money this how I feed my muafuckin daughter! I'll straight black the fuck out on a bitch I swearda God. That bitch gone end up straight up hurt fuckin wit my ass Ion't give a fuck if the bitch know howda fight or not. That aint gone mean shit once these bullets start flyin aroun nis muafucka. Yall better let that bitch know I'm not the one. An I'm not thinkin about no consequences once I get the spazzin out on a bitch neither. So we gone end up dead an in jail while I'm somewhurr cryin talm bout sorry. Yall might wanna make sure a bitch mentally stable before yall keep allowin nis ho to come at me sideways knowin I got this gun on me. Cuz the muafucka do got me hella unstabled bitch I be ready to pop off. I mean it aint like I'm one a these bitches that be hoppin aroun na muafuckin club puttin my hands whurr my fist at bitch I'm a boss! That's jus not what the fuck I be on. Ion't even carry myself like that, fuck yall thought this was?" she vented before I bust out laughing unable to hold it in any longer. Now I was just driving around quiet listening to her vent so she could get it all out at first but when she said "sheon't be hoppin aroun na club puttin her hands whurr her fist at," it got hard to keep a straight face cuz that shit was funny as fuck to me.

"Naw foreal cuz the bitch steady comin at me like that's the type a time I be on. What the fuck do I look like," she said finally cracking a smile and laughing herself.

"Baby you fuckin crazy I jus love yo sexy ass tho," I said keeping one hand on the wheel as I drove and grabbing her pussy with the other like I always did. "Ion't give a fuck tho baby she had you fucked up an if a muafucka got a problem witchu they got a problem wit me flatout. The bitch should'nt have no problem witchu no way. She act like she wanna suck my dick asumn. Whyda fuck is you steady comin for my bitch knowin she not the one fuckin wit Hustle. Then Hustle whyda fuck is you actin like you can't control yo ho alla sudden Ion't get it," I added letting her know I had her back 100%.

"Wasup bruh, " I said finally answering the phone after silencing the back to back calls I was getting from Hustle, not wanting to interrupt Babydoll during her raging rant. Hell if I would've answered the phone as mad as she was aint no telling what the fuck would've came out her mouth. So I just waited until I knew she had calmed down enough to let me talk to Hustle myself.

"Tell Babydoll ass I'm lightin nat muafuckin car up next time I see that muafucka too while she call herself popin off," Hustle said with Latoya ass all in the background tryna play victim. Knowing damn well she had all her friends standing by ready to pounce on my bitch soon as the fight kicked off. Nobody expected Babydoll to react so irrationally with the gun like she did though. Especially knowing all the niggas standing around out thurr most likely had thumpas on em too. But that just goes to show she wasn't bullshittin when she said she be blackin out an not thinkin about no consequences.

Luckily all the niggas outside was obviously my peoples too so nobody was out thurr taking sides. They was to entertained by Babydoll being my new bitch and already poppin off on Hustle's. Everybody was just pretty much enjoying the show amazed with all the drama and how quickly it was escalating.

"Fuck you mean bruh? So what we at each other head now? Cuz I'm in nis muafucka too an you know how I'm rockin homie jus lemme know," I replied making the situation more about me and him since he was steady tryna come for my bitch like a ho for some reason.

"Nigga you met this bitch yesterday!" Hustle yelled sarcastically with rage "Fuck you mean is we at each other head!?! Nigga she jus shot at my muafuckin babymama bruh!" he ranted feeling appalled that I was actually willing to go to war with him for Babydoll after knowing her for only a few days.

"Nigga! the bitch steady walkin up on na mutha fuckin car bruh! Whyda fuck is you lettin yo bitch keep comin for mines tryna fight when you sposed to be my nigga anyway! An whyda fuck you not questionin why she steady comin for my bitch knowin she not the one that was fuckin witchu in na first place? fuck outta hurr bruh!" I yelled before hanging up in his face without giving him a chance to answer.

"This nigga actin like a straight Rudy," Hustle said looking at the phone realizing I had just hung up on his silly ass.

"I seen nis shit comin bruh I swear. Now yall into it cuz they into it," Rambo said shaking his head in disappointment feeling like we both oughta be ashamed of ourselves for letting some females take control of the situation instead of handling the shit ourselves.

"Babydoll ass just got the nigga head sprung asumn cuz he actin like he been fuckin wit that bitch for years," Chad said not really wanting to take sides but noticing a change in my behavior. He knew it was only gone get worse the more time me and Babydoll spent together too.

"Yall niggas jus sposed to have more control over the situation bruh. These is some females at the end of the day an ney sposed to respect what yall say if they down witchu. Yall should've deaded this shit before it even got started foreal. It definitely shouldn't've got this far. Now it's puttin both a yall ass in a uncomfortable position when na whole sitatuion could've been avoided," Heavy said giving Hustle his lil words of wisdom.

"Naw fuck that Heavy! That bitch jus shot at me. Dashon ass should've avoided that shit. An since he wanna take her side like she really somebody to be goin to war for fuck both a they ass," Latoya butted in tryna see if her and Hustle could turn the whole hood against me because of what had happened.

"Why you walk up on na car again after she had already bucked the burner out last night tho Latoya?" DonDon asked with a smile already ready to crack jokes about the shit.

"It'ont matter bruh foreal, he shouldn't've pulled up wit her ass after that shit no way," Hustle interrupted before Latoya even got a chance to answer.

"Yeah Hustle but if that's who he wit that's who he pullin up wit. That's why yall ladies sposed to respect each other outta respect for yall," Dre said tryna be the voice of reason.

"Howda fuck I'ma respect her when she jus fuckin shot at me Dre?" Latoya asked annoyed that everybody wasn't a hundred percent on her side and blaming me and Babydoll for the whole incident.

"Man I aint respectin shit fuck both they ass straight up. Cummon baby," Hustle blurted out before leaving with Latoya.

"Damn, Babydoll straight thugged out. It 'ont even seem like she'll do all that," Lil Rodney responded when I pulled up telling him the entire story from start to finish.

"Man can't nobody tell you you can't pullup on na set wit cho bitch, Hustle know that," he added calmly as he smiled amused with the whole Latoya and Babydoll beef like everybody else.

"That's all I'm sayin bruh! So by you knowin nat shit you shoulda jus squashed that lil beef before they even bumped heads again. But naw, yo big fat ass wanna yell out (Aye Latoya say Babydoll can't come on Gamble.) So you basicly gotta take yo bitch an shake cuz my bitch don't like her," I replied with rage, mocking Hustle while Lil Rodney stood thurr trying not to laugh.

"You hear about this shit man?" Rambo asked when Lil Rodney picked up his phone in the midst of me entertaining him with the news about all the drama going on.

"Yeah man na nigga ova hurr hot bruh, this nigga hella funny tho I swear," Lil Rodney answered before putting the phone on speaker so I could hear whatever Rambo had to say about the shit.

"Come on bruh, yall straight lettin some females take control of this whole situation! Man if yall 'ont put these bitches in check an smack the shit outta they ass if they'ont fall in line yall crazy," Rambo advised making Lil Rodney bust out laughing, unable to keep a serious demeanor like he usually did.

"So yall really finna let them make yall stop fuckin wit each other?" Chad asked soon as I picked up my phone in the midst of me and Lil Rodney laughing about what Rambo was sayin.

"Whurr that nigga Hustle at anyway? What he talm about?" Lil Rodney asked outta curiosity amused by the whole conversation.

"Man he ova thurr gettin high wit Heavy an DonDon nem. They tryna calm his big ass down wit the drugs cuz he mad then a muafucka too. These niggas trippin," Rambo answered rolling his eyes bout ready for the drama to come to a end.

"Yeah that nigga feelin some type a way an Latoya all mad talm bout we sposed to be her brothers but we not even takin her side over a new bitch you jus met." Chad added annoyed once I put him on speaker so he could join in on the conversation me, Lil Rodney and Rambo was having. Chad was more annoyed than anybody cuz he was hella close to Hustle and Latoya too but wasn't really a big fan of Babydoll. He felt like she was just coming right in changing shit and basically taking over my whole life. He would still never go against me for nobody though.

Despite his dislike for Babydoll if it ever really came down to it Chad was rocking with me regardless. That's not what he wanted though, he felt like he was the one who could talk some sense into our stubborn asses if nobody else could. He knew how awkward it would be for him to end up having to pick a side so he really just wanted us to go ahead and squash the beef.

"Man jus let the girls calm down for right now cuz the situation way too fresh at this point. Let that tension die out a lil bit first then you an Hustle can handle the shit the way yall sposed to. This shit silly tho foreal," Rambo advised hoping the beef would just eventually blow over once me and Hustle had time to sit back and think. We was both way to stubborn though.

BROS BEFORE HOES

It took months for us to go ahead and talk it out. I wasn't really worried about getting back cool with Hustle cuz I was spending all my time with Babydoll anyway. While me and Babydoll grew closer to each other, Hustle and Latoya did too. They even officially got married which was something I thought Hustle would never do just knowing the type of nigga he was.

"Cum up to the courthouse wit me an Latoya bruh, we finna go ahead an tie the knot," Hustle said to Chad hoping Chad would fill that void he felt with me and him still not being cool at the time. I aint even gone lie I felt a lil void myself but the girls was treating us like kings for having they back and going to war with each other for they asses. So we basically just kept it how it was.

"Yeah man of course I'll go nigga! Black love, I support that shit fa sho. I think you need the whole squad up in nat muafucka whichu tho, this a big day for you homie. You should hit Dashon ass up an tell em to pop out for yall big day. Squash all that bullshit this shit important," Chad answered feeling just about fed up with the two of us going so long without speaking.

"Shshsh, man please don't let Latoya ass hear you say that nigga name. I'm so sick a hearin about a muafuckin Babyboll I swear," Hustle whispered hoping Latoya wouldn't over hear the conversation.

"Lets jus go up thurr bruh, that shit thurr is dead tho trust me," He added with his head hanging down looking all sad and shit.

"Yall niggas straight trippin I swear" Chad said shaking his head in disappointment. "Come on tho nigga cheer up you sposed to be lit. This a big day for you son you finna be a man now," Chad said pushing him playfully tryna change the mood.

"Aye we finna make you niggas talk flatout," Heavy said soon as I picked up the phone when he called.

"Man fuck that nigga, Chad told me him an Latoya ass ran off an got married an shit. Silly ass nigga can't even control the damn girl but wanna marry her," I replied with a smile feeling like it was about time we went ahead and talked about the shit myself cuz I was nowhurr near as mad as I was before.

"Man fuck all that nigga pullup right now an leave Babydoll ass at home too bruh straight up, aint no females out hurr," Rambo demanded letting me know they was most likely posted on Gamble tryna get me to pull up over thurr.

"Yeah bruh, or you gone have to see me when I catch you nigga straight like that homie," DonDon said playfully as him and Dre laughed.

"Foreal tho bruh, you need to pullup," Dre added ready for me and Hustle to finally squash the beef and kill all that tension we had floating around.

"Fuck you Don, nigga you always talkin shit," I said as DonDon laughed.

"Cumon bruh we on G code pullup," Heavy stated, not willing to take no for a answer.

"Iight hurr I come I aint far," I said before hanging up the phone and heading towards Gamble.

"Aye Chad pullup wit Hustle bruh, if yall wit Latoya drop her ass off first but hurry up," Rambo directed soon as Chad picked up the phone when Rambo called. He knew Chad was with Hustle at the time cuz he had just got up out the car with them niggas.

"Iight we right aroun na corner hurr we come," Chad said before hanging up the phone, already knowing the game plan.

"Yeah cuz I'm bout sick a dis shit. Both a them niggas actin like some straightup Rudys. This shit been goin on long enough," Heavy said as Lil Rodney pulled down Gamble in the truck.

"Wasup bruh? Whatchu finna get on?" Rambo asked walking up to the truck and shaking Lil Rodney hand through the window to greet him.

"Shit jus finna bus these coupla lil moves real quick. What chall niggas out hurr on?" Lil Rodney asked curious as to why everybody was out posted on Gamble like they was waiting on somebody to pull up or something.

"Shid I need to hop in ner witchu foreal but we waitin on Dashon an Hustle nem to pullup right now tho. Im jus tryna make sure these silly ass niggas squash this petty ass beef first. I'm gettin sick a that shit man," Rambo answered not really wanting to slide out until me and Hustle finally talked about the shit like we should've did months ago in his opinion.

"Aw yeah, I'm definitely stickin aroun for that. We can jus slide out after they pullup. I aint missin nis convo tho nigga I'm hurr for that shit," Lil Rodney said jokingly but seriously willing to stick around just to see me and Hustle finally talk face to face after all the time we spent avoiding each other.

Lil Rodney pulled the truck over to the curb before hopping out as I was pulling up with Drako. Drako was tired of hearing about all the drama too cuz I had talked his muafuckin ear off about the shit by then. I was just ready to talk to Hustle about it at that point though. Me talking to everybody else about the situation just wasn't enough no more.

"Look, you niggas finna talk today foreal cuz this some bullshit. You jus got married so be a man an holla at cho boy. That's yo brother man holla at em," DonDon announced once me and Hustle was out the car and face to face while everybody else stood around in silence.

"Wasup," Hustle said hunching his shoulders feeling just as tired of the bullshit as everybody else and ready for us to finally talk it out.

"Ok look I got a question homie. Who all you know finna let a bitch- a female, tell them who they can or can't pull up wit on ney set? But wait before you answer cuz I'm not even done. We talkin bout a bitch- a female, that they not fuckin, never fucked an don't wanna fuck. This they potna bitch. He sayin he can't control what she do an how she act tho so whateva she say jus goes. Who all you know goin for that shit bruh?" I asked breaking the silence as me and Hustle stood thurr face to face for the first time in months.

"Iight maybe you right, I guess I should've handled the shit different. I mean if I would've nipped the shit in na bud that first night it prolly wouldnt've escalated like it did," Hustle admitted owning up to the part he played in us falling out the way we did.

"That's all I was sayin bruh. That first night took a left turn but it wasn't really nothin we couldn't fix nigga. All we had to do was get rid a Bre ass then link Latoya an Babydoll up so they could endup gettin cool! Whyda fuck is my bitch an yo bitch beefin bruh? They 'ont even know each other. An at the end a the day Hustle Babydoll aint have no control over what you an Bre had goin on. She aint owe nobody no explanation about the shit or nothin so she wasn't really in na wrong. I mean I get whurr the tension was comin from cuz Bre is Babydoll homegirl an all but we still could've smoothed that shit out ourselves. I know that for a fact cuz my bitch jus gone follow my lead. That's why I fuck wit her so tuff she laid back as fuck. She'ont be on all that messy shit bruh. It aint like she was on some big ol Bre gone be wit me regardless no matter what, or fuck what Hustle got goin on cuz this my muafuckin rollie type shit. Naw, she jus reacted to Latoya comin up to the car the way she did. Then when she did it again the next day talm bout fightin Babydoll jus blacked out. You know she wasn't tryna kill Latoya foreal bruh. She not even really like that the bitch jus kinda crazy sometimes. She wasn't even herself that day shid the bitch upped the banga on me she was so turnt up," I explained before everybody outside burst into laughter tryna picture Babydoll having me at gun point.

"Babydoll a straight savage that shit hella funny," Lil Rodney said as he laughed.

"Damn bruh, I aint even know she did all that. Yall might wanna check Babydoll background nigga have she ever been lockedup?" DonDon joked while holding his side from laughing so hard.

"Yeah this the first I'm hearin about this part hurr. The nigga must've been kinda scared, you was jus too embarrassed to mention that part huh," Chad said making everybody outside laugh even harder including me. It was the way his ugly ass was looking when he said it.

"Man Babydoll ass goin on na next lick fuck that," Heavy said playfully as we all continued to laugh.

"That shit hella funny bruh, you sposed to have more control over that type a situation tho nigga. Howda fuck you let her up the banga on yo ass?" Rambo said wiping a tear out his eye from laughing so hard about the shit.

"Yall niggas jus need to be a lil more dominate an assertive so they ass can fall in line," Drako said giving us a lil helpful advise to keep us both on the same page moving forward.

"Take em out together, like a double date asumn. They jus need to get to know each other a lil bit. Shid they might end up the best a friends once they apologize to each other an move on from that shit you never know. It's definitely worth a shot tho," Dre suggested, hoping the girls could form some type a friendship so the brotherhood me and Hustle had would go back to the way it was.

"Yeah bruh, we should take em out so they can apologize to each other an squash that shit. But chu gotta talk to Latoya first cuz she can't be askin about Bre an shit. That'll fuck aroun an start a problem all over again," I added stressing how important it was to make sure both the girls came with a new type of energy and willing to put the past behind them.

"Yeah I'ma showl let her ass know like look, this my muafuckin peoples an Ion't need you beefin wit his bitch straightup. They jus gotta get past that shit cuz I can't have this catty ass drama they got goin on keep gettin in na way of what im tryna do. We finna build a fuckin empire shid I'm tryna take over the streets foreal. Everybody jus need to be on na same page an work together so we all can eat you feel me?" Hustle preached explaining his true ulterior motive so everybody could stay on board and not let all the drama get in the way. "I done let Latoya ass start gettin high wit me an shit man she 'ont even hold it together like Bre used to tho. I mean Bre kinda knew howda keep it cute when she got high wit a nigga. But Latoya ass be hurt man, mouth all open, hunched over lookin a mess bruh. I hate that shit. It is easier to direct her ass when she gripped tho. So I jus be lettin her do her thang shid that's on her ass if she wanna be out hurr lookin crazy. That shit straight silly tho I aint even gone stunt," Hustle explained regretting the day he ever even pasted her the bottle.

"Yeah I heard about that shit bruh, Nikki said she be straight zombie mode now. She better be careful out hurr tho, you know how niggas be lampin an shit. Muafuckas already know who she is an ney know she most likely got some paper on her, niggas be plottin. An these hoes aint no better so you need to keep a eye on her ass if she gone be out hurr like that foreal," Lil Rodney advised warning Hustle about the dangers that awaited his new wife if he didn't keep a close watch on that particular situation.

"Yeah man Latoya aint really got no tolerance for the shit foreal. She be big hurt," Heavy added, voicing his concern about it.

"I'm tellin you bruh, a muafucka can size Latoya ass up so quick I swear. She jus be way to gripped. Ion't think she can handle that shit man. Tyresha said they put down one pack the otha day an next thing she know Latoya ass was bent all over on na porch wit her mouth hangin open. Straight standin ner noddin off for like five minutes straight. Tyresha had to wake her ass up cuz some lil kids was walkin past laughin tryna record her an shit. She said she jus took her upstairs an let her sleep it off in na house but everybody not finna lookout for Latoya like that bruh. You know these hoes be slick hatin on na low," DonDon explained stressing to Hustle how bad the situation had gotten since Hustle was steady tryna brush the shit off like it wasn't that big of a deal.

"Yeah an Tyresha said she ran na shit out that pack so Latoya aint even get that much. Ion't know howda fuck she was that fucked up bruh. She just can't handle that shit obviously," Dre added, reminding Hustle how low his wife's tolerance for the shit actually was.

"That's straight fucked up bruh, you gotta get a handle on nat shit before it get outta control man. Bitches be strungout fuckin wit this shit nigga," Rambo said voicing his concern.

"Man fuck all that shid long as I gotta handle on her ass she can figure all that otha shit out on her own cuz she stressin me the fuck out straightup," Hustle replied secretly embarrassed about how bad the situation had gotten.

"Well go holla at Latoya bruh, I'ma talk to Babydoll. Jus call my phone when yall ready to link up. We can take em to see Straight Outta Compton. She was jus tryna get me to take her to see that yesterday," I suggested hoping a double date to the movies would help break the ice enough for the girls to get back off on the right foot.

Once Hustle talked to Latoya he hit me right up. "Ay meet me on G code bruh. Me an Latoya jus had a conversation bout the shit. She finna apologize to Babydoll an just straighten na shit out. I had to let her ass know she was fuckin up the movement wit all that bullshit. She aint on no bullshit now tho. Jus pullup wit Babydoll so they can gone talk it out homie it's all good," he said ready to put our plan into motion before clicking over to take another call.

I aint waste no time at all. I hung right up and went straight in the house ready to convince Babydoll to do whatever I wanted her to do. I started by licking her pussy real good then fucked her real good from the back. After that I told her to get dressed so I could take her to the movies like she wanted me to do the night before. I aint even mention Latoya, I just rolled a couple blunts while Babydoll was in the shower. I wanted to make sure she stayed nice and mellow knowing she was already in a pretty good mood. When we pulled up on Gamble I finally let her know what was going on feeling confident that she would just follow my lead and make peace with Latoya for the sake of me an Hustle friendship.

"I need to go holla at Hustle real quick baby, Latoya aint on no bullshit trust me. She jus finna come sit in na car witchu so yall can talk it out an apologize to each other. Everybody jus wanna kill all this tension me an Hustle got goin on behind yall beef," I explained hoping she would hear me out and be willing to squash the beef with Latoya since Latoya was willing to. "Can you please talk to her for me baby? I'll lick yo pussy for two hours like I did that one time if you do," I said playfully tryna loosen her up a lil more before she talked to Latoya.

"Naw cuz you do it too hard. You act like you can't lick it soft like you know whatchu doin so naw," she said softly with a smile teasing me about not knowing how to lick her pussy as good as I thought I did.

"I'ma lick it however you tell me to baby, I love yo sexy ass," I said before kissing her softly to show my affection.

"Ok baby you can have yo friend back I know you miss Hustle. I'll talk to Latoya an straighten everything out don't worry," Babydoll said picking up the half a blunt she left in the ashtray hoping to make the conversation a little less awkward and uncomfortable by smoking with her while they talked.

"Gone head get in Latoya," I said after hopping out the driver's seat encouraging Latoya to take my spot so they could finally talk it out without all the bullshit. So Latoya sat down in the driver's seat ready to lay they beef to rest once and for all.

"Hey Babydoll, I jus wanna say sorry for tryna fight chu I really am. The stuff Hustle be tryna do behind my back is not cho fault an it wasn't right for me to keep basically blamin you for what was goin on. I hope you can forgive me," Latoya said apologizing to Babydoll for the sake of her new marriage.

"I'm sorry too Latoya, I never would've been able to live wit myself if that bullet would've actually hit chu. I would never wanna take somebody away from they kids like that so please forgive me cuz I definitely took it way too far that day," Babydoll responded sincerely feeling guilty about the way she was kinda devaluing Latoya's life in the heat of the moment at the time. She felt like apologizing to Latoya was the best thing she could've did to ease her guilt at that point. She was low-key happy to have the opportunity thanks to me and Hustle. Letting go of all that drama and animosity felt good after holding on to the shit for so long.

    I was happier than I had been in months, it felt good to be back cool with that nigga I aint even gone stunt. Babydoll could tell too, she kept making jokes about how happy I was all asudden but it made her feel even better about squashing the beef. Me and Hustle took the girls out once they agreed to respect each other and be cordial so everything worked out perfect. Me and Hustle was back in motion and everybody was happy. Now hurr come Crystle calling...

BABYMAMA VS BABYDOLL

"I keep hearin about this new bitch you call yoself havin. Is she the reason you aint brought cho ass back home yet?" she said bitterly soon as I answered the phone. We had got back on good terms after she apologized about the bullshit she was on before I left Michigan. But I still wasn't tripping off her ass no more and she could tell.

"Come on Crystle I'm in na streets, this not even no good time to be callin tryna talk to me about that bullshit. I need to be focused on what the fuck I'm doin out hurr. I aint got time to be holdin nis phone to my ear arguin witchu bitch, whurr my kids at?" I asked tryna change the subject so I wouldn't have to hear her mouth about Babydoll or explain who she was.

"Who is the bitch!" she screamed as I moved the phone away from my ear with a smile.

"Man I'm finna hang up on yo ass you trippin. Whurr my kids at Crystle?" I asked amused with her tone and curiosity about Babydoll.

"Don't worry about my muafuckin kids while you tryna play house wit a whole new bitch! I heard she got a daughter too so yo ass down ner playin step daddy an sum mo shit! Do she know about how you was just all on my line tellin me you miss yo family an wanna come back home nigga? Yo dusty ass steady lyin talm bout chu miss yo kids an wanna be back wit cho family but really rather ride aroun wit a random stripper bitch all day. That's straight fucked up too cuz yo kids down hurr jus missin yo sorry ass. You'ont give a fuck about us!" she yelled tryna make me feel guilty about leaving her and the kids in Michigan when it was really her fault I moved back in the first place.

"Man fuck you bitch, whatchu want some money asumn?" I replied with a smile hoping that would get me off the hook and get her worsm ass the fuck off my line.

"Damn right I want some money, you down ner gettin bitches hair an nails done like you'ont got kids down hurr that need shit!" she answered still furious.

"Now whyda fuck is you that mad about me gettin a bitch hair an nails done Crystle? What the fuck that got to do wit me takin care a my kids?" I asked even more amused that she knew so much about what me and Babydoll had going on.

"Cuz yo muafuckin kids need that money while you trickin off to this nothin ass bitch that aint even cute nigga! She'ont even look like shit while you doin all that bitch!" she answered feeling outraged.

"Whatchu want me to get cho hair an nails done too?" I replied making a joke out the whole conversation.

"Yep, run me all that shit! When you sendin my money?" she asked knowing she would feel a lot better about the situation once I did.

"I'm finna moneygram that shit right now I'ma call you when I'm leavin Walmart wit the confirmation code," I said before hanging up in her face hella eager to get the fuck off the phone cuz the bitch was giving me a full-blown headache.

"Um whyda fuck yo babymama call me today talm bout chu sent her some money to get her hair an nails done an you goin back to Michigan soon as you get cho bread up an yall gone always fuck aroun no matter who you talk to? Like what the fuck is yall on? Youon't see my babydaddy callin doin alla that cuz weon't fuck aroun no more, so I kinda jus wanna know wasup from you," Babydoll finally blurted out after giving me the silent treatment all day.

"I knew you was actin funny," I replied amused. "Crystle know I'm not goin back down ner baby. She already know about chu," I added hoping that would be the end of conversation. (yeah right)

"She was sayin you be tellin her that I'm just yo homegirl an you keep me aroun cuz you gotta keep swhichin cars to duck the police," she replied with her face all frowned up annoyed after trippin off the shit all day.

"Baby Crystle just sayin shit tryna run you off," I said before she interrupted.

"So did you send her some money to get her hair an nails done or not?" she asked with a serious face, eager to hear my answer.

"Baby you just crazy, so you tellin me outta all the bullshit you said she was sayin that's what's botherin you more than anything? Yall females be fuckin me up I swear," I answered playfully tryna laugh my way out of answering her question.

"Did you send her the money for her hair an nails or not?" She asked again, ready to get a yes or no answer.

"Yeah baby I mean why not? She been takin care a the kids by herself since I left from down ner. I give you money for yo hair an nails too so what's the big deal," I answered hoping she would respect my honesty.

"So what you an yo babymama got some type a open ass long distance relationship goin on asumn?" she asked offended wanting just a lil bit more clarity about me and Crystle relationship status.

"Naw baby you jus trippin fa no reason," I replied with a evil grin.

"Well you smilin like yall do. An you payin for the bitch hair an nails to get done like she me so I guess you call yoself fuckin wit both of us right," she asked curious to see if I would even deny it or not.

"Baby how I'ma fuck wit her an she allaway in Michigan," I asked still smiling and amused by the whole conversation.

"Well she said she comin down hurr in a couple weeks. So how this finna go? Is yall finna be fuckin aroun or what?" she asked ready to find out if me and Crystle was gone keep fucking around no matter what like Crystle had said.

"We all gone be fuckin aroun baby, yall gone like eachother cuz both a yall real cute," I answered playfully but hoping she would actually be with the shit for real.

"First of all bitch I'm not finna be fuckin witchu an yo dusty-ass babymama. She can have yo dirty ass! Howda fuck she get my number anyway?" she asked curiously not knowing Crystle home girl got it from Latoya and gave it to her. "You aint even nothin to be doin all that for no way nigga. I was jus fuckin wit cho ass for fun. I'm surprised I been fuckin witchu this long. You ride aroun wit Hustle ass all day while he makin all that fuckin money but cho dumbass jus makin enough to get high. So you takin all these penitentiary ass chances by runnin na fuckin streets 24-7 instead a takin yo broke ass to work. Bitch get a job! You grown as fuck! Then yo pants always saggin to yo knees. Draws always showin like that shit cute. You wakeup tryna get high every damn day so you can nod off in na middle of a fuckin conversation. You stand out on nat dirty-ass street every chance you get. An you literally keep Chad in yo back pocket everyday of yo life so we never even alone together like two adults in a fuckin relationship. Plus youon't even know howda lick my pussy no way. That bitch can actually have you really!" she yelled before storming to her car and pulling off.

    I must've called Babydoll phone a hundred times that day. I'm not even exaggerating. I called that muafucka so many times she straight changed her number on my ass I was hurt. I aint have no way of getting in contact with her. She got the keys to her new apartment the next day and I aint even know whurr that muafucka was at. I tried to get Bre ass to give me her new number or tell me whurr she moved cuz her and Hustle had started back talking after a while but Babydoll had already told Bre not to.

    Bre had start acting like she wanted me to fuck her though. Ion't know if she was tryna get back at Hustle for kicking her to the curb like he did or what but she was coming on pretty strong about the shit. She might've even been tryna get back at Babydoll for being so distant once me and Hustle made Latoya and Babydoll get cool. But either way I knew I was gone end up finding Babydoll some type a way and getting back together with her. So I aint even entertain Bre with the dick like I could've as easy as that would've been. I was just ready to get back with Babydoll and I aint want no extra bullshit like me fucking Bre getting in the way cuz I was missing her like crazy. I always rode past the nail shop she went to knowing I would catch her car parked out thurr sooner or later and one day I did.

    "You not gone be able to shake me Babydoll, I'ma always find yo ass cuz you my bitch. Niggas already know I'll kill sumn ova that pussy. I'm fucked up in na head ova yo ass," I said with a grin when she walked out the nail shop smiling at her nails infatuated with the color and design.

"Shit," she said dropping the smile the moment she heard my voice and looked up to see me standing thurr waiting in front of her car.

"Look I'm not finna share you wit a bitch jus cuz yall got kids an still in love or whatever the fuck yall got goin on! What the fuck I look like? You got me fucked up she can have you like I said!" she yelled pushing right past me to get to her car.

"Babydoll stop actin crazy we is not still in love. I'm in love witchu, why you keep actin like you'ont know that," I said pulling her closer to me.

"Well if yall not still in love whyda fuck is she callin me wit all that bullshit she was sayin? An whyda fuck is you doin na same shit you do for me for her too?" she responded as she looked me in my eyes getting a whiff of my one million cologne she loved so much. She start realizing how much she missed me then but was nowhurr near willing to admit it at that point.

"Baby you is so crazy. You jus do not wanna share this dick wit nobody, I get it it's too good so you want it all to yo self okay," I said arrogantly with a smile.

"I gotta go," she said still making her way to the car.

"Iight," I said before snatching her phone out her hands an quickly calling my phone so I could have her new number.

"Gimme my fuckin phone Dashon!" she yelled before snatching her phone back out my hand and slapping me as hard as she could. "I'ma block yo number anyway stupid!" she yelled before getting in the car and pulling off.

I still called her phone from a million different numbers tryna get her to talk to me after she blocked my number though. That is until she got her whole number changed on my ass again. I was pissed. The next time I seen her car parked at the nail shop I was with Chad so instead of waiting outside I went in. I was really just tryna avoid hearing Chad mouth about chasing Babydoll down. He already knew why I was always swarming around the nail shop and how bad I wanted her back. I always downplayed the situation to everybody else making it seem like Babydoll was only calling me at night to get some dick. Chad knew I wasn't in contact with her at all though. I was getting hella frustrated cuz everybody kept asking about her ass and I did not wanna let nobody know what was really going on with us for some reason.

"You know even if you did end up goin to another nailshop to avoid me I'll still find you right?" I said calmly walking up behind her and picking up her phone as she sat thurr getting her old nails soaked off. She had a whole new phone that was way better than her old one. I noticed it was brand new soon as I picked it up.

"Look Dashon, I'm just gone change the fuckin number again so go ahead Ion't even care," she said rolling her eyes as I started to dial my number.

"I mean you gone have to! You gone have to keep changin nis muafucka til you get tired a changin it cuz me not havin yo number don't even make sense. You my bitch, I should be able to call yo phone even if it's just to make sure you okay an check up on you," I said dialing my number in her new phone before realizing she already had it saved. "Baby why you save my number under Dusty Dick," I asked surprise she took the time out to lock my number in her new phone at all. "Baby you is sooo crazy, why it always gotta have sumn to do wit my dick? That's all the fuck you be worried about," I said playfully as I laughed.

"Cuz you hella dusty an yo dick was really the only reason I was even talkin to you but I'm over it now so leave me the hell alone," she answered with a smile as the lady that was doing her nails bust out laughing at the two of us.

"Girl you aint neva gone be ova this dick. That's why I'ma getcho ass pregnant next time I fuck you. You steady tryna run off an shit, I shoulda been gotcho ass pregnant foreal this shit jus too stressful I swear," I said after sitting down in the empty chair beside her.

"You probably the last person on nis earth I would wanna be pregnant by honestly," she replied rolling her eyes at the thought.

"But I got a job like you wanid me to so you can be happy," I answered with a smile. "Matter fact you should pick me up from work tomorrow so I can prove it," I added hoping that would give me the opportunity to get her back on my team.

"Why would you get the job just to make me happy? Why not jus get it to better yoself so you won't end up dead or locked up?" Babydoll asked feeling flattered that I said I had got the job to make her happy but knowing I wouldn't keep it if I aint want it for myself.

"Well I jus want you to be happy baby. I miss yo ass an I know you be missin me too. I can feel it every time I see you. That's why I'm always lookin for yo ass Ion't want nobody else," I explained hoping she could tell how sincere I was about everything I was saying to her.

"I mean I do miss you Dashon but I still don't feel like we should be together. Bre told me how you be fuckin wit all them different bitches. An when yo babymama came down hurr she was stayin witchu at cho mama house so I know you still fuckin wit her ass too. I jus rather you be her problem shid she the one that got kids an history. I'm not finna come second to her basic ass jus cuz she been aroun longer an got kids witchu tho, it's not even that serious I'll be okay. I mean we have no ties to each other at all. An what we had was fun but it's not somethin I wanna keep holdin on to when we not even mentally on na same page. You be worried about hangin out wit cho friends all day but I kinda feel like we gettin a lil too old for that shit. An you gettin too old for yo draws to always be showin like that too. Look, you got a fuckin belt on right now an yo draws still showin," she said pointing to the Gucci belt I bought from Chad. "When na fuck are you gone grow outta that shit? An not only that you really need to slow down wit them dems too. You already hella skinny you gone be lookin like one a Hustle geeks in a minute if you don't," she continued, giving me a lot to think about cuz I was curious to know exactly how she felt about me for some reason.

"Baby why we can't just work on all this shit together? Ion't wanna keep doin nis. Let's jus work it out. I'll change all that shit if that's what chu want," I replied, just wanting a second chance to get things back to the way they was.

"But if that's not somethin you wanna do on yo own you never gone change. I want chu to change that shit cuz you growin, not cuz I'm makin you," she responded as Chad walked in the nail shop furious.

"Nigga what the fuck, you been in nis muafucka damn near a whole hour. I thought chu was in hurr gettin yo shit done damn! Babydoll can he please call yo phone a sumn cuz this shit just don't make no damn sense. It aint never this serious bruh," he complained feeling like he had just about had it with both of our asses.

"He has my number Chad trust me" Babydoll said rolling her eyes as I put her new phone back down on the table whurr it was.

"I'ma work on nat shit so we can be back together baby you still my bitch tho. Don't forget that shit, I'll straight hurt sumn ova you on my kids," I said before heading back out to the car with Chad.

Jessica Whitfield

NO GAME PLAN

"Man nis nigga Grip got me so fucked up on everything I love he do," Hustle complained once me and Chad pulled up on Gamble whurr he was posted up looking mad as hell.

"What happened? What he do?" I asked curiously as I got out the driver's seat and stood by the car with him and Chad.

"Man nis nigga took me aroun na corner to get some dems from nis one bitch then stole a lil petty ass six pills out my cup holder bruh. I guess he was feelin some type a way cuz I said I wasn't puttin down a pack wit em. Niggas always think you gota get high wit they ass jus cuz they showin you whurr da fuck to go. But why the fuck is you takin some beans tho bruh? This a lil sell I had put together on some quick shit. What the fuck you finna do wit em? These geeks aint finna trust yo ass wit no dope. They already know this aint cho lane so they automatically gone think you tryna gank they ass. So what chu want wit the beans bruh?.... Man nat nigga gone fuck aroun an snort that shit hisself, straight tweakin, on my mama!" Hustle vented making us question whether or not the dems was even enough for Grip anymore cuz he was nowhurr to be found after taking off with Hustle dope.

"Damn Grip, that's how you rockin now?" Chad said with a smile confident about the allegations and suspicion. "He is always stealin shit like a geek, maybe the nigga done graduated. Shid I wouldn't be surprised if he did," he added feeling pretty sure Hustle was right but not knowing they would find Grip dead in his room the next day. He ended up overdosing off the same pills Hustle was bitchin about.

"Yeah that nigga trippin," I said still thinking about what Babydoll was saying when I talked to her at the nail shop.

"What's wrong witchu nigga? Seem like you kinda stressin homie wasup?" Hustle asked changing the subject after noticing how I wasn't really giving much feedback about Grip. I would've been talking my ass off about that type a shit any other day

"Man nis ol sucka fa love ass nigga steady chasin Babydoll ass down every chance he get. That nigga aint worried about shit else trust me. I'm so sick a they ass I swear," Chad blurted out feeling annoyed with me for not acting like myself knowing Babydoll was the reason why.

She had me even more stressed out once I found out she changed her number on me again. But she was about as stressed out as I was when she changed it that time though. She had just found out she was pregnant by the nigga that lived upstairs from her in the apartments she moved to. An she aint want me calling her phone making the situation more confusing for her I guess.

She knew I had her heart by then so me calling her phone would've made her feel ten times worse. She aint even like the nigga she was pregnant by for real but he was happy about it though. He was ready to start a lil family with her but she already knew if she had dude baby things would never be the same with us. So she wasn't really sure if she wanted to terminate the pregnancy or not until dude girlfriend of six years came knocking on the door letting her know that she was pregnant too. After Babydoll talked to his girl she was sure she wasn't gone go through with the pregnancy. She was leaning more towards keeping it at first but felt like that was a sign that she shouldn't. So she made the appointment to get it done as soon as possible. Dude still wanted Babydoll to keep his baby making her a lil unsure about the procedure but she ended up going up thurr anyway. He even showed up at the door on her way out begging her to have a change of heart and reconsider. But it was nothing he could do or say to stop her at that point. When she laid down on the table at the clinic the guilt was almost too much to bare. Tears start flowing down her face once the thought of her killing the innocent life she created crossed her mind. It made her feel like she aint deserve to live herself. She finally realized how irrational she was being by letting that nigga fuck her raw just to get even with me. Bre hating ass was letting her know about all the random bitches I was entertaining but aint give a fuck about. Plus Crystle and the kids staying at my mama house when they came down to visit. I was chasing Babydoll ass down the whole time Crystle was ova thurr though.

Even she knew how crazy I was about the damn girl. She was in Babydoll ear the whole time cuz they called theyselves getting cool after me and Babydoll broke up. Babydoll claimed she only befriended Crystle to prove she was over me. But she really just wanted to be sure that me and Crystle was still fuckin around so it would be easier for her to move on. Crystle was only playing into the friendship to try and keep Babydoll away from me. So neither one of they asses had good intentions or really trusted each other. They both crazy as fuck for real. Crystle knew damn well I aint want her ass unless I could have em both. And Badydoll just wasn't tryna share the dick with nobody. She aint wanna fuck with me at all unless I cut Crystle ass completely off but I knew Babydoll was missing the dick. She must've had a lil weak moment cuz she called me hella late one Saturday night most likely drunk. I was high as fuck, knocked out cold on my mama couch and missed the call though. I was hella mad when I woke up. That was around the time she got pregnant too. So it fuck around would've been my baby had I answered. She probably wouldn't've even been sure had it went that route though, so I guess it all played out like it did for a reason.

She laid thurr praying for forgiveness and mercy while contemplating on whether to live with the guilt for the rest of her life or just get up off the table while she still had a chance. She was feeling scared and unsure about altering God's plan if the baby was really meant to be born. She was praying God wasn't too angry about her choosing to kill the baby but was still worried about feeling his wrath if what she was doing was just too unforgivable for his mercy. That moment she made a promise never to even have sex again unless she got married. That way she would never end up in that predicament again. Keeping that promise was her peace of mind, a shield of protection from the karma she knew she deserved. It was like making a deal with the author and finisher of her fate so that the fear of getting what she had coming to her would go away after the procedure. She still felt the guilt but convinced herself that as long as she kept her promise the cold hearted sacrifice she made for her own happiness would go unpunished.

The next time I saw Babydoll she was in her dad's old neighborhood over thurr by 20th whurr Chucky and nem raised hell before getting theyselves booked. Everybody was out swarming around the northside like bees scattered all over the city. Gamble was just too hot to be lingering around thurr at the time. The police must've been feeling a lil lazy that day cuz they was patrolling and posted up over thurr like we aint know better than to just stay the hell away until they found something better to do.

"Wasup BabyD," Hustle said pulling up on Babydoll with Twin in the passenger's side. Twin had just got out the joint for a gun case he caught for the second or third time in a row. So the hood was hella happy to finally see him back out on the pavement again. We called him Twin cuz he had a twin a sister. But he was a pretty boy type. His light brown eyes, caramel skin, and deep waves had the bitches willing to do whatever the fuck he wanted em to. He knew the ladies like the back of his hand because of his twin sister which made it a hell of a lot easier to direct they ass from prison.

"Damn who is that bruh?" Twin asked when Hustle let down his window to say what's up to Babydoll.

"Thats Dashon lil joint bruh, he gone hurt sumn ova that trust me," Hustle answered with a smile.

"Hustle please stop sayin nat me an Dashon is not together no more," she said annoyed as Hustle's eyes widened like he had no idea.

"Damn BabyD, you gone do em like that?" Hustle asked smiling an amused.

"Aye fuck what he talm bout shorty, if yall ova wit wasup wit me an you?" Twin said turning on the charm before Babydoll rolled her eyes and walked away.

"Babydoll ova thurr on na crusher bruh," Hustle said after pulling off with Twin and calling my phone immediately. We start calling 20th street the crusher after Chucky nem went over thurr and crushed they ass on some trigger happy hothead shit.

"Aye pullup at Fairground Park real quick bruh," I said anxiously tryna hurry up and get Chad out the car with me and in the car with them so I could go pull up on Babydoll ass alone.

"Cumon Tyler, lets go to the store an get some rellos," Babydoll said to her big gay friend ready to tell him all about how much of a selfish bitch she was for killing her baby knowing the dude she was pregnant by wanted her to keep it. "I just been kinda goin thru it lately Tyler," she admitted as they both got settled in the car. She was feeling so down and depressed about the situation she couldn't even wait until she sparked up a blunt to talk about the shit.

"I feel hella fucked up for killin nat baby. Plus I been talkin to Cryslte tryna see what Dashon ass been on an that aint makin me feel no better cuz I kinda miss him. I feel like he the only one that can make me feel better right now but he still on some bullshit wit her. I'm really startin to feel like I should've jus kept my baby an moved on. Crystle say she pregnant again an all," Babydoll vented knowing Tyler was all ears just waiting to give some type of feedback or advise.

"Girl you an his thirsty ass babymama is hella fuckin funny I swear," Tyler replied loving the drama and entertainment. He already knew about everything that was going on with us up until Babydoll had got the abortion. "But I would not trust her tho Babydoll she still want him. Howda fuck she come down hurr one time for a couple muafuckin days now alla sudden she pregnant by Dashon. Like she aint been fuckin nobody else the whole time he been down hurr. That 'ont even sound right, aint no way she sure that baby his an nat's if she even pregnant foreal. That damn girl jus tryna make sure you'ont start back fuckin wit her babydaddy. She know his ass still tryna get chu back," Tyler continued warning Babydoll about what Crystle's true intentions was.

"Yeah I be feelin like that too tho. She always talm bout how he be tellin her he love her an comin back home but be all in my face tryna get back wit me every time we see each other. I mean sumn not addin up. If he was really tryna come home whyda fuck is he steady tryna rekindle what the fuck we had goin on. It's just not makin sense," she agreed before looking over to see Lil Rodney and Rambo crazy ass on the side of her.

"Flocka, flocka, flocka. That's how we pullin up if you keep duckin my boy Babydoll," Rambo said jokingly using his bare hand to pretend like he was shooting at her from the passenger's side as Lil Rodney sat thurr smiling and amused.

"Rambo stop playin like that, you is so fucked up in na head," Babydoll replied with a smile trying not to laugh about how they caught her so off guard.

"Shid you fucked up ina head too Babydoll that's why you tied in. It's only one way out this shit tho," Lil Rodney said playfully as Rambo laughed.

"Yeah BabyD! You can't duck no real street nigga remember that sis. He gone find yo ass trust me," Rambo said letting the window up slowly with a smile as Lil Rodney pulled off in front of her.

"Damn he got all his peoples pullin up on yo ass, it's gone be him in a minute," Tyler said entertained.

"Them niggas play too much I swear, all they ass," Babydoll said pulling up to the gas station amused.

"Aye wasup BabyD? Why you trippin wit my mans? He say you been duckin!" DonDon yelled from across the parking lot with his hands up.

"Don't keep playin wit my nigga heart Babydoll cuz when he spaz out on yo ass I'ma have to fuck em up!" Heavy yelled playfully before Babydoll put her middle finger up with a smile then headed in the gas station. Once she got back to Tyler crib I pulled right up as she was getting out the car.

"Get the fuck away from me Dashon, I do not wanna talk to you," she said rolling her eyes as I approached.

"Get in na car wit me, we need to talk," I replied reaching for her keys with a smile.

"Ok jus let me let the top up," she said before getting back in the driver's seat and quickly pulling off on my ass.

"She so fuckin silly," I said before running back to my mama beamer so I could chase her crazy ass down behind the wheel.

"You know for this to be yo old neighborhood you showl don't know yo way around real well," I said after trapping her on a dead end street.

"Okay what the hell do you want from me Dashon, just let me know," she replied after getting out the car finally willing to talk face to face.

"I see you got the car painted, I hope you aint think that was gone make you invisible," I said acknowledging the fact that she had changed the color of her car from silver to black since the last time I saw her.

"Maybe I'm just tired of you pullin up at my nail shop every time you see my car outside," she said shrugging her shoulders with her arms folded.

"Well jus talk to me Babydoll I mean damn I miss you, I miss us. I straight love yo ass. I can't keep goin everyday witout seein you, talkin to you, touchin you, kissin you, not even knowin if you okay," I vented hoping she would finally hear me out and understand how hard it was for me to live without her. "I need us to be together so I can know you ok Babydoll. I told you Ion't want nobody else, so what chu want me to do?" I continued, ready for us to finally get back on the same page so we could move on with our relationship cuz that was seriously all I really wanted.

"If you love me so much why are you steady tellin yo babymama somethin different? Why you steady tellin her you love an wanna be wit her knowin you can't have both of us? Why the fuck are you makin it seem like you wanna go back home to her if us workin shit out is that important to you?" she replied ready to get to the bottom of the whole me and Crystle situation once an for all

CHANGING THE GAME

"Baby Crystle know I'm not goin back down ner. She know you got my heart, that's why she tell you a bunch a shit to make you feel like you don't. Everybody know you got my heart baby," I explained trying my hardest to express how sincere and honest I was being.

"Well let her know cuz she on na phone right now," Babydoll said putting the phone on speaker after letting Crystle listen to everything I was saying the whole time without me knowing.

"Its cool nigga go ahead shid. You the one steady lyin tellin me this an nat but then go chasin bitches down to fuck wit them. Boy fuck you! An don't worry about my muafuckin kids cuz you'ont give a fuck about em no way. Fuck you!" Crystle shouted before hanging up the phone.

"Ion't care baby. I'll tell her ass straight to her face, I just wanna be witchu. That's all I want," I said as she looked into my eyes finally willing to give in and get our lives together back on track.

"Well we can talk it out an see whurr it go but it's still a couple things we need to work on. I been missin you too tho honestly," she said with a smile. "Let's just start over an take it slow this time," she added as I grabbed and kissed her for the first time in months unable to hold it back any longer.

"Hurr this my number, I'm not gone change it this time cuz I actually want chu to call," she said playfully while locking her new number in my phone.

"It's been a lot goin on wit me lately so it'll be nice to hear yo voice on a daily basis an see you sometimes cuz you always have been able to make me happy," she said as she handed me back my phone suddenly feeling concerned. That was when she realized how much our relationship would change if she kept her promise and didn't have sex with me until I married her. Lord knows we was seriously overdue for some makeup sex after being apart for so long. So that was starting to stress her out more than anything at that point.

"See that's what I'm talm bout baby, Ion't even know what's been goin on witchu wasup?" I asked ready to just hold her in my arms so she could tell me all about it while she laid on my chest like she used to.

"We can talk about it later I'll be okay. Just call me whenever babe," she answered not even knowing how to explain that particular situation.

When I came to the lil apartments she moved in she told me about everything that had happened from start to finish. Luckily the nigga had already moved out from upstairs cuz I would've been on all bullshit with his ass.

"So this nigga got chu pregnant an now you won't fuck me," I said bluntly after she explained the situation.

"Youon't have to be a dick about it Dashon. I mean how you gone get mad cuz Ion't wanna fuck nobody til I get married now," she replied annoyed with my lack of compassion and understanding.

"Babydoll who does this shit? How you just gone stop fuckin me til we get married? How long you think that's gone last?" I asked hoping to God it wouldn't take too long cuz I wanted to fuck her ass so bad.

"You might as well just move on Dashon, I'll figure this out on my own," she said getting off the couch and heading to the door to let me out.

"Figure out what baby? I jus don't understand why I can't fuck you jus cuz a lame-ass nigga nutted in yo pussy an got chu pregnant, that's all I'm sayin," I said stopping her in her tracks before she got to the door.

"I just need to figure out my life an whurr it's goin right now. Ion't like who I am, I just wanna be different! Don't nobody understand what I'm goin thru. Just leave me alone an let me figure it out!" she vented as tears started rolling down her face like a waterfall.

"Baby please stop cryin, you overreactin. Why you gettin so emotional, I hate seein you cry," I said holding her in my arms tryna calm her down.

"Cuz I hate myself, I hate my life, I wish I was somebody else!" she continued definitely having some type of mental break down or something cuz she was hysterical.

"Baby why would you wanna be somebody else? You perfect, how you hate yoself? That'ont even make sense," I said still holding her closely while she cried.

"Cuz that wasn't even my first time doin nat shit. When my daughter was like six months I got pregnant again" she admitted as the tears continued to flow. "I was straight pregnant wit twins at 16 wit a six month old daughter already. I couldn't imagine havin three kids at that age especially after seein how much time an attention she needed on her own plus finances. I was steady runnin back to my babydaddy tryna be wit him then fuckin wit my highschool boyfriend at the same time. So I wasn't even sure which one a them I was pregnant by which made it even worse. Then a couple years ago I got pregnant by the dude I was wit before I start fuckin wit Curtis, I'm so fucked up I aint even eat shit after I found out I was pregnant wit his baby. So I had a miscarriage wit that one but I basically kilt that baby too cuz I wasn't eatin shit on purpose. I aint even have a good enough reason to do that shit neither cuz I was actually in love wit the nigga. My ass was just to scared he was gone change up an stop likin me once I had the baby like my first babydaddy did," she continued as she wiped the constant tears runnin down her face. "I just feel like…what's wrong wit me? It just seem like I'm never gone get it together I feel so hopeless," she said trying her best to calm down and pull herself together.

"Look baby, we gone get it together okay. I'ma get cho ring wit my income tax an til then its whatever you wanna do. Shid if you'ont wanna fuck me I aint gone force you to. I'ma jus lick yo pussy til you nut on my face," I said with a evil grin tryna change the mood a lil bit so she could cheer up and start acting like herself again.

"No cuz you'on't do it right," she replied wiping the tears off her face and finally cracking a lil smile.

"I'ma learn tonight cummer," I said pulling the basketball shorts she stole from me before we broke up down to her ankles and lying her down on the couch. After I laid her down I opened her legs, spread her pussy open, then licked real soft on the tip of her clit in a circle. I had never made her nut by licking her pussy before but that night I knew I did. Her legs start shaking when it came down then I tasted it. She started talking to me right before she came and while she was cummin like she did when I used to fuck her. And that shit was satisfying as fuck to me for some reason.

She was always the queen of sucking my dick real good but once I start eating her pussy like that she got hella nasty with that shit. She would always suck my dick until I came then keep going while it shot all down her throat making me even more crazy about her ass. She was sucking my dick all the time too, like everyday all day and would never spit it out. That's all she ever wanted to do. The shit started getting kinda frustrating after a while though. It always just made me extra horny and I still wanted to fuck her hella bad but she would not fuck me for shit. No matter how many times I licked her pussy, no matter how hard I was tryna get her to break, she just would not give in and let me fuck her. So I ended up sneaking off and fucking one of my potnas lil sister out of spite and aggravation. I mean a whole year had past by and we was living together and everything. Shid I had moved in soon as we got back together. So the bitch was basically just torturing me for a whole year straight before I went behind her back and got some pussy. She had me fucked up.

Kayla was a lil hood bitch that used to always be geeked up about getting high with me and her brother. She was kinda skinny but was still real cute and naïve. So it was easy for me to knock her lil ass off after we got high without feeling like she was gone be a threat to me and Babydoll relationship. Babydoll wouldn't've even had to worry about me fucking the bitch if she was coming up off some pussy herself though. I felt like I had a damn good excuse and Babydoll knew it too. She suspected I was fucking the bitch soon as she seen her lil ass but never even confronted me about it.

She wasn't sure but didn't really wanna be either. She would always say lil slick shit to me about Kayla just to let me know she wasn't stupid. But she wouldn't dare start a problem with me about it knowing I was itching to blow her ass down about not fucking me herself. I was still crazy over Babydoll but sleeping next to her half naked body every night and her sucking my dick like she was doing made me fuck the shit out of Kayla ass. I was just way too horney shid I wasn't even wearing a condom when I was fucking her. And I was nuttin all in her pussy like she was my bitch. I aint stop fuckin with her ass until she told me she was pregnant. After a while I told Babydoll what was up though so she made me take a blood test for the baby once she talked to Kayla herself.

When we found out the baby wasn't mine Babydoll chunked the whole situation up and we moved on. Her crazy ass still aint start back fucking me. The bitch a straight up fucking psychopath I swear.

It was about two years after we had stopped fucking at this point and Babydoll psycho ass still wasn't willing to fuck me. She would always just blame everything on me for not getting her a ring like I said I would. But us not having sex made the relationship so toxic that neither one of us was sure if we really wanted to get married. All we knew was that we loved each other, and we knew the love was real cuz neither one of us was willing to just let it go and move on.

I still couldn't imagine not seeing her ass everyday and she couldn't stand the ideal of somebody else holding her at night. She knew another nigga wasn't gone love her crazy ass like I did. I was just tired of trying so hard to make her happy and still not being able to fuck her though. Hell I felt like I deserved to fuck another bitch an get away with it. She said she aint want me selling dope wit Hustle so I got a job. She said she aint want me hanging out on Gamble so much so I cut back on that and start spending more time with her. She wanted me to go to church with her so I started going to church with her. She wanted me to stop getting high so I cut back as much as I could. I was bending over backwards to make that damn girl happy and she still would not fuck me. It was ridiculous.

Chad had got caught lackin on Gamble with a gun he bought from lil Beezy and ended up getting locked up for a couple of years. So he wasn't around all the time no more and I know she was happy about that. I had made her quit working at the strip club after a while cuz I start feeling some type a way about all them goofy ass white boys being able to touch and grab all on her ass every night. Then she start working a regular job like me which made it a lot harder for us to keep up wit the rent and all the bills. That put even more stress and strain on the relationship. But we still never considered just giving up and going our separate ways cuz the love we had was so solid.

Hustle and Latoya aint feel like our love was worth the struggle though. Hustle felt like I was a damn fool and let me know every chance he got while Latoya would just flex on Babydoll with all her designer clothes and new shoes every chance she got. "Why the fuck you tell Latoya I'm not fuckin you

Babydoll," I asked furiously after Hustle start clowning me about the shit when I seen him on Gamble. We had just took her and Latoya to this fancy lil restaurant in the casino the night before for Valentine's day and I guess Babydoll must've start telling the bitch all our business when me and Hustle left them alone together to duck off and get some more dems before we headed out.

"I mean yall the ones wanid us to be friends it was just girl talk damn. I can't tell the bitch about my spiritual journey but you can force me to be cool wit her ass?" she replied rolling her eyes as she looked in the mirror rubbing lip gloss on her lips like she did alla time.

"Bitch you talk too much damn! Certain shit I jus don't want they ass to know! Whyda fuck would I want my potna knowin another nigga nutted in my bitch an got her pregnant so I haven't fucked this dinky bitch in two years!" I yelled feeling outraged.

"Ok first of all you nutted in a random bitch an supposedly got her pregnant too. Second of all yo lame ass be too worried about what Hustle think when he don't even got a bitch that love him like I love you. He actually married her ass tho, howda fuck Latoya even remember what the fuck I was talkin about when her dope fein ass was steady noddin out the whole time anyway. Plus she probably fuckin everybody but Hustle drove ass, you want us to be like them so bad tho you stupid as fuck! Hustle an Latoya aint got no type a structure an don't even know what the fuck to do wit all that money. They aint even got no fuckin furniture in ney crib! They won't even put no plates on ney car! I mean at least our crib fully furnished an our car legit wit up to date tags! You aint worried about that type a shit tho cuz you to worried about all they clothes an shoes. You stupid as fuck I swear! Go get chu a bitch like Hustle got since he always makin you feel like you aint got nothin special wit me. Just cuz we not takin na same stupid ass penitentiary ass chances they takin. Fuck you!" she screamed before I stormed back out the door slamming it behind me.

GAME TIME

"Man Babydoll ass drivin me crazy we always fuckin arguin I'm sick a that shit," I said as I got out the car to greet Rambo after pulling up on Gamble.

"Shid yall a couple years in now of course yall always arguin. That honeymoon shit been dead an ova wit," Rambo replied before hitting the blunt he had just sparked up then passing it to me.

"Yeah I'm tired a her ass tryna control everything tho, some shit finna have to change I'm not bullshitin," I said before hitting the blunt a couple times then passing it back to him.

"Yeah you seen Lil Rodney tho?" he asked randomly changing the subject with a mouth fulla smoke.

"Naw not today why? What's goin on wit him?" I asked curiously, realizing it must've been a reason why he just bust out asking about Lil Rodney out the blue. Rambo had to be trippin off something for him to just be posted up on Gamble by hisself anyway cuz nobody else out thurr at the time. Gamble was like a second home to all of us no matter what. That's whurr we went to get away and clear our minds usually. It was easy to take our minds off certain shit cuz it was always so much going on. It just gave us a sense of freedom and independence knowing it was no rules in the jungle ova thurr.

Pow pow pow pow pow!

"Damn bruh, who the fuck was that?" I asked ducking down while Rambo dumped back at the black Buick Regal zooming off at top speed. "I can't believe I'm out hurr lackin on nis muafucka like Ion't know whurr the fuck I'm at," I added feeling hella rookied out for not having my thumpa on me at the time.

"Thats them Tallaban niggas bruh, we at each other head cuz they know I kilt they lil peoples an shit," Rambo answered still watching the corner they was shooting from. "Lil Rodney got mad talm bout I'm puttin him in na middle of the shit an I aint heard from his ass since," Rambo explained as he looked around cautiously with his gun cocked ready to shoot up anything moving out of instinct and fear.

"Damn bruh, yall got all that goin on? That's crazy, I thought yall been squashed that lil rival beef yall had goin on," I replied feeling kinda lame for not knowing what was going on in the neighborhood like I used to.

"Yeah man it's real in na field right now homeboy. I been knockin nem niggas off one by one. Lil Rodney don't even know all that but he sposed to be rockin wit me no matter what anyway. I'm feelin some type a way about that shit I aint even gone stunt," Rambo revealed stressin how frustrated he was with Lil Rodney for being all mad instead of just having his back.

"That shit is hella messy tho bruh, he do business wit them niggas so it do kinda put em in na middle a the shit. He the one gotta squash that shit foreal but for right now jus lay low for a minute. Sometimes you gota let certain shit die down for a while its time to take a break homie. If Lil Rodney wasn't so mad he'll tell yo ass the same thing shid you see how he had to duck off for a minute after that shit happened wit him an Trouble back in na day. You just got to when its too much goin on like this nigga the streets gone be hurr when you get back. You gotta chill out for a minute tho I'm tellin you. It's way too much heat on yo ass right now an too close to home. Listen to what I'm sayin cuz I aint gone tell you nothin wrong," I said warning him about how the situation would only get worse if his hotheaded ass didn't take my advice.

"Yeah you right bruh. I'm jus gone duck off for a lil minute then, hold it down nigga faces up," he said before shaking my hand goodbye and heading to his car.

"Waddup fool, you stayin out past curfew? I know Babydoll want cho ass back before the streetlights come on," Hustle said playfully as he pulled up next to my car. "Daaamn what happened nigga? You straight got bullet holes in yo shit wasup?" Hustle blurted out in shock noticing the windshield.

"Yeah man ova hurr fuckin aroun wit Rambo lil hot ass. Niggas done came thru an shot my shit up," I said looking at the windshield feeling even more pissed off about it.

"Daaamn bruh, do Babydoll know yet?" Hustle asked with a smile making me feel ten times worse. I hadn't even told her ass about the shit yet cuz I aint wanna hear her mouth.

"Man fuck naw, I aint even tryna deal wit Babydoll ass right now. I aint neva gone hear the end a this shit bruh I already know," I answered hoping to avoid that headache as long as possible.

"Yeah she gone be mad then a muafucka, you might as well gone hop in wit me. I know you scared to go home nigga that's why you still out hurr now," Hustle said as he laughed.

"Man fuck you bruh," I said with a smile as I hopped in the passenger's side.

"Yo ass out hurr lackin like a muafucka too aint chu? Damn thumpa somewhurr at home wit Babydoll ass," Hustle teased knowing I aint have it on me cuz I most definitely would've had that muafucka out an in my hand after all that.

"Man nis muafucka jus be too hot I wasn't even plannin on sittin out hurr that long. Shid I was jus tryna slide thru an get high real quick so I could go tune Babydoll ass out foreal. Rambo was the only muafucka outside tho an he aint even have no dems. We had jus smoked a lil blunt before that shit popped off," I explained knowing damn well that wasn't a good enough reason to not have my gun pulling up on Gamble.

"What that nigga Rambo have on em?" Hustle asked curiously wishing he was thurr to catch a piece a the action hisself.

"He had a mack on em, he was on point wit that muafucka too shid he fuck aroun an hit sumbody cuz they showl took off hella quick," I answered reassuring him that at least one of our asses was armed and dangerous at the time even though it wasn't me.

"An yo ass jus out hurr naked in na trenches. I can't believe you bruh man hurr," he said playfully before handing me a glock to ease my embarrassment.

"What the fuck happened to you bruh. Babydoll dun turnt cho silly ass into a straightup lemon," he added still giving me a hard time about not having a thumpa on me in the first place.

"You need to go get chu a phone nigga, I'll turn nat muafucka up witchu man that goin to work shit dead homie. We can straight be gettin nis bag an runnin it up it's too much paper out hurr bruh. Niggas steady gettin kilt an locked up wit they phones an shit, it's all money floatin aroun nis muafucka. Fuck what Babydoll talm bout nigga jus hand her ass the money an she gone fall in line trust me. You gotta get this bag tho man foreal," Hustle preached trying his best to get me back in the streets regardless of what Babydoll wanted.

"I think you right bruh, it's time for me to get this bag. I'm sick a Babydoll thinkin she runnin shit anyway. I'm on a whole new mission from now on nigga it's a new day," I said with pride, confident that I was making the right move despite what Babydoll would think about it.

"Bout time nigga! I been waitin on yo ass to snap up out that shit homie," Hustle said proudly, happy to finally have me back to my normal self after all the time I spent stuck up Babydoll's ass instead of running the streets with him.

After that I quit my job and was back in the car with Hustle everyday passing out dope and giving out my new number. Babydoll hated the ideal of me quitting my job outa nowhurr and being gone with Hustle most of the time. But all she did was constantly call my phone while I was out moving around begging me to come home with her so she wouldn't be so worried. She was always calling my phone. Hustle just thought that shit was so annoying and pointless though. He would talk a million dollars worth a shit every time he heard us on the phone.

"Nigga get cho Rudy-ass off the phone man nat shit straight sickenin bruh. Yall live together damn this the same girl you finna see soon as you get home. It is not that serious bruh it aint neva that deep," Hustle would say loud enough for Babydoll to hear making her hate him more and more every time she called. They couldn't stand each other for shit I swear.

"Man nis nigga can't go nowhurr witout Babydoll ass that shit sad bruh," Hustle said carelessly as me and Babydoll walked through the door together. We had came to his house that day and Babydoll was the only female thurr amongst a house fulla niggas counting money, weighing up dope, and directing everybody that called to the alley in the back of Hustle crib. "Nigga do you see Latoya, or Bre, or anybody else bitch up in nis muafucka right now?" Hustle asked tryna make me feel like a lemon for pulling up with Babydoll knowing everybody thurr was trappin.

"Kiss my ass Hustle if I say I'm goin I'm goin," Babydoll said with a smile walking right past him before sitting down on the crate they was using for a chair in the living room.

"Come on BabyD, why you wanna be in na mix so bad? You sposed to be somewhurr shoppin all this money bein made," Hustle replied with a smile while looking her up an down noticing her new wardrobe.

"Hustle would you please stop callin me BabyD? Damn you got everybody yall know callin me that shit. You jus not gone be happy til you change everything about my life is you?" Babydoll said playfully picking a fight with Hustle since he was always talking shit.

"Yeah you wanna be a street nigga so bad so you need a street nigga name," Hustle said playfully as Babydoll put her middle finger up trying not to laugh.

"Damn yo nails was just all blue, howda fuck they turnin purple?" Hustle asked realizing her nails was mostly purple all asudden.

"Its mood change nail polish Hustle, the color changin cuz you pissin me off," Babydoll said jokingly as she laughed.

"Damn you showl got real Hollywood on a nigga all asudden, that shit hard tho I aint even gone stunt," Hustle replied before answering his phone.

"What the fuck you mean yo PO locked chu up!" Hustle blurted out after hearing what Latoya had to say when she called. "Howda fuck you finna do ahunnit an twenty days in jail. We got kids Latoya, I can't just take care of our kids by myself fa four months like I aint got shit goin on. This some bullshit!" Hustle complained before Latoya hung up in his face out of frustration "Man Latoya ass just got booked for a punkass probation violation. She straight gotta do a 120. Now what the fuck I'm sposed to do for four months witout her stupid ass doin what she sposed to be doin wit the kids on a daily basis," Hustle said after slamming the phone down on the table.

"Damn, what she dropped dirty?" Twin asked out of curiosity but feeling pretty sure that was the reason her probation officer cuffed her ass.

"Hell yeah she droped dirty, that shit'll getchu booked quick. Ion't know why Latoya went up thurr playin wit them people like they won't lock her ass up," Heavy interrupted already knowing that was probably what happened too.

"Man Latoya ass fuck aroun an went up thurr high," DonDon added as he laughed.

"Betta call Bre ass, she'll hold it down for a few months for you. Whatchu think Babydoll?" Heavy suggested with a smile.

"Yeah BabyD, holla at cho girl real quick, tell her it's time to step up to the plate," DonDon added playfully.

"Yeah I don't really wanna be involved, I'm already forced to be a fake ass bitch cuz yall wanid me an Latoya to be cool so bad. I haven't talked to Bre in hellas. Yo secret safe wit me tho bro, we jus gone leave it at that," Babydoll replied with her eyebrows raised reassuring Hustle that she wouldn't run her mouth about it if that's what he decided to do.

"Bre is pretty much exactly what a nigga need right now. I mean she showl keep quiet about the shit me an her be havin goin on. I fuck aroun an hit her ass up foreal," Hustle said feeling like Bre was the perfect candidate to play Latoya roll while she was gone.

TEAM PLAYER

"Yeah you need to let her ass fill in shid that's the whole point of havin a side bitch. Bre aint even got no kids so I know she got the time on her hands. Tell the kids her name TT. Latoya gone think you got one a yo geeks watchin ney ass," I encouraged as everybody laughed.

"I'm hip bruh she need to come thru," Hustle said dialing Bre number right then and thurr.

"We straight been fuckin wit these crazy ass niggas fa three years Baby-doll. Howda fuck that happen?" Bre blurted out as me, her, Babydoll, and Hustle sat on the back porch smoking a blunt together. Hustle had paid for a cab to drop Bre off at his crib that day.

"Damn it's been three years? It 'ont even seem like it's been three years since we met chall. That shit crazy," Hustle interrupted amazed with how fast the three years went by.

"An I aint even like this nigga at first, that's the crazy part," Babydoll commented with a smile as I handed her the blunt Hustle passed me.

"Right, you aint like Dashon ass for shit. I straight had to talk her bougie ass inta linkin up wit chall. She love the nigga dirty draws now tho so I guess my ass jus cupid," Bre added taking credit for the whole relationship escalating the way it did.

"Yeah an I'm jus stupid," Babydoll replied handing her the blunt as they laughed.

"That's yall new names too, Cupid an Stupid," Hustle said jokingly making me and the girls laugh even harder.

"I knew I was gone get cho ass tho baby, I wasn't worried bout chu not likin me girl you'ont run shit," I said giving Babydoll a quick kiss as Hustle rolled his eyes.

"An I should've been got cho ass pregnant Bre, lemme find out chu snuck off an kilt my baby behind my back," Hustle said playfully cutting his eyes at Bre.

"Boy you know damn well I would've kept cho baby. You the one busted out an got married on my dumbass. Hell I still woulda had that lil muafucka tho I aint even gone stunt," Bre replied with a smile before Twin pulled back up and ran to the back door.

"My dumbass dun left my trap phone ova hurr bruh," he said before dashing in the house hoping nobody hadn't swiped that muafucka cuz it was a house fulla niggas over thurr earlier that day.

"Loose ass nigga, you better hope aint nobody snatch that muafucka. If I'da seen yo shit just layin aroun in ner unattended I'da had all yo people callin my phone by now," Hustle said jokingly but really just tryna warn Twin about how quick a nigga would take his phone and serve all his people if he wasn't careful.

"Man fuck you nigga, bet it won't happen again," Twin replied playfully coming out the back door with his phone in his hand. He was definitely lucky nobody noticed he had left it in thurr.

"Yeah it bet not happen again cuz I'ma getchu next time bruh. Everybody on yo line gone have my number an ima be answerin yo shit," I added jokingly knowing he would be a lil more cautious with his phone since me and Hustle was giving him such a hard time about it.

"You niggas lousy bruh, yall won't get me tho," Twin replied as we laughed. "Faces up yall, safe sex an pay checks ladies," he added as he ran back to the car while the girl that had to drive him back over thurr sat impatiently in the driver's seat waiting.

"Aye why I run inta that nigga Rello earlier you remember him? He went to school wit us back in na day, the lil nigga that was already trappin," Hustle asked tryna jog my memory.

"Yeah wit the mohawk, had all the lil hoes on em. I remember that fool what he on now?" I asked feeling sure I knew exactly who he was talking about cuz the lil nigga was trappin before any of us start fucking with the shit. Shid he was the reason everybody wanted to get off in the dope game in the first place.

"Shit, same shit. He got a lil team behind'm now tho they tryna linkup wit us tomorrow," Hustle answered as he hit the blunt one last time before throwing the roach in the grass. "He say he want some mo niggas like us rockin wit em, he remember who you is too. We jus need to get up under they ass long enough to grab some a they people foreal tho. Them niggas got like six phones each bruh. They can't even keep up wit all them people," Hustle explained letting me know the game plan before we even went to link up with they asses.

"Iight cool. We jus gone play into the shit, double our clientele, then branch back off on our own shit simple, " I replied letting him know I understood the motive so he could know we was both on the same page with the shit.

So the next day we linked up with the niggas eager to see how Rello was running his lil operation only to find out them niggas really was making way more money than they could keep up with. Rello only had two niggas working for him and they was so in over they heads that Rello was practically begging us to step in and help em out. He knew we would bring more to the table after seeing how well we was keeping up with our own phones. We only had two but they was still always ringing and we always had enough pills to serve all our people no matter what. His squad on the other hand kept running out and having to go get back in the lab to make more.

Rello never really helped em out in the lab and he never really wanted to go serve the people himself. So he convinced me and Hustle to knock all the dope we had off on his phone then get in the lab with his squad. It was kinda hard to turn down too cuz we was knockin off a whole day's worth in like a hour and we was putting hella more people on our line. It got to a point whurr it was a lil too much to keep up with even for us.

After a while my ass had forgot all about the original plan. Hustle was ready to branch off from them niggas but I felt like we was straight getting rich fucking with they ass. I aint really see no reason to branch off from the niggas. Once Hustle realized they had access to all his geeks just like we had access to all theirs he was more worried than I was cuz Hustle had a lot of big dog geeks. Geeks that spent like 8 or 9 hunnit at a time but the people I had on my phone never really called with more than like two or three. I just felt like as long as I was knocking off more dope and making more money nothing else mattered. I mean I had doubled my clientele and tripled my income just by jamming with these niggas everyday. So I wasn't in a rush to change up our everyday routine at all.

Rello ass was making his money without even having to do shit. The nigga kept all four of us high though. He always had a bunch of dems in his pocket before anything so we was getting high every day without ever even having to pay for shit. I was saving hella money. Plus he introduced us to dirty Sprite, that's promethazine mixed with Sprite and that shit had us faded on a whole nother level.

"You know that nigga Chucky jus touched back down. They done finally let his crazy ass up out that muafucka," I said to Hustle after my mama called reminding me to make sure I came to his lil homecoming party she was in the process of cooking a bunch of food for.

"See that's what I'm talm bout nigga. We can build our own lil team now. They finna let Cutthroat back up out that muafucka too. We got Twin, Don-Don, Heavy, Dre. We can jus takeover Rello shit foreal," Hustle replied taking the opportunity to stress how bad he wanted to branch off from Rello nem.

"Man nat nigga Chucky ass not even comin home on no paperchase like I thought he would. That nigga aint even hisself no more right now. An aint no tellin what Cutthroat ass finna be on when he touch back down. I think niggas jus be needin a lil time to adjust back into the real world after bein gone nat long. I talked to that nigga Chucky the otha day an na nigga on some whole otha shit I swear," I said warning Hustle that building a team like Rello did just wouldn't be so easy.

"Whatchu mean he on some whole otha shit bruh?" Hustle asked with a smile amused and curious about how serious I was. Once we got to my mama house he was able to see himself how serious I was about Chucky being completely different. He was a full blown Muslim wearing some glasses he aint really need and some sort of dashiki shirt oddly enough.

"Wasup Kings," Chucky greeted as me and Hustle walked through the door.

"Wasup bruh? They done finally let a real nigga up out that muafucka huh?" Hustle replied disregarding his unusual outfit and weird approach.

"Aw naw my uneducated brother, they let a king free on nis day. You see they want us to refer to ourselves as real niggas so we won't realize how powerful we are as black kings of this world," Chucky replied as I rolled my eyes with a smile.

"Man fuck all that bruh when we takin nis nigga shoppin? What the fuck you got on homie?" Hustle responded as he laughed.

"Yeah nigga when na fuck you start wearin glasses fool? You tellin me jail be fuckin up niggas vision now?" I asked playfully as me and Hustle laughed.

"You the one blinded brother, I'm seein more clearly than I ever did," Chucky answered with a prideful smile.

"Well it aint them fake ass glasses helpin you see more clearly that's fa damn sho," I said jokingly having a good time teasing my lil brother after so long.

"Foreal tho man when you tryna hit the mall fool? We finna hook you up. We can hit that muafucka tomorrow if you want to," Hustle said hoping some new clothes would make him start acting more like his old self again.

"Brother save yo money, you gotta stop lettin na white man make you his bitch wit all these designer tags an labels. That's just a way for them to put us back in na mind a slavery by makin us work like a dog for a label that don't even mean shit. They wanna take you back to workin for nothin after comin so far from havin to do that shit. Look at all the chances you takin to wear that shit Hustle. You gamblin yo whole life for somethin that has absolutely no value whatsoever in all reality. What yall need to do is go wit me to one a these sermons so yall can get the knowledge yall need as black kings an leaders of society," Chucky preached as me and Hustle rolled our eyes wondering how long this phase would last.

"I heard they let a real nigga up out that muafucka," DonDon yelled out walking up to my mama porch whurr we was all standing around eating our plates forced to listen to Chucky lecture us about being black and more powerful than we realized.

"Bout muafuckin time too foreal," Dre added after getting out the driver's seat as Tyresha big ass got up out the back.

"They freed a king brother, they locked up a real nigga an released a king more powerful than they could ever imagine," Chucky replied proudly as me and Hustle kept eating hoping he wouldn't lecture DonDon and Dre as much as he lectured us.

"Now what the fuck done happened to yo ass Mohammad? Whatchu muslim now nigga?" DonDon asked as him and Dre laughed.

"Baby go fix me a plate," DonDon said to Tyresha brushing the bullshit Chucky was talking about off with a laugh.

"Yeah then go downstairs wit Babydoll nem the porch reserved fa street niggas. Aint no females out hurr," Hustle said playfully just talking shit tryna piss Tyresha off for no reason.

"Hustle shut cho fat ass up! Don't nobody wanna sit aroun yall ass no way. I'm tryna sit at the damn table an eat I'm hungry as hell," Tyresha replied making her way in the house to make Don plate an get him out the way so she could make hers.

"Wasup mama?" DonDon said answering his phone when she called. "Damn mama foreal?" he replied holding the phone looking disappointed after hearing what she had to say.

'Wasup bruh? Whats wrong?" I asked curiously as we all stood around him waiting to hear the news.

"Heavy jus got booked, she said Task Force boxed him in when he was comin out the alley," Don answered feeling crushed about the news his mama had just called with out the blue. "Ok mama I'ma call you back. Love you," he said before hanging up the phone heartbroken.

"Damn nis nigga done got caught lackin in nat hot ass stolo that fuckin quick. I started not to even give it to his ass too. That muafucka was jus way too hot bruh, I kept tellin his ass that shit damn,…talm bout he gone take em, knowin his fatass can't drive. I hate I gave em that muafucka I aint even gone stunt," Hustle said feeling just as disappointed and somewhat responsible for Heavy getting booked.

Twin sold Hustle that car after this green ass bitch left it running at the gas station. He hopped right in that muafucka and we trapped that bitch out for hellas. I mean we had high speeded that car so many times aint no way they wasn't gone end up boxin that muafucka in eventually. Plus that hot ass car was already getting passed around the hood before Hustle even bought it.

"So Heavy jus got booked?" Tyresha announced coming out the house with DonDon plate in one hand and holding her phone to her ear with the other. "Don't cry sis, its gone be okay boo," she said handing DonDon his plate as she listened to how upset Heavy baby mama was about the whole situation on the phone.

"Tell her to calm down, we gone make sure she straight til my nigga touch down," Dre assured before Tyresha headed back in the house to try an comfort her some more.

"Damn man, Cutthroat finna touch back down an Heavy get booked. Chucky back home but Chad ass booked. Soon as Twin came home that nigga Drako got booked. Niggas can't stay up out that muafucka for shit," DonDon complained, playing around with the food on his plate not really having much of a appetite anymore. "Shid you a damn lie brotha I aint goin back, an you can bet cho ass on nat," Chucky blurted out making everybody but DonDon bust out laughing changing the mood a lil bit.

"Cumon Don cheer up homie you know how this shit go nigga. Heavy gone do his time come home an it's gone be like he never even left. Just let the shit play out like it's gone play out anyway. Stressin off it aint gone do you no good," I said tryna cheer his ass up a lil bit. It was kinda weird seeing the lil nigga all down and depressed knowing he was usually the one who was always playing and joking around.

"Let's just hope he'ont come home actin like this nigga Chucky tho foreal," Hustle blurted out making even DonDon goofy ass bust out laughing.

SWITCHIN UP

"Wasup homie? I see you finally back on na bricks. How you feel after fuckin up all them racks on a nigga," I said teasing Cutthroat about us missing out on all the money he got locked up with when they finally let his ass out.

"Yeah man, I been trippin off that shit for damn ner five years now nigga. That shit was a epic fail bruh. I should've tucked that muafuckin money in a bush some muafuckin whurr asumn. Ion't know what the fuck I was on," Cutthroat replied laughing the whole incident off as he shook my hand to greet me.

"Wasup fool, I think it's time to hit the mall homie you back outside now nigga wasup?" Hustle said as Cutthroat shook his hand to greet him. He was happy to see me and Hustle out, alive, and racked up after hitting that lick with the two of us and Chad then doing damn near five years in the joint behind that shit. An we was just happy we had the money to look out for him like we did.

"Aye whurr yall at bruh? I need you and Hustle to get in na lab wit these niggas man. It's too much goin on ova hurr an we aint got enough hands to keep up," Rello explained in a panic soon as I answered his call.

"Damn bruh, all them pills gone already? Shid we on our way to the mall right now tho. The homie jus did a lil five peice so we finna make sure he straight real quick since he back outside an shit," I replied explaining why me and Hustle wasn't able to come help em out right then and thurr like he needed us to.

"Man it aint no time for that type a shit right now bruh it's all people callin, jus slide that nigga sum paper asumn. It aint neva that serious to be doin nat type a shit while all this goin on!" Rello yelled as Hustle grabbed the phone after overhearing what Rello was saying.

"Look bruh! My nigga jus did a whole five piece! We finna go get his ass together flatout we gone holla at chu in a minute homie!" Hustle yelled before hanging up smack dead in the nigga face pissed. "Fuck you thought nigga," he added with his face all frowned up feeling bothered. "That nigga straight be thinkin he runnin shit, I aint one a them yes man-ass niggas he be keepin up under his ass. An you aint neither bruh so don't let that clown-ass nigga think he directin shit ova hurr homie foreal," he continued feeling outraged with the nerve and audacity Rello had when he called.

"Man you know why we rockin wit that nigga fool. These phones aint never did the numbers they do now, it's all new people on our shit," I replied reminding him how beneficial it was to link up with Rello nem on a daily basis. "Fuck naw that nigga aint directin shit ova hurr, that's why I deal wit the nigga when I want to. I aint finna sit hurr an act like Ion't get shit outta fuckin wit they ass tho cuz I do," I added tryna get Hustle to look at the situation from my point of view.

"Man you still pullup on nem niggas every day bruh, it aint neva that serious when we already got a phone fulla they geeks homie," Hustle said feeling annoyed with how involved I still was with Rello when he had already started to shy away.

"Yeah why the hell not? When I be jammin wit them niggas I'm guaranteed to knock off all the dope I got on me, stay high for free, an I be cuffin some a the sells I buck for his ass. That shit gravy bruh you trippin. We jammin outta his cars, steady switchin em up so Task Force don't even know what the fuck to hop down on unless you movin all slow an sloppy. An you know damn well that aint how I'm rockin out. That's why Rello scary-ass always sendin me to buck his hooks inna first place. Muafuckas know how smooth an professional I be wit the shit," I said with a smile as Cutthroat chuckled shaking my hand to encourage me.

"Shid by the time I branch off from nem niggas I got a pocket fulla money, no dope, an I'm hoppin back in my own shit. The whole time I'm out trappin nat muafucka been sittin somewhurr parked all day, well outside the police radar. Damn right I'm pullin up on nem niggas everyday bruh. Fuck you mean?" I added as I laughed. "Now don't that sound like a go Cutthroat?" I asked feeling like Hustle needed a third opinion on the situation so his stubborn ass could actually hear me out.

"Damn right, who is this nigga?" Cutthroat asked curiously entertained by the whole conversation.

"Man nis lame ass nigga we went to school wit bruh. A straight Rudy on my kids. Dude so scary he aint even got no business fuckin wit the dope game foreal," Hustle answered, hoping that was enough information for Cutthroat to come up with some diabolical plan to take Rello ass out like he would've did back in na day.

After we took Cutthroat shopping we gave him a couple hunnit then I branched off on my own to go fuck with Rello nem. Cutthroat stayed with Hustle but Hustle was even more annoyed and irritated when I left cuz I was steady branching off with Rello every chance I got. He just couldn't understand why I aint wanna stick to the original plan and branch off from them niggas at that point.

"Damn man nis nigga Rambo jus hit me up in na dice game homie. Lemme hold sumn so I can win my money back real quick bruh," Cutthroat said to Hustle after shooting dice with Rambo for damn near a hour in the midst of Hustle bussin all his hooks.

"Fuck naw, you better tell that nigga to jus give you yo money back. I aint got shit else for you homie straight up," Hustle answered loudly feeling even more frustrated with Cutthroat cuz he really just wanted to be left alone.

"Shiiid I jus gave that nigga his money back twice. I'm gone bruh," Rambo interrupted with a laugh sensing Hustle wasn't really in the mood for company anymore.

"We gone try again tomorrow tho Cut, I'm jus finna flip this real quick then run it back to you homie. I aint gone wanna shoot wit cho ass no mo if I give it back this time tho nigga," Rambo said with a smile as he headed out the door.

"Damn man a nigga can't even go get shit to eat now bruh? Lemme get some a them noodles homie," Cutthroat said as Hustle was putting the flavor packet in the noodles he had just made for himself.

"Man fuck naw nigga, I aint wit all that jailhouse ass shit bruh. You better get out hurr an get chu some paper homie you aint my son. I aint finna be carryin yo ass like I'm yo daddy nigga you might as well gone shake foreal. Shid it aint even no point a yo ass sittin aroun a nigga like me if you aint tryna get no money straight the fuck up," Hustle replied harshly while stirring up the noodles before takin his first bite.

"You da one on some jailhouse shit nigga, yo ass eatin noodles in nis muafucka knowin that's all this man know," Twin said playfully as he laughed.

"Whurr you at bruh?" I asked when I called Hustle phone tryna pull up on him wit Rello ass. I was hoping to kill the tension between the two of them so it wouldn't get outa hand. I knew Rello scary ass would be a lil more humble pulling up in our territory so I figured I'd go that route rather than tryna get Hustle to pull up on Rello.

"I'm at the crib bruh pullup," Hustle answered before hanging up the phone still eating his noodles with no intentions of sharing whatsoever.

"Whurr the fuck is you at Dashon? I'm off," Babydoll said when she called my phone pissed that I wasn't sitting in the lot waiting to pick her up already. She had just got her bartending license and was working at the strip club as a bartender. They had her working the day shift while it was kinda slow so she wouldn't be in thurr fucking up them people drinks cuz she still aint really know what the hell she was doing.

"Damn its nine a clock already? Time be rollin, my bad baby I dun got inna car wit Rello ass an straight forgot. The damn car still parked at his crib," I answered knowing she was bout to snap on my ass regardless of what excuse I had for not being thurr.

"What the fuck you mean you forgot! You left me stranded on na east side at the most dangerous strip club in na world to hop yo dusty-ass in na car wit Rello ass! Who the fuck is this nigga! I'm sick a this dude, I never even met this clown while you blowin me off to ride aroun wit his ass. Like yall just the best a fuckin friends asumn, you wouldn't even pull this shit ridin aroun wit fuckin Hustle. What the fuck is wrong wit cho dusty ass? I look hella stupid walkin outta hurr thinkin you already sittin outside waitin on me to get off. This some bullshit!" she yelled being over the top and hella dramatic like always.

"Man can we please go pick my bitch up from na slip real quick? She jus got off work an I straight forgot to go get her ass," I asked Rello rolling my eyes annoyed.

"Damn yo bitch work at the Pink Slip?" Rello asked surprised, assuming she was a stripper of course.

"Yeah she just the bartender tho bruh. She all pissed off cuz I was supposed to be up thurr at nine a clock to pick her up," I explained with the phone down to muffle our conversation while Babydoll kept going on and on knowing damn well I wasn't paying her ass no attention.

"Yeah nigga a course, that's wifey aint it?" Rello answered tapping the dude who was driving on the shoulder to let him know to head to the Pink Slip instead of pulling up at Hustle crib. He was curious to see how Babydoll looked anyway, and he showl wasn't in no rush to pull up on Hustle moody ass. He aint want it to be so much tension between the two of them neither tho. He knew if it got any worse it would eventually affect me and his friendship putting him in a position whurr he couldn't even trust me no more. He definitely aint want it to get to that point cuz I already knew way too much about his ass by then.

'I'm on my way baby," I said before hanging up in Babydoll face so I wouldn't have to hear her mouth the whole way thurr. When we pulled up she walked to the truck with a lil attitude. I opened the door to let her in then she got in the third row of the Tahoe without saying a word. She sat thurr comfortably with her legs crossed and arms folded giving me the silent treatment. But that was really right up my alley cuz I aint feel like hearing her muafuckin mouth no way.

"Is you cumin in baby?" I asked once we pulled up to Hustle crib after me and Rello hopped out. She was so pissed off she didn't even answer me. She just rolled her eyes with her face all frowned up wishing we was alone so she could go off on my ass like she wanted to. "Iight I see you wanna be a bitch just stay in ner wit them then," I said before shutting the door and leaving her ass in the back row mad. The other two niggas was in the front playing music and talking amongst themselves so it aint like I left her ass out thurr alone. I aint really give a damn if she came in or not for real.

"Aye whurr that nigga Rambo ass at man I know his lil hot ass back outside in na streets," I said when me and Rello walked in through the back door. Hustle, Cutthroat, and Twin was all sitting around the living room lookin at the new trap music videos on Youtube. We always wanted to see who had the most views and whurr the niggas was from cuz a few of they asses was from St. Louis. It's always some street niggas dropping new music tryna make it out the dope game. Hell even Rello ass was on that muafucka flashing all his guns with all his money and phones all out in the camera. All you really need is enough views to get noticed by somebody that can hook yo ass up with a record deal.

"That nigga Rambo jus left wit all my fuckin money. The nigga must got some loaded dice asumn cuz his ass just cleaned me out quick," Cutthroat answered as Hustle rolled his eyes.

"Man if them dice was loaded you woulda hit too fool. Them na same dice you was shootin wit," Twin blurted out as he laughed.

"That nigga be hittin everybody bruh I swear. That's why Ion't even shoot wit Rambo ass," I added with a smile while calling Rambo phone just to talk shit and make his ass feel bad about taking all Cutthroat money knowing he had just got out.

"He must be ducked off wit a lil bitch asumn now, trickin all yo lil money off nasty bastard," I said playfully after getting the voicemail.

"I'm showl waitin on my lil bitch to pullup, I been waitin on nis ho for damn near a hour tho. I'm bout ready to curve her ass by now shid if I call this otha bitch she pullin up in ten minutes tops on my mama. Matter fact I'm finna hit her ass up," Twin said before pulling out his phone and calling the other bitch just to prove his point.

"Baby come pick me up from Hustle crib I'm tryna fuck," he said bluntly once the other bitch answered the phone.

"I'm showl right by Hustle crib, is you ready tho? Cuz I aint really tryna sit ova thurr. It be to many different niggas swarmin aroun nat muafucka for me," she answered hoping he would come right out soon as she pulled up. She was right though, Hustle crib was trapped the fuck out especially after Latoya went to jail. The kids was never thurr and it was always a house fulla niggas with a pocket fulla dope constantly running back to the alley behind his crib to serve the endless cycle of geeks that was always pulling up.

"What I tell you bruh, this bitch finna pull right up. The only fucked up part about it is I rather fuck the bitch that's bullshittin. Her lil bougie ass got me fucked up tho so fuck it," Twin explained when he hung up the phone.

"Aye my bad about earlier tho Hustle, it be a lotta pressure on a nigga once them phones get tha ringin an it aint enough dope to serve everybody ya know. Yall was lookin out for yall peoples tho I respect that shit. Matter fact welcome home homie," Rello said cutting the tension in the room by apologizing to Hustle and acknowledging Cutthroat with a handshake. "That's for you my nigga. Lil sumn for yo pockets bruh," he added handing Cutthroat a hundred dollar bill just to let him know he aint mean no harm.

"Good lookin out bruh," Cutthroat replied putting the hundred dollar bill in his pocket relieved he was able to get back at least some of the money he fucked off.

"Yall can take this nigga wit chall foreal. Aint no kids in nis muafucka. This the real world homie you gotta get out hurr an get it. Fuck a nigga handin you some money to blow," Hustle blurted out still giving Cutthroat a hard time about asking him for some more money after he had already gave him some and took him shopping earlier that day.

"It's all good I'm finna slide out now. Shid I'm jus glad a nigga got some money to eat wit. I'll end up killin sumn before I starve to death, the real world a jungle. I aint been gone long enough to forget that shit. Either you eat or you die an I'ma eat fuck that," Cutthroat replied before heading to the door.

"Yeah well holla at me once you do that then nigga flatout," Hustle replied carelessly before putting the last of the noodles in his mouth unbothered.

"Aye Twin, it's some hoes outside talkin to each other about chu bruh. One of em told me to tell you to come outside when I pulled up then na otha bitch was like "Why? Who is you?" then they start talkin so I just hurried up an ran in hurr," DonDon announced after busting in through the back door with a big ass smile on his face already entertained with the drama he had just walked into.

"Damn bruh, what they was sayin? Go tell the one in nat blue Altima to shake cuz I'm gone. I'm tryna get in nat white Infinity wit ol babe," Twin responded in a panic peeking out the window hoping neither one of them would see.

"Hell naw nigga, every female out thurr on bullshit right now. I jus walked up to that Tahoe tryna see who was all up in nat muafucka an Babydoll ass jus let down na window tellin me to fuck off for no reason. You aint finna send me back out thurr wit a bunch a angry black women nigga," DonDon answered playfully. "What the hell yall done did to Babydoll anyway?" he asked still smiling and amused.

"That shit thurr jus don't make no damn sense man foreal. I swear this nigga keep Babydoll ass wit em like they just met, that shit jus sickenin bruh foreal," Hustle said giving me a hard time about having Babydoll with me like always.

"Nigga shut up, we had to go pick her up from work. Shid I damn near forgot that's why she in ner mad now. I was hella late," I said with a smile as Hustle shook his head still shaming me anyway.

"What the fuck is they out thurr talm bout bruh, I can't hear shit," Twin said in a hushed tone still peeking out the window trying not to be seen.

"I'm finna jus call Dre he still out in na car. He talkin to his babymama tho so he might not even answer, the conversation sounded kinda serious," DonDon said calling Dre phone. "Yeah he aint answer, he fuck aroun finna have to slide out. His babymama at the hospital talkin to the doctor bout the baby right now," DonDon announced after getting Dre voicemail.

"Damn now the nigga gettin out the car, he still on na phone tho," Twin blurted out not knowing how to go about handling the situation.

"Aye can you see if Twin in ner for me? Tell em I'm outside," one of the girls yelled out to Dre as he was walking to the back door.

"Aye Twin nem hoes out thurr lookin for you homie. Drop me off real quick Don, she want me to come up thurr so I can drive her back home," Dre said quickly after putting the phone on mute for a couple seconds so his baby mama could feel like she still had his full attention.

"Iight cumon, whatchu want me to tell em bruh?" DonDon asked Twin with a smile as he was heading to the door.

"Fuck you Don! Tell em to suck my dick," Twin answered jokingly.

"Naw foreal tho, act like you tryna hop down on ol babe in na Infinity but jus tell her I'm finna call her phone low key. This bitch in na Altima callin my shit back to back I need to spin her ass myself," Twin answered watching

219

his phone ring after putting it on silent so he could think about his next move without hearing the phone constantly goin off.

"Hello," Twin said finally answering his phone tryna sound like he wasn't aware or worried about the situation at hand.

"Whurr you at? I'm outside, who is this bitch in nis white Infinity tho?" the girl in the Altima replied immediately ready to curse his ass out if he had anything to do with the other bitch pulling up too.

"Damn I forgot you was finna pullup baby, I had to slide out wit Rambo ass real quick. We gotta handle some shit ASAP. I'ma have him drop me off whurreva you at when we done tho so I'll be callin you inna minute," Twin answered before hanging up in the bitch face without giving her a chance to respond to the bullshit he was feeding her ass just so she would leave.

"Up, now ol babe in na Infinity pullin off, they both finna shake on yo ass," I announced peeking out the window entertained myself. We was all just curious to see how the shit was gone play out for him.

"Baby pullup to the front real quick, I'm finna come out now," Twin directed after calling the girl in the Infinity before she got too far away.

"You got me fucked up nigga don't be havin me pullup an you got some other bitches waitin on yo dusty ass to come outside. I coulda stayed whurr the fuck I was at!" she answered feeling pissed off and offended.

"Baby that bitch a stalker I aint tell her ass to pullup. Jus pullup to the front boo. I wanna see you hella bad, been thinkin bout chu all day," he lied but was so convincing that she turned right back around like he told her to. That's basically all it took for her to cooperate instead of leaving his ass over thurr looking stupid. Once Twin left me and Rello headed out too. So Hustle was finally alone like he wanted.

Latoya had court the next morning and the lawyer Hustle hired assured him that she would be released right after they talked to the judge. He was happy too cuz he did kinda miss her ass. He knew she was coming home clean like she was back when they first fell in love. They relationship was never the same once Latoya start getting high so he was looking forward to having everything back to normal. He wasn't really worried about Bre cuz she kept going back and forth from him to Corey crazy ass not knowing what Hustle was gone be on once Latoya was released. An Latoya was in that muafucka doing squats, sit-ups, and anything else she could do to keep her body on point and perfect. She wanted to make sure she was the center of attention like she was before she start falling off fucking with them dems.

Hustle crunched down a pack of pills, mixed it with the NyQuil an Kool-Aid then gulped down the whole bottle before heading upstairs to his room to sleep alone for the last night. He was looking forward to seeing his wife the next day but was still enjoying the fuck out of his high uninterrupted before he nodded off.

CUTTHROAT CITY

"Wake yo ass up nigga! You finna get all the rest you need inna minute homie," Cutthroat said waking Hustle up with a forty to his head.

"What the fuck yall on man yall trippin wasup?" Hustle shouted in a panic waking up instantly while Cutthroat and Beezy big brother Murder stood over his bed with they guns pointed at him.

"It's that time bruh, you had a good run now it's my turn nigga," Cutthroat replied calmly as Hustle looked into his eyes speechless and terrified.

"Man what chall want? Yall can take everything I got up in nis muafucka jus leave me my dems bruh," Hustle answered after working up the courage to respond.

"You see…it aint that simple Hustle. When niggas like you in na way, niggas like us gotta move em. That mean we gotta put chu in na ground homie, it's bout time we took ova. Now help us clean nis muafucka up so you can clock out," Cutthroat explained heartlessly as Hustle mind start racing a million miles a minute.

"Whurr the stash at nigga," Murder asked bluntly as Hustle tried to gather his thoughts. But Hustle aint know what to say or do.

"Man lemme take a shit my muafuckin stomach bubblin an shit. Yall trippin off this lil petty as shit in hurr like it's really sumn in hurr to be doin all that ova bruh. This sum bullshit!" Hustle blurted out, rubbing his stomach just saying the first thing that came to his mind.

"Nigga you gone shit when you die, now tell us whurr all this lil petty shit is before I finish you right hurr in yo draws," Murder replied pointing the gun closer to Hustle head as he talked.

"Iight, that shit downstairs homie. Jus lemme put my pants on so yall can get it," Hustle said looking around for the pants he took off right before he hopped in the bed and nodded off.

"Fuck naw nigga, yo ass goin right back to sleep. Jus get the fuck down na stairs an get the shit bruh. I aint finna play wit chu neither, you make one wrong move an I'm parkin yo ass on na spot flatout," Murder said warning Hustle not to try and escape.

"This shit don't even make no sense man I got kids an some mo shit. Yall know this some bullshit," Hustle preached walking down the stairs tempted to try an dash right out the front door soon as he got to the bottom of the steps. Cutthroat and Murder came in through the back door after kicking it off the hinges without being seen or heard with the music still blasting. The front door was still locked so Hustle was sure they would kill him before he was able to unlock the door, open it up, and run outside. So it was really no way to escape.

"Lemme get these dems first," Hustle said reaching for the gun that was tucked under the pillow on the couch.

Pow! Pow! Pow!

One in the arm, chest, and stomach right then and thurr. Murder aint hesitate at all not even a lil bit. "See I was gone make it easy for yo ass an give you a head shot but now I'ma just let chu bleed out slowly," Cutthroat said carelessly as he picked up the gun Hustle was reaching for and put it on his waist. Hustle struggled to crawl away heading for the front door while Murder start looking around for anything he could find hisself. Meanwhile Cutthroat stood over Hustle watching him reach for the doorknob before collapsing back down to the floor weaker than ever.

"Like I said yo time up nigga," Cutthroat said before shooting Hustle in the back of his neck, shoulder, and head, then heading out the back door with Murder. The next morning Rambo came over thurr bright and early after dropping off the lil bitch he was ducked off with all night. He knocked on the front door ready to brag about how much of a freak she was but didn't get a answer so he went around back. He noticed that the door had been kicked opened then closed back so he took out his gun and headed in the house with caution.

"Hustle!" Rambo shouted as he walked through the kitchen already sensing something had gone terribly wrong out of instinct. "Hustle! Bruh what the fuck! Who did this shit nigga?" Rambo yelled after running up to Hustle's dead body appalled. "What the fuck man this some straight bullshit," he shouted before pulling out his phone and calling me.

I was still wit Rello at the time cuz I aint even feel like dealin with Babydoll attitude having ass. I had just dropped her off at the car then pulled up at this nice ass hotel room wit Rello nem. He had got the room for one of his lil stripper bitch's birthday and she had all her lil stripper friends up in that muafucka too. So I got drunk and crashed out right thurr with them shid Babydoll calling herself being mad was right up my alley that night. She was so mad she wasn't even calling blowing up my phone like she usually did too. That shit worked out perfectly for me though I can't even stunt.

"Wasup early bird? You out hurr gettin nat worm I see," I said with a smile when I answered the phone.

"Aye pullup at Hustle crib bruh, " Rambo replied with tears running down his face like a waterfall.

"Nigga is you cryin? Wasup wit chu?" I said after hopping up realizing something had to be seriously wrong for Rambo to call me crying telling me to pull up at Hustle crib with no explanation.

"Jus pullup bruh," he answered before hanging up the phone leaving me clueless.

"Woah nigga slow down whurr you rushin off to homie?" Rello asked as I looked around frantically for my keys. I forgot Babydoll had took the car home with her the night before.

"I aint got time for this shit man I gotta go. Whurr the fuck is my keys?" I yelled outa frustration.

"Calm down nigga, Babydoll got the car bruh jus tell me whurr you gotta go," Rello replied calmly and confused.

"Hustle crib, take me to Hustle crib real quick bruh. I gotta drive tho gimme yo keys an cumon," I said before heading to the truck eager to get behind the wheel so I could make it ova thurr as quick as possible. When we pulled up at Hustle crib Rambo was sitting on the front porch crying so I already knew it had to be the worse case scenario.

"Wasup whurr he at bruh?" I asked after hopping out the driver's seat.

"He in ner man," Rambo answered as I immediately headed to the back door. When I saw the back door had been kicked off the hinges damn near I knew for sure what to expect going in. But when I saw Hustle lying thurr face down in his draws I just couldn't believe what my eyes was seeing. It seemed so unreal to be looking down at Hustle's lifeless body knowing he couldn't explain what happened.

"What the fuck bruh? Man cum on nis how they do you? Howda fuck you let this shit happen bruh? Who the fuck did this shit man? This some straightup bullshit on God," I vented as I pulled out my phone to call Babydoll for comfort. Ion't really know why I felt the need to hear her voice at that moment but I did. Hustle not being able to talk back to me just made me feel real alone so I needed her.

"What the fuck do you want Dashon? You aint even come home last night or call so don't tryda fuckin call me now fuck you," she said soon as she picked up the phone before I even had a chance to say a word.

"Baby they…somebody straight kilt Hustle. He jus layin hurr fuckin dead an Ion't even know what happened," I replied hoping she could ease my pain some kinda way despite how mad she was at the time.

"Oh my God! Are you fuckin serious? Where are you?" she responded feeling shocked and overwhelmed.

"I'm at his house baby, he jus layin hurr by the front door. Ion't even understand why this shit happenin right now. He got kids, Latoya gettin out today, his manma don't even know this shit den happened to em yet or nothin," I answered feeling sympathy for his family knowing they was all about to feel the same pain I was feeling when they found out. "It's dried up blood all on na floor an doorknob, bullet holes all in his back an shit. This shit jus crazy baby iton't even feel real," I added feeling like I was on the verge of having a nervous or breakdown or something.

"Look baby calm down, we gone get past this okay. I just want you to get up out that house tho before the police pullup. Come home baby, you need to be at home wit me right now. I miss you an I jus want chu hurr, everything gone be okay. You still got me, an I'ma love you forever no matter what," she said wishing she could just make the pain I was feeling go away somehow but couldn't.

"Cumon bruh we gotta slide out, his peoples on ney way so I know the police comin," Rello announced after coming in the house unfazed by Hustle's dead body. I went outside and stood across the street with Rambo as Hustle's family started to pull up anxious to see if the horrific news was actually true with they own eyes. When DonDon pulled up with Tyresha crying her eyes out in the car, he got out and stood across the street with me and Rambo instead of going in the house.

By that time Hustle whole family was out thurr including his mom and dad. Most of em stood outside tryna comfort his daughter who was screaming and crying hysterically cuz she was definitely old enough to know what was going on. His son was a few years older than her so he knew how real shit had just got too but he reacted differently. He just stood thurr speechless showing no emotion whatsoever. He was most likely more devastated than anybody but never said a word. All he could do was hug his lil sister as she cried. Dre pulled up with his baby mama, Chucky pulled up with my sister, and Lil Rodney pulled up with Nikki. By the time Twin pulled up with the lil bitch he left with the night before the whole block was filled with cars, and a big ass crowd of people surrounded Hustle crib.

"Man who the fuck did this shit bruh?" Rambo blurted out feeling angry and confused.

"Ion't know, I do know that shit gone come to the light tho for sure. Jus give it a lil time, shit like this neva take to long to reveal it'self trust me" Chucky said calmly encouraging everybody to just be patient until the truth about what actually happened finally came out.

"This shit fucked up bruh, I got a feelin its somebody he trusted too," Lil Rodney said sympathetically as Twin walked up after parking ole girl car down the street in the first parking spot he could find.

"This some straight bullshit man, who the fuck did this shit!" Twin yelled full of anger and rage.

"Calm down bruh, we tryna figure this shit out now cuz it was most likely a muafucka that knew when to catch Hustle by hisself. He hardly ever up in nat muafucka alone," DonDon explained as we all stood around wondering who it might've been. "I know damn well he aint have that back door unlocked if he was in ner by hisself" Dre said tryna figure out how somebody got in the house without Hustle being alarmed.

"Naw that muafucka was kicked off the hinges so it had to be locked," Rambo stated but still feeling clueless about everything else.

"Howda fuck he aint hear a muafucka kick the door off the hinges?" Savage asked chiming in on the conversation after popping up outa no whurr.

"Hustle fat ass probably nodded off on na couch high wit the music still blastin. He was laid out by the front door so he had to be curlt on na couch when ney came in," I answered still feeling frustrated about not knowing exactly what happened and how everything went down.

"Man aint no way he was sleepin on na couch bruh. He keep that 40 right thurr under that pillow. I know damn well he wasn't sleepin nat muafuckin hard to whurr he couldn'tve hopped up an grabbed that muafucka real quick," DonDon said feeling certain that Hustle would've had enough time to get the gun if he was already on the couch whether he was sleep or not.

"Yeah that muafuckin 40 is always under that pillow on na couch. Member Twin almost blew his fuckin head off ploppin down ova thurr drunk that day," Dre agreed recalling the exact incident cuz he was thurr.

"Yeah I did that shit twice, Hustle used to stay gettin on my head about ploppin down ova thurr like that cuz the muafuckin gun was always right thurr," Twin added knowing the gun had to be right whurr it always was even though Hustle never made it over thurr to it.

"So howda fuck they get the ups on na nigga if he was right thurr by the fuckin gun? It shoulda been a whole shootout in nat muafucka," Savage replied confused.

"Man don't nobody even know how many niggas even went up in nat bitch. Shid it was probably somebody that already knew the fuckin gun was right thurr Ion't know. Whurr Cutthroat at?" I asked realizing he wasn't out thurr brainstorming the whole situation with the rest of us for some odd reason.

"I aint seen em today but he was showl ova hurr last night tho. I tow his ass up in na dice game before I left," Rambo answered shrugging his shoulders unsure about why Cutthroat was missing in action all asudden too. It definitely made everybody wonder cuz Hustle death traveled like lightning so Cutthroat had to have heard about the shit by then. I mean the whole hood was literally outside of Hustle house at that point. It seem like everybody that knew Hustle pulled right up, especially the niggas that used to be over thurr.

"Yeah Cutthroat ass was ova hurr last night, whyda fuck he aint ova hurr now? Fuck that, call his ass up. Why the fuck you on ghost mode homie whatchu now," Twin blurted out already jumping to conclusions because of Cutthroat's absence at that particular moment.

"No answer," DonDon announced after calling Cutthroat phone and getting his voicemail within the first 3 or 4 rings.

"That's a red flag if he was just ova hurr last night tho. Shid if he'ont call back he must do know sumn," Chucky stated making everybody around us even more suspicious about the situation.

"I swearda God if he had sumn to do wit this shit I'm killin'm. I'ma hunt his ass down an punish that nigga on my mama. He already know I'm comin for that ass once I find out who did Hustle like this man let that nigga know flatout!" Twin yelled making a even bigger scene than before.

"Calm down bruh, I'ma know wasup soon as I talk to that nigga. He gone keep it ahunnit wit me fa sho. I'll get to the bottom of the shit trust me," Savage assured him before walking back to his car to call Cutthroat privately. Once that the coroner pulled up and got Hustle body out the house everybody else start leaving too. I had been told Rello nem I would just link up with them later so I hopped in the car with my sister and Chucky.

"Take me to the crib so I can get the car sis," I said after the three of us got settled in the car and pulled off.

"This shit so crazy man, mama was jus tellin me she had a dream Hustle got kilt like three nights ago, that shit just creepy," Tasha said as she headed towards my crib so I could get the keys from Babydoll and hit the streets alone to clear my head.

"Yeah mama was showl tellin Babydoll that shit the other day when she called cryin bout chu neva bein at home cuz you always wit Hustle nem," Chucky added letting me know about Babydoll calling and complaining about me to my mama after eavesdropping in on they conversation.

"Babydoll get on my fuckin nerve wit that shit, she always got mama all in our business that shit blows me," I replied annoyed. I just always wanted my mama to think we was happy in love and safe. So Babydoll calling crying to her about me runnin the streets with Hustle all the time kinda pissed me off cuz that's what made her worry. She wasn't really worried about me when I was ducked off up under Babydoll ass all day but knowing I was back runnin around with Hustle on a daily basis was sure to stress her out.

"They say Latoya on Gamble, after I drop you off I'ma go pullup on her an see how she doin. You need to pullup on her too cuz I know she freakin out behind nis shit. Hell she need all the love an support she can get right about now," my sister said feeling sympathy for Hustle wife and kids knowing he was the one who supported them.

"Yeah I'ma go pullup on her inna minute," I replied hoping me droppin off a couple hunnit for the kids would make her feel like everything was still gone be okay some kinda way. Once my sister dropped me off at my crib I picked a fight wit Babydoll for calling my mama crying about me never being at home. That was actually the perfect excuse to leave right back out. She was mad but didn't even put up too much of a fight about it. She aint wanna make me mad enough to not come home again that night so she just let me go peacefully.

"I love you Dashon," she said before I rolled my eyes and headed out the door. I was low key feeling hella bad about fakin a fallout with her just to leave but left anyway without thinkin twice. When I pulled up on Gamble to see Latoya she just bust out crying soon as she saw me. I gave her a hug to comfort her but the way she was holding me back made me feel like she wanted or needed my comfort more than anybody's for some reason.

"Hurr Latoya, get whatever you an na kids need for right now an just call my phone when yall need sumn from now on," I said after reaching in my pocket and peeling off about six hundred dollars from the big knot of money I had like it was nothing.

"Thank you Dashon, I thank God I still gotchu like foreal," she replied taking the money appreciatively.

"Man nat's fucked up what happened to Hustle bruh. I got my ear to da streets tho, we gone find out who done nat shit to em sooner or later," Rello said when I pulled up on him after I left from off Gamble.

"Yeah I think I know who might've done nat shit, I aint really sure yet tho," I replied after realizing Cutthroat still hadn't called my phone yet and nobody I talked to on Gamble had heard from his ass yet neither. "Wasup bruh, whats the word?" I said quickly answering the phone soon as I seen Savage number pop up. I knew he was calling with some information about what actually happened cuz Cutthroat Savage real blood cousin so I was sure they had talked by then.

"Yeah that's what it was bruh, he said Hustle was talkin down to'm an shit. Then he pulled up on Murder tellin'm about how Hustle was doggin'm out so they ended up pullin up ova thurr last night. He said they heard the music blastin when ney got to the back door but they aint see nobody else car outside so they kicked that muafucka open. Hustle was upstairs in his bed still sleep when ney went in ner. But they woke'm up, told'm what was bout to go down, then walked'm downstairs so he could show em whurr the stash was at. When ney got downstairs he say Hustle tried to reach for that gun on na couch he had stashed on some quick shit so Murder hit em up an Cutthroat finished em off before they left. He said they aint get shit but a couple guns, a few racks out the nigga pocket, an alla dope an dems he had on em. Cut say it wasn't about the money tho, he said it was the lack a respect Hustle was showin'm. He said Hustle was tryna make him feel like he was less of a man cuz he aint have no money," Savage explained as I held the phone listening to every word he was saying without interrupting. I had already suspected Cutthroat had did that shit but when Savage confirmed it I was still in a state of shock for some reason. "He told me to let chu know that what happened was between him an Hustle an don't nobody really need to be takin sides. I told him what Twin was sayin but he jus said he'll cross that bridge once he get to that muafucka, he aint tryna cross that bridge wit everybody tho. I advised'm to jus fall back for a lil while like Lil Rodney did after he kilt Trouble. I know muafuckas need time to grieve in order to really get past sum shit like that. But he wanid me to tell yall not to take it too personal," Savage added speaking on Cutthroat's behalf since he was the only one Cutthroat had opened up to about it.

"He aint have to do Hustle like that man nat nigga talk shit to everybody like that bruh. That's jus how Hustle is, muafuckas know that shit man nis shit crazy" I replied feeling disappointed and even more heartbroken than I was before. I kept thinking about how betrayed Hustle must've felt in the moments before he died and how heartless Cutthroat was for snaking him out so quick without even thinking it over for real. The situation was similar to the whole Lil Rodney and Trouble episode but this one hurr definitely cut a lot deeper since me and Hustle was so close. I felt like I couldn't trust a soul after talking to Savage I swear. When I got off the phone with him I sat thurr in silence letting all the memories me and Hustle shared cloud my mind until Latoya texted my phone. She was asking me to help her get the kids a fly lil fit to wear to Hustle funeral so they could be looking nice and fresh like Hustle would've wanted.

{Don't worry bout it I got chu,} I texted back hoping my response was just the comfort she needed for her to feel as less stress as possible.

{Thanks boo, I'm so thankful Hustle left me somebody like you,} she sent back with a heart emoji and a smiley face.

{Yeah he 'ont want chu entertainin none a these thirsty-ass niggas for shit so keep curvin ney asses like you been doin. LOL,} I texted back hoping that would brighten her mood and maybe put a smile on her face when she read it.

{Yeah I think he just want me to be yours now so you can give me everything else I need too, you know some things money just can't buy unless niggas out here sellin theyself for a couple dollars I guess. LOL,} she responded with a wink emoji blowing a kiss.

I sat thurr frozen feeling unsure about what to text back after reading her message, I knew I had to text back something though so I just decided to go with the flow pretty much.

LOYALTY AND LUST

{Yeah well don't get nobody fucked up LOL,} I replied letting her know the ball was in her court if she really wanted to take it thurr.

{When you droppin the money off for the kids clothes?} she replied changing the subject just to turn down the heat a lil bit I guess. I mean the conversation was getting heated and I was feeling kinda crazy cuz I actually liked it a lot more than I thought I would.

{I'll be ova there in bout 20 minutes. I'ma call you when I'm pullin up,} I texted as I got in the car with Rello nem so we could bus the couple hooks we had lined up.

"Pullup on Gamble bruh, I'm finna drop this lil dust off to Latoya for the kid's clothes an shit," I said to Rello after we served all the people we had waiting on us. When we pulled up on Gamble Latoya was sitting on Hustle mama porch alone. So instead of calling I just let down my window. "You iight?" I asked once she realized it was me and Rello pulling up in the Tahoe.

"Yeah I'm cool, I just be a lil zoned out whenever I'm alone you know," she answered after walking up to the truck and taking the 1200 dollars I had wrapped up in a rubber band for her.

"Sorry for yo loss baby girl," Rello said before pulling a stack a hundreds out his bag, counting out 10, then handing em to her through the window.

"You let me know if it's anything else I can do for you sweetheart," he said charmingly with a lil sneaky smile. After we pulled off I got another text from Latoya {Why you aint come by yo self?} It said wit 3 sad face emojis and three question marks in a separate text

{So Rello ass could give you some money too. I knew he would shid sometimes you just gotta take advantage of the situation and get all you can get, that's free bands,} I replied, with a evil grin emoji.

{Why you wanid me to pullup by myself tho?} I asked in a separate text just tryna see whurr her head was really at.

{Pull up by yo self an find out. I need to talk to you but it's kinda personal so Ion't want nobody else around,} she sent back letting me know she was definitely ready to take it thurr despite how scandalous and fucked up it was. Hustle had jus got murdered the night before but I knew she hadn't had no dick in four months and was probably sexually frustrated. It was obvious she needed to relieve some stress and tension with everything she had going on. I wasn't sure if I would be helping her move on with her life or just taking advantage of the situation. I needed to relieve some stress at the moment my damn self though. I know I could've hooked up with almost anybody but Babydoll ass of course. I guess I jus felt like it was a reason why she was coming for me outa everybody she could've had so it was up to me to give her what she wanted.

{When I get back in my car I'ma call you. It won't be long. I'll see you soon,} I texted back as Rello commented on how sexy Latoya was looking. "I damn ner forgot that was Hustle wife for a minute," He joked, like her being Hustle wife really made her off limits to him. When I pulled up on Latoya she came right outside and got in the car.

"So whurr we goin?" she asked with a cute lil smirk as she got settled in the front seat.

"Whurr you wanna go?" I asked with a evil grin.

"Whurr you wann take me?" She asked playfully looking back at me with a smile.

"Shid I'm finna go get this room for the night, Babydoll dun pissed me off so I aint really tryna go home foreal," I answered tryna see exactly what all she was really willing to do.

"Boy don't do Babydoll, you know you love that girl," she said pushing me playfully as I brushed her comment off with a laugh while heading to the nearest hotel. When we got to the room we got right to it. I mean we aint waste no time at all. I kinda thought it was gone be a lil awkward at first but we was moving so fast we aint even have time to think about whether it was awkward or not. I think the sex was so good cuz we knew we was wrong for doing it but we showl didn't hesitate to at all. Babydoll was calling my phone back to back the whole time and the thought of me doing something I knew she wouldn't want me doing made the sex more of a thrill for some reason. After we got done I silenced my phone to ease the guilt I was finally feeling then laid in the bed with Latoya shameless and comfortable.

"So what now? You just gone keep cheatin on yo girlfriend wit me?" Latoya asked breaking the silence. Babydoll was still calling nonstop thinking the worse like I was somewhurr dead rather than laid up with another girl, especially Hustle wife.

"Babydoll gone deal wit whatever I make her deal wit you aint gotta worry bout that," I answered as Latoya rolled her eyes unsatisfied with my answer. At that point she just wanted to get Babydoll completely out the picture so she could have me all to herself.

"Well why would you want her to deal wit somethin like this? Don't chu love her?" she asked fishing to see how easy it would be to get Babydoll out her way so she wouldn't be considered a side bitch after being Hustle wife.

"Yeah I love her but she still gone deal wit whatever I make her deal wit. She aint cumin up off no pussy so she already know I'ma be fuckin somebody else," I said bluntly reminding her why I was cheating on Babydoll so carelessly in the first place.

"So you tellin me you jus gone keep fuckin me like that then goin home to her? Why you was lickin my pussy like that at first? You'ont think she'll be hella mad if she ever found out about that?" she asked with a smirk.

"Naw she won't be mad shid I do that to her allatime cuz thats all her lil dinky ass eva let me do," I answered with a smile, entertained by how much she was concerned about me and Babydoll all asudden.

"Mmm whatever, that's a shame tho I guess you an Hustle aint no different. Maybe that's why yall was so cool," she said rolling her eyes with a attitude. "I know he was out hurr cheatin na whole time I was locked up wasn't he?" she asked putting me on the spot tryna see how much I would tell her I guess.

"Jus cuz a nigga cheat don't mean heon't love you Latoya," I said avoiding the question before she rolled her eyes and turned away from me. After she turned around on me I moved over thurr closer to her before forcing my dick back up in her pussy from behind. Then I fucked her like that until I nutted without saying another word. When I got home the next day Babydoll was sitting up on the couch with the phone in her hand looking like she had just nodded off without ever even laying down. She woke right up soon as she heard the door close relieved to see I was actually okay.

"Baby I was so worried about chu don't do that to me no more. Whatever I did I'm sorry baby I really am I love you. Just stop bein mad cuz I can't take it no more, Ion't wanna fight wit chu, Ion't want chu to keep ignorin me an makin me sleep alone. Ion't even sleep when you not hurr an not answerin na phone for me it's just to stressful baby. I just want chu to come home an answer the phone when I call. It feel like you givin up on us but if you knew how much I really love you you wouldn't. Jus don't give up on me baby I can't live witout chu," she vented with tears constantly flowing down her face since the moment she opened her eyes and saw me. She stood to her feet and wrapped her arms around me as she cried making me feel like shit. So I grabbed her face and kissed her lips softly.

"I'll never leave you Babydoll," I said looking in her eyes as the tears continued to flow. I kissed her again before pulling the basketball shorts she had on down to her ankles. Then I laid her down on the couch and licked her pussy until she came all on my face like she always did. After she nutted I laid on the couch holding her close while she drifted off into a deep sleep. I nodded off with her for a lil minute too but soon as I hopped up to go get in the shower her lil ass woke right up.

"Whurr you goin baby?" she asked as I headed towards the bathroom.

"I gotta get in na shower bae, I can't jus aroun an sleep all day. My phone still constantly ringin I jus got it on silent cuz I aint really feel like bein bothered. We still got bills tho so it's time for me to turn my phone back on. Hell life goes on, it's time to get back to work," I answered as she got off the couch and slipped the basketball shorts right back on in a hurry.

"Now why would you turn yo phone off last night knowin I was finna be callin too. Damn you could've at least called me," she said following me to the bathroom as I turned the shower on and got undressed.

"Baby I fell asleep at Rello crib we was gettin so high I forgot. Now can you please stop bein worsm an get me a towel, gimme a wash rag too," I said as she stood at the bathroom door watching me get undressed.

"Okay babe, but soon as you get out the shower I'ma get in na shower so I can jus go wit chu when you leave," she said before eagerly walking to the closet to get my towel and rag.

"No baby it's too much goin on in na streets, yo ass need to be at home. That's yo fuckin problem you always tryna run na streets wit me. That shit dead!" I said as the energy she previously had suddenly disappeared the moment I raised my voice at her. When she handed me my towel and rag looking like she wanted to cry again I felt kinda bad and changed my tone tho.

"Bae don't be lookin like that stressin me out you always wit me. But sometimes it's just better for you to be at home damn. This nigga dun kilt Hustle now he want static wit the whole damn hood includin me. Why would I wanna have you wit me in na midst a all that goin on?" I said setting the folded towel she handed me down on the toilet then stepping in the shower.

"Well why would I want chu in na midst of all that? An who kilt Hustle? Why he got a problem wit chu?" she asked stepping in the bathroom and sitting on the toilet whurr my towel was at.

"Baby close the door it's hella cold an don't worry about all that, you jus need to worry about what I'm eatin tonight. Why you can't stay home an cook me sum dinner asumn," I said letting the water hit my body as she quickly shut the door then sat back down on the toilet.

"Watchu mean don't worry about it Dashon? I can't help but to worry about the shit. I'm not always wit chu no more cuz you always wit Hustle an Rello nem," she said before she paused realizing she jus mentioned Hustle's name without even trying to. She knew me hearing her bitchin about me always being with him had to sting a lil bit considering Hustle was gone forever.

"Baby look I'm sorry all this goin on, I know you hurtin right now but maybe it'll be better if you cling to me instead a the streets. I mean I actually love you an na streets don't. I just want chu to be wit me so I can know you safe. I need you wit me cuz I need to know you okay an outta harms way. Remember you used to say that to me everytime I wanid to breakup?" she said poking her head around the shower curtain with a smile.

"Baby you might as well jus get in hurr wit me damn. I need you to wash my back anyway," I said loving her irresistible charm even though she was being annoying. So she quickly took off the basketball shorts, tank top, and bra she was wearing before stepping in the shower without hesitation. After she washed my back she turned me around and start sucking my dick while the water massaged my back and trickled down my body relaxing me from head to toe til I nutted. When we got out the shower I licked her pussy again so she wouldn't give me a hard time about leaving without her but that shit aint even work.

"Baby please lemme go wit chu? I won't get on yo nerves I swear. I won't even talk I jus wanna be wit chu," she said hopping up soon as she seen me putting on my shoes.

"Baby can I just leave please this phone steady ringin. I gotta go pullup on na plug all type a shit goin on today. Matter fact, I'm finna jus hop in a rental real quick. Can you maybe call Latoya an go pullup on her to see if she okay? You know she goin thru it right now she need a good friend bae," I said tryna get Babydoll and Latoya as close as possible before Babydoll found out what was going on cuz I knew she would eventually.

"Okay I'll go check on her," Babydoll said rolling her eyes wishing she could just go with me instead. She felt sorry for Latoya and the kids and all but she had already sensed that Latoya was gone end up wanting me to kinda step in an play Hustle role since he was gone. So she wasn't really too thrilled about being around Latoya. But she still went ahead and pulled up on her just because she told me she would when I asked her to. She never in a million years would've thought me and Latoya hooked up just the night before though. Once she pulled up on Latoya she noticed a weird vibe the moment the two of them stood face to face.

"What Dashon ass been on? I heard him an Hustle was on all bullshit wit these hoes the whole time I was locked up," Latoya said tryna get as much information she could from Babydoll about how well our relationship was holding up.

"He been kinda distant I guess. He a lil harder to read then he used to be. It got even worse since all this happened," Babydoll answered vaguely.

"What about you since all this happened?" she asked tryna fill Latoya out a lil more and see whurr her head was really at.

"Ion't know Babydoll, I jus feel kinda lost witout Hustle. It's like Ion't really know whurr to go from hurr. I mean Dashon nem been lookin out for me financially so that make me feel a lil more secure. But I still be feelin like I need a muafucka to hold me, I hate bein alone," Latoya answered tryna make Babydoll question if I was gone be the one she wanted to hold her once she decided to move on. It did make Babydoll wonder but surely no time soon she assumed. That was a bridge Babydoll felt like she would have to cross later on down the line. Hustle wasn't even in a casket yet so she certainly aint feel like that was something she would have to worry about right away.

"Well let me know if you ever wanna go to church wit me asumn. I mean you could probably use some spiritual guidance right about now. I know that's not really what chu used to but it has got me thru some pretty rough times in my life so jus think about it okay?" Babydoll replied before giving Latoya a fake ass hug goodbye and leaving. Babydoll knew it was only a matter a time before Latoya became a problem. But she was unsure about how I would respond once Latoya let me know she wanted me to fuck her.

On the day of Hustle funeral I woke up feeling like shit, I aint even wanna go. "Baby get up an get dressed. Aint no way in hell you jus gone not go. Hustle was yo best friend an you need closure. Don't worry I'ma be right thurr witchu like always. It's gone be okay alright," Babydoll said after getting out the shower an realizing I was still laying down. She told me to get up before she even got in but I had already told her I didn't wanna go. She aint know I meant literally.

"Damn baby this stupid! You always tryna make me do some shit Ion't even wanna do," I said getting out the bed and heading to the bathroom annoyed.

"Yo rag an towel already folded up on na toilet. Get in na shower baby I'll pick you out sumn to wear," she replied as I rolled my eyes and shut the bathroom door behind me. When we got to Hustle funeral Babydoll noticed Latoya strutting around in the tight fitted long red dress and fashionable heels almost instantly. She was a lil intimidated knowing I had to have noticed how flawless Latoya was looking. Her Chinese bangs was cut perfectly and her weave was hella long with an expensive glow blowing in the breeze. This was hands down the cutest she had ever seen Latoya look. But Babydoll still convinced herself that Latoya was too busy mourning the loss of her husband to be worried about me. It wasn't long before she suspected otherwise though. After watching Latoya like a hawk the whole time, studying her every move and paying close attention to her body language, Babydoll realized Latoya wasn't that fucked up about Hustle being gone after all. It was just something real fake and phony about the performance she was putting on once they finally closed the casket. Babydoll knew it wasn't really as genuine as Latoya tried to make it seem an she couldn't help but wonder if I had anything to do with that. She wasn't a hundred percent sure if that's what it was but she did feel like something just wasn't right. So she decided to go ahead and bring it to my attention despite how crazy it might've made her look cuz it was killing her not to speak on that shit for real.

"I gotta talk to you baby. Somethin been kinda heavy on my mind since Hustle died an I jus wanna talk to you about it," Babydoll blurted out after we left the funeral on the way to the repast.

"Whatchu gota talk to me about crazy ass girl?" I asked after turning down the music so she could let me know what was so heavy on her mind. I already knew what she was finna say cuz I know the damn girl like the back of my fuckin hand.

"Um I kinda feel like Latoya gone tryda fuck you at some point, like what would you do? Would you fuck her if she told you she wanid you to?" she asked bluntly making me bust out laughing at how right I was about her. "Foreal baby? I literally got a feelin she wanna fuck you an I jus really wanna know if you would do it or not. Would you?" she asked again as I continued to laugh.

"Baby why is you so crazy, damn? Why would that girl be worried about me an her husband jus died. She aint worried about no dick you jus crazy," I replied tryna play on her intelligence so she wouldn't realize how right she was about Latoya wanting to fuck. "I mean she know I'm not fuckin you an I always get this weird vibe from her every time yo name come up. Like she'll tryda sneak an fuck you jus to shit on me asumn. She already told me she had a crush on you when yall was little before she got wit Hustle. It's almost like she want me to know she would fuck you just to see if it'll make me insecure.

An she told me that bullshit when Hustle was still alive right before yall took us out for Valentines day. I wasn't really worried about it then cuz she knew I could've easily jus retaliated by tryna fuck Hustle. But now she know if yall was to actually fuck it wouldn't really be nothin I could do to get back at her, which it kinda wouldn't foreal," she explained tryna convince me that she wasn't crazy so I could start taking the conversation a lil more serious.

"You see what happen when you tell people our business? That shit'll come back an bite chu in na ass won't it? An Hustle knew I'll hurt sumn ova yo ass girl, aint no way he would've had the balls to fuck you Babydoll," I replied playfully making Babydoll feel irritated and annoyed with me for steady joking around about it.

"So whatchu sayin you would fuck her if she tried to sneak an fuck you Dashon?" she asked seriously not finding a damn thing funny and waiting for a honest answer to her question.

"Naw I'm jus sayin stop tellin people our business an you won't have to worry about a bitch knowin whatchu not doin. But the damn girl not worried about me tho bae, she was prolly jus tryna make you feel like that cuz she knew Hustle wanid to fuck you. Hell Ion't know why she told you that shit. I know one thing that's probably the last thing on her mind right now tho," I said lying through my damn teeth just to calm her down and throw her off a lil bit cuz she was getting a lil riled up talking about the shit after a while. It made me a lil nervous about her ever even finding out about what had already happened. But all I could really do was wait until the shit came to the light and handle it the best way I could from thurr.

After the repast everybody pulled up at Hustle mama crib on Gamble. The hood was hella poppin like Hustle would've wanted. Everybody came out for his ass. We was blasting all his favorite songs, popping bottles, and getting high. Latoya was shaking her ass and making twerk videos while the whole hood hyped her up. That made Babydoll even more sure about Latoya not wasting no time before moving on from Hustle. She was paying close attention to Latoya whole vibe and realized Latoya wanted my attention. Latoya kept giving me a certain look every time she walked past shamelessly letting Babydoll know something was definitely going on with me and her without a doubt. Babydoll sat back analyzing everything without saying another word. It was no use bringing the shit to my attention again cuz she knew I would have to be a fool not to notice Latoya letting me know she wanted the dick by then. It was no way in hell I could've convinced her that Latoya wasn't tripping off me, all that shit went right out the window.

    Babydoll was quiet as a mouse for the rest of the day cuz the situation was a lil too much for her to swallow. Being so certain about what was going on basically had her speechless. It was pretty clear that Latoya wanted Babydoll to know what was goin on. I guess she figured Babydoll would maybe fall back so she could step in and completely take over without looking like a side bitch once everybody else found out. I mean she knew Babydoll was watching and she was really putting on a show. Shid I'm surprised aint nobody else pick up on what was going on that day. She was over the whole I'm sad and grieving act soon as she took off the red dress she wore to the funeral. By the time we got to Hustle mama house she had slipped on some skimpy ass cut up true religion shorts with a white tank top that showed half her stomach and some fresh white jays. She was clearly seeking attention rather than sympathy once Hustle was in the ground and out the way completely. And she definitely got what she wanted cuz all eyes was on her while she danced around with all the other neighborhood hoes who was pretty much clueless. They all just assumed she had a lil too much to drink but was happy to see she wasn't moping around like you would think she'd be. Everybody was just focused on having a good time.

Jessica Whitfield

A DIRTY GAME

Pow! pow! pow! pow! pow!

Somebody just bust out and hit Murder lil brother Beezy outa no whurr. Shot him dead right thurr in front of Hustle mama crib. Beezy aint even know what was going on neither. He was completely clueless about what Cutthroat and his brother had did. Hell all he knew was somebody killed Hustle. The whole hood damn near knew what went down since Cutthroat cocky ass called himself bragging about the shit to Savage. Somebody seen Beezy lil ass out thurr and hit'm up on the spot really just to let Murder know they was looking for him. Murder had been missing in action since the night they killed Hustle and he had enough sense not to speak on the shit to nobody.

He aint even know Cutthroat had spoke on the shit but I'm pretty sure he put two and two together once he found out Bezzy got killed in front of Hustle mama crib right after the funeral. I aint even gone lie I felt kinda bad for lil Beezy when that shit happened to him cuz he was a good lil dude man. He definitely looked up to Hustle and probably would've been hella disappointed in his brother if he hada known what really happened. Dude was young as fuck and the only reason his life got cut so short is simply because he was Murder lil brother. The shit was just sad man for real.

After watching Beezy get gunned down and seeing Latoya confirm what she had already suspected Babydoll was mentally and emotionally drained. So she aint put up a fight at all when I finally dropped her ass off at home. She felt defeated and must've slipped into some kinda depression cuz she wasn't even acting like herself no more. The situation with me and Latoya was constantly on her mind 24-7 but she never even wanted to speak on the shit for some reason. It was weird cuz she never really wanted to speak on nothing no more.

She was a lot more quiet and soft spoken than what I was used to which let me know something was most likely wrong with her mental state of mind. She was losing all weight and she always looked like she was bout to cry. I knew the situation was taking a real toll on her mental health cuz her confidence was completely gone and she was nothing like the girl I met. Latoya was more confident than she had ever been tho thanks to me. I was steady sneaking off to give her some dick every chance I got so she wasn't even worried about what happened to Hustle ass no more.

Babydoll already knew what I was up to at that point but was too scared to confront me about it I guess. She knew I wouldn't admit to the shit and it would only lead to a argument that was gone push me further and further away. After a while I kinda wanted her to lash out at me about the shit. I guess the guilt was finally weighing me down and the way she was dealing with what I was doing made me not even wanna be around her as much.

It felt like she was a whole different person. I just wanted some kinda normal reaction from her ass or at least see how much she would let me get away with since she was acting so passive. In the perfect world I could've had both of them around me without either of em having a problem with it. So I decided to just go ahead and shoot my shot with that. I figured once I did I would at least feel better not having to sneak around behind Babydoll's back to fuck with Latoya. Latoya was already hooked on the dick so I knew she wasn't going no whurr. Plus she had started back getting high so her ass was pretty much gone go for just about anything. All I needed was for Babydoll to get with the shit really.

"Baby I'm finna go pick up Latoya she said she wanna go to church wit chu in na mornin," I said when I called her phone one Saturday night after trappin with Rello nem all day.

"Um okay…but wouldn't I just pick her up in na mornin before I go?" she replied feeling a mixture of rage and confusion but tryna stay as calm as possible so she could finally see whurr the bullshit was going once and for all.

"Naw baby I'm finna pullup at her house right now but I gotta answer this other line tho money callin. I'ma see you ina minute boo," I said before clicking over to take my other call. Babydoll never called back to question my motive so I knew it wasn't gone be a problem when I pulled up with Latoya that night.

Babydoll was furious but she was more curious about how the night was finna go. So she played it cool and just waited for us to finally put everything out on the table despite how fucked up the whole situation was with Hustle's death still being so fresh. When me and Latoya pulled up at the house Babydoll watched us walk up to the door from the balcony. She lit up one of the Newport cigarettes she had just recently start smoking then calmly waited for everything she already suspected to unfold. Once we got in the house she stood at the balcony door nonchalantly smoking the cigarette while giving Latoya a dirty look.

"Wasup baby," I said before kissing her softly on the lips pretending not to notice the dirty look she was giving Latoya and the fact that she hadn't looked over at me not one time even when I kissed her.

"Hey boo," Latoya said smugly as I headed to the bedroom to put up my bag and get comfortable.

"Hey....you wearin that to church? I noticed you aint have a bag I mean do you even plan on changin yo panties? or is the rest of yo clothes in na car wit hopefully a toothbrush at least?" Babydoll said being catty just to let Latoya know she wasn't blind to the bullshit that was going on.

"Oh don't worry about that boo I'm not wearin any panties. But I guess Dashon jus gone have to take me home in na mornin so I can get a change a clothes," Latoya replied arrogantly with a evil grin.

"Wow! Who knew Hustle wife had such class, but how weird is the fact that you plan on spinnin na night witout even a toothbrush to wakeup to," Babydoll said sarcastically rolling her eyes.

"I'm sure Dashon can get me a toothbrush, I mean he give me everything else I need so that shouldn't be a problem," Latoya said as Babydoll stood thurr with the cigarette burning unsure about how far I would really go to keep Latoya ass around at that point.

"You look comfortable," Babydoll said turning her attention to me as I walked out the bedroom in some basketball shorts and no shirt.

"Of course I look comfortable baby I'm at home," I replied pretending not to even notice the way her face was all frowned up as I took the cigarette out her hand and finished it off myself.

"Come crunch down nis pack Latoya," I said setting a bag of perks and a half a bottle of NyQuil down on the kitchen table so I could get her high like she had been begging me to do since I picked her up from her mama house that night.

"Baby roll this blunt," I said to Babydoll as I put the big ass bag of weed I had down on the table with a pack of rellos. I was hoping that would cut the tension in the room so the girls could start acting a lil more friendly and maybe catch a vibe with each other. I just wanted them both to be okay with what was going on and have fun with it. I figured if I could get em both to get along and on the same page I'd be happier than I had ever been. Babydoll was just ready for us to admit what was going on though. She smoked the blunt while me and Latoya got high off the pack we put down quietly observing the two of us until we nodded off. By that time she was losing her patience. She wanted to confront the situation hella bad but not until me and Latoya actually confirmed what had been going on with all the details leading up to how it all got started. So she just decided to confirm what had been going on herself then simply see what we had to say about it. She took my phone out my pocket, typed in the code and went right to me and Latoya messages.

"So this really what chu want? Yall be tellin each other yall love each other an askin for kisses an shit? How long you been fuckin wit her rachet ass? Damn Hustle aint been in na fuckin ground five minutes. Yall scandalous as fuck!" Babydoll said furiously waking us both up after reading me and Latoya's text messages.

"Man cummer," I said pulling her to the bedroom after hopping up off the couch once she threw the damn phone at my face as hard as she could.

"Naw don't act like you want some privacy now. You brought this bitch hurr for a reason so let's talk about the shit. Why you even doin nis? Hustle was yo best friend! This his fuckin wife Dashon. You mean to tell me you like this bitch enough to let me know? I mean damn if you aint wanna be wit me no more why you aint jus say that?" Babydoll shouted as tears ran down her face while she talked.

"Baby I'll never leave you, sometimes you jus gotta follow my lead an go wit the flo tho. Lay back an keep gettin yo pussy licked like you been doin. Stop stressin out about what I'm doin cuz I'm not goin nowhurr bae," I said before she slapped me in my face as hard as she could.

"You know what Latoya you can have his dusty ass okay. Maybe this the closest you gone get to havin yo husband back so go ahead. Both a yall can go to hell tho cuz aint shit good gone come outta what the fuck yall got goin on no way! You an Hustle got kids together an all! Howda fuck you think they gone feel once they realize you fuckin a nigga that they used to see aroun ney daddy every day? How you think Hustle family gone feel once they find out about this shit? That shit embarassin as fuck, Hustle probably turnin in his fuckin grave. He'ont deserve to get did like this soon as he fuckin die!" Babydoll yelled turning her attention to Latoya who was suddenly regretful about Babydoll finding out about us after hearing what she had to say.

"Don't nobody gotta know about this Babydoll. We could jus keep this between the three of us like adults," Latoya replied feeling a lil nervous about Hustle family and kids finding out about what was going on after all. She hadn't even thought that part through yet obviously. Hell she was just worried about me giving her some dick and keeping her ass high up until that point.

"Yeah baby, whateva we got goin on in nis muafucka need to be between us. I told you about tellin people all our business now calm down so we can jus work this shit out altogether," I said as I sat down on the couch next to Latoya pulling Babydoll hand in a attempt to convince her to sit down on the couch so the three of us could talk it out without being confrontational.

"Fuck you Dashon!" She yelled before storming to the bedroom and quickly taking all the money out my bag so she wouldn't leave empty handed. I decided to just fall back and let her ass calm down for a minute at that point. I knew it would only get worse if I kept tryna force it by then. Plus I was way too high with no whurr near enough energy to convince her to stay. So I just let her go hoping she would cool off a lil bit then come back and discuss the situation a lil more calmly. I mean the last thing I needed was the police pulling up in that racist as neighborhood due to a noise complaint. That would've been a whole nother problem and a worse one at that.

"Dashon what the hell is Babydoll talkin about? She is literally hysterical seriously what's goin on son? This shit jus look crazy. Babydoll dun posted you, her, Latoya an Hustle club picture on Facebook talm bout you an Latoya some snakes for fuckin aroun behind her an Hustle back. You in hurr layin on na couch wit Latoya like its normal. I can't get Babydoll to take the damn picture down for shit. People probably thinkin you took Hustle ass out the way yall movin. I know everybody talkin about the shit by now. This is not good son it just don't look right," my mama said walking in the house with my dad feeling concerned, worried, and confused. "Get up son! I'm hurr to help you get yo stuff together cuz Babydoll said if yall still hurr by the time she get back she shootin both a yall," she added willing to do anything she could to stop the situation from escalating to something that drastic.

"Mama that damn girl aint gone shoot nobody, an I'm not leavin my house like Ion't pay bills hurr," I said before heading to the bedroom to get my phone from my bag not realizing it was right thurr on the couch whurr it landed after Babydoll threw the muafucka at my face. "Man nis bitch took all my fuckin money! An whurr the fuck is my phone!" I yelled furiously after looking in my bag and seeing that the only thing inside was my gun and an extra clip.

"Hell Ion't really blame her son, you got Latoya all in hurr laid up knowin yall been messin aroun. Shid yall kicked back in nis muafucka like Babydoll don't even live hurr. Yo name not even on nis lease son. You think these crackers give a damn about chu payin bills hurr? No they do not. If Babydoll did come back in hurr shootin they is not takin her ass to jail cuz first of all her gun is legal an na only names on nis lease is hers an her daughter's. You sitin hurr talm bout she aint gone shoot nobody. Boy that damn girl is emotionally unstable right now, thats probably why she left. I think she would do somethin like that in na state a mind she in. Haven't she shot at Latoya before?" my mama scolded as Latoya rolled her eyes.

"I know one thing everybody need to get the fuck up outta my daughter shit before this locksmith get hurr. She said take all yo shit cuz once these locks get changed you not comin back an you not finna have access to her house either so get the steppin," Babydoll mama said walking through the door with her boyfriend who was about twelve years younger than her trailing right behind looking like somebody bodyguard.

"Ma'am I'm not leavin my house. I pay bills hurr," I replied feeling even more pissed off at Babydoll for putting both of our mamas all in our business along with everybody on Facebook. I felt like she had blown the situation way out of proportion and the shit was just getting way too out of control with both of our mamas over thurr knowing what was going on.

"Look you little frog face bug eyed bastard, you got this lil hussy all up in my daughter shit an you got the audacity to tell me you not gone leave! You outta yo rabbit ass mind! Everybody finna get the fuck outta this bitch or I'm callin na goddamn police cuz yo upside down mop lookin ass not even on this fuckin lease," her mama yelled feeling outraged with me for refusing to leave.

"Hold on you not finna be talkin to my son like that ma'am, he finna get his things an leave. Cumon son get cho stuff cuz I feel like this bitch got me fucked up now an I'm not the one," my mama said feeling offended by all the funny ass shit Babydoll mama was saying about me cuz she felt like it was disrespectful to her.

"Bitch Ion't give a fuck about havin you fucked up ho! Yo funny lookin ass son got my daughter fucked up so he gotta go!" her mama yelled as they got all up in each other face ready to fight.

"Okay mama I'ma go, let's jus go," I said standing in between them as my dad pulled my mama closer to him. "It's all good tell her she can keep that money I'll make it back," I said before packing up all my shit.

"I'm not hurr to relay no got damn messages, I'm hurr to make sure yall get the fuck up outta this house before my daughter end up goin to jail for killin a bitch okay," her mama replied as my mom and dad helped me carry out my shit.

Babydoll called me furious once her mama told her how she got into it with mine of course. "Bitch yo mama got my mama fucked up. Fuck that bitch an I hope you get kilt like Hustle did since you wanna choose his bad luck ass wife over me wit cho lame ass! Yo dusty ass gone end up dead or in jail anyway fuck you! An you is not stylin wit that bitch cuz both a yall some fuckin dope feins from nat dusty ass hood yall always in. It's only a matter a time before you end up dead like her real husband you fake-ass wannabe Hustle. That's why Hustle was better than you cuz you wanid his bitch the whole time but couldn't even get her ass til he died! An I'ma suck Rambo dick! You can go ahead and let em know I'm on nat now so he won't be surprised when I call him tryna link up. You not even na cutest one, the bitch prolly jus tryna get back at me fa shootin at her wit cho drove ass. Twin look better than you, Lil Rodney cuter than you, an DonDon is. You jus the only one lame enough to keep cashin na bitch out. She still gone end up fuckin na rest a them niggas too tho while you thinkin you special. You gone be lookin so stupid when nis whole situation blowup in yo face watch. An don't come lookin for me cuz I'm done wit cho ass forever. I never even wanna see you again. I hope you die!" she yelled before hanging up the phone without giving me a chance to say a single word.

I knew she was just tryna make me jealous by telling me she was gone suck Rambo dick. So I aint really take the shit serious for real but Rambo dick was the last dick she would've wanted to suck little did she know. I was pretty sure Rambo wouldn'tve entertained her ass knowing she would obviously be tryna use him to make me jealous anyway. Especially if she just hit him up tryna suck his dick out the blue.

The whole me and Latoya situation definitely wasn't no secret no more thanks to Babydoll's Facebook post. That muafucka had me and Latoya phone ringing nonstop. The whole damn city knew what was going on by the end of the day.

{Wasup bruh, Babydoll ass trippin on Facebook. You seen this shit?} Don-Don texted with a screenshot of the post Babydoll made with a picture me, her, Latoya and Hustle took at the club together one night.

{Yo bruh what Babydoll on? Nikki say she on facbook trippin out} Lil Rodney sent in a text with the same damn screenshot DonDon had just sent.

{Aye Babydoll spazin on the book bruh what the fuck is this???} Dre texted with the same fucking screenshot.

Everybody wanted me or Latoya to confirm the shit so bad but I wasn't really in the mood to explain what was going on so I never even responded. I jus ended up turning my phone completely off. Me and Latoya stayed ducked off in my mama basement gettin high and fuckin for the rest of the night. After a while we aint give a fuck what nobody had to say about it. Latoya was able to help me put my shit together so I could serve my people cuz she always helped Hustle in the lab when he needed it. Her already knowing what to do was hella beneficial cuz once the word got out about Hustle to his geeks they automatically start calling my phone on top of all my people. It definitely got hard to keep up with by myself so her ass was hella useful. Besides, them dems had Latoya all extra freaky 24-7 and I was back getting pussy whenever I wanted without having to sneak around. I wasn't really worried about going back home to Babydoll at that point. An once everybody else realized I wasn't finna give nobody a explanation about the shit they just stopped tryna get one. It was still the talk of the town when we wasn't around though.

"So you really jus gone leave me for Hustle wife like that? Muafuckas steady talm bout yall call yallself together now. How is this bitch able to jus snatch you right the fuck away from me soon as Hustle die? You know how this make me look Dashon? This shit hurt hella bad I thought chu loved me. You really willin to let me go after everything we been thru. We was supposed to be together forever but now you wanna be wit her when she don't even love you like I do. I get so mad every time I think about you an her together I swearda God. I never felt like this before in my life like why you wanna hurt me this bad? I jus don't get it," Babydoll said when she finally broke down and called my phone trying her hardest not to cry but couldn't help but shed the tears building up in her eyes as she talked.

"I'll never stop lovin you Babydoll, you know I hate when you cry baby jus calm down," I replied realizing how much I actually missed her even though I still wasn't willing to stop fucking Latoya and go back home. I knew Babydoll still had my heart though cuz making her cry like that just gave me the urge to hold her close and tell her it was gone be okay. "Don't ever think Ion't love you no more baby, you my rib I can't even live witout cho ass. It's just gettin kinda hard to be aroun you allatime cuz you always suckin my dick like that an it make me hella horny bae. I know you make this dick nut every time you put it in yo mouth an all but I still be wantin to fuck you Babydoll. I'm a man, you sleep wit cho ass pressed up against me every night. Then walk aroun na house in yo lil matchin bra an panties n shit but expect me not to wanna fuck you allatime. That's not even realistic baby that shit'll straight drive a nigga crazy after a while. That's why I aint really worried about comin back home jus so you know. That'ont mean I stopped lovin you tho," I explained hoping she would have a better understanding about why I never tried to come back home to her after she put me out.

"Well you the one keep lyin talm bout chu gone get my ring wit cho income tax but never do. We was sposed to been an got married," she said still tryna put the blame on me even though she did understand whurr I was coming from after listening to what I had to say.

"Baby we gone get married when the timin right stop tryna rush everything. When we get married we both gone be ready then you gone have my son. But for right now we need to jus keep livin, don't worry I'm still gone keep my bills paid an make you happy. Matter fact I'm finna come drop this money off an lick yo lil pussy like you like so get naked," I said tryna make her laugh and put her in a better mood so she wouldn't keep feeling so depressed about me and Latoya.

"No cuz I'ma keep thinkin about how you be lickin her pussy like that an it's gone make me mad," she said in a cute lil pouty voice making me miss her even more.

"Baby you jus crazy, that's why I love yo ass I swear. I jus love you lil girl," I replied knowing I could still control the way she felt about me just by licking her pussy. It was just like giving her some dick. I always got off by being able to control her with sex for some reason, that's how I knew she was my bitch. Little did she know I wasn't finna let her ass get over me whether she broke down and called that day or not. When she called I felt like that was a good time to let her know I still wasn't willing to let her go tho. So soon as I got over thurr I put the 4000 dollars in 20s on the kitchen table then laid her on the couch and licked her pussy like I planned to. She was craving the shit so bad that she nutted in like three minutes but I wasn't really surprised cuz she never really lasted more than like ten. After she came I kissed her softly on her lips then headed for the door.

"Baby whurr you goin? You jus got hurr an I wanna drink it," she said with a smirk. "Lemme drink it," she said seductively pulling me back towards the couch while tryna unzip my jeans.

"Baby I can't, I left my phones in na car wit Latoya. I jus need you to go pay my bills right now I'll be back later. It's hella people waitin on me to pullup," I said stopping her in her tracks as her eyes instantly filled with tears soon as I said Latoya name.

"Baby why is you doin nis? She is not me, why is she wit chu? I fuckin hate her. All she want is yo money baby she don't even love you. Why you actin like she me an keepin her wit chu allatime?" she wined as the tears started to fall down her face while she talked. "Do you love her?" she asked looking in my eyes desperately wanting a honest answer so she could know exactly how serious I was about the bitch I guess. But I just gave her another kiss before leaving without given her a answer at all. I couldn't stand seeing her cry knowing it was nothing I could've really said that would've made her feel different. It aint like she would've believed me if I hada said no so I just walked away. I was just hoping she would realize that I still loved her no matter what. I did feel bad about jus leaving her standing thurr heartbroken and pretty much defeated but after I got high Babydoll's feelings was the last thing on my mind.

PLAYING DIRTY

"Why do you like her Dashon?" Babydoll asked when she bust out and called my phone a couple days later pissed that I hadn't tried to call her since I dropped off that money, licked her pussy hella good, then left with Latoya like it was no big deal. "You think she cuter than me? Do she suck yo dick better than I do? The only reason you think her pussy so good is cuz you haven't felt mine in so long. You crazy if you think her pussy better than mine cuz she'll give that shit to anybody wit some money or dems so I know her shit ran thru," she said feeling bitter and completely fed up with the fact that everybody thought Latoya was my new bitch. But I was happy Babydoll called cuz she had just crossed my mind a few moments before my phone rang ironically.

"Fuck naw Latoya aint cuter than you baby everybody know that. An I remember how yo pussy feel lil girl. That pussy don't belong to nobody but me, I already know aint nobody pussy better than mines. Can't nobody suck my dick better than you neither that's why I'll kill sumn ova yo ass. Ion't jus be sayin nat shit you'll get somebody fucked up playin wit me," I said amused with her jealousy but still wanting to set the record straight so she wouldn't be so insecure about Latoya at the same time.

"Whatever Dashon, you so fulla shit I swear. What is you even doin? Whurr you at? Why you always got that bitch aroun you instead a me?" she asked feeling annoyed with not being a part a my everyday life anymore knowing Latoya was.

"I jus left DonDon crib baby, I'm finna come pick you an Latoya up so we can all go shoppin so get ready to come outside," I answered with a smile tryna make it so that I wouldn't keep feeling like I couldn't have her around me because of Latoya. I was starting to miss Babydoll's presence on a daily basis but Latoya's presence was way too helpful and convenient to let go. I was determined to have em both at the end of the day.

"I'm not goin shoppin wit that bitch I hate her! You shouldn't even be takin her shoppin you disloyal as fuck! You'ont do shit but tear me down an build her up when she don't even deserve all that. I'm hella loyal to you. I haven't been fuckin wit nobody since you left me cuz Ion't even want nobody else. You really think she anything like me after what she did to Hustle soon as he died? What makes you think she'll have more loyalty an respect for you than she had for her own husband who she got kids an straight history wit. She wasn't even loyal to Hustle when he was alive an takin care a her ass so why would she be any more loyal to you? Why put her on nis pedestal an just kick me to the curb like Ion't mean nothin to you? Howda hell you expect me to feel like you actually still love me like you say when you jus keepin me on na backburner. All so this bitch can feel like she took a muafucka away from me, you straight won't even come back home," Babydoll replied feeling outraged.

"Baby shutup that girl did not take me away from you. I already told you I aint came back home yet cuz you aint comin up off no pussy an I'm sick of it. Plus you the one put me out. So as long as them fuckin bills stay paid you shouldn't be worried about whether I'm thurr or not," I responded defensively reminding her exactly why I left home in the first place. I did understand whurr she was coming from though. She was kinda making me feel bad when she called herself going off so I had to come back with something.

'Okay Dashon, jus keep yo so called bitch on na sideline while you treat Hustle bitch like she yo wifey. Give her everything I'm sposed to have just because I'm not okay wit chu fuckin na bitch an lickin her pussy. Let the bitch keep shittin on me wit the only nigga I give a fuck about, go ahead," she said sarcastically making me feel even worse.

"Baby cut it out, you my wife aint nobody shittin on you. Just come outside an get the money when I pullup witcho dramatic ass," I said before hanging up the phone soon as I seen Latoya walking to the car.

"Say hi to Babydoll when she come outside so I can take yall shoppin together," I said to Latoya tryna get her to help me convince Babydoll that it wouldn't be so bad if the three of us was rockin out altogether without all the drama.

"Why I gotta say hi to the bitch? Ion't even want her ass to go," Latoya replied rolling her eyes with a attitude.

"Get off that bullshit Latoya yall jus need to be friends. I aint got time for yall hoes to be fightin," I said as I pulled up to the luxurious apartment complex Babydoll insisted we move to. The damn rent was more than we would've paid for a whole house so we was kinda stupid for living thurr but it was nice though.

"Ion't know why you still deal wit the bitch anyway. It aint like yall got kids together an she not helpin you get this money like I am neither so it's really kinda pointless if you ask me," Latoya replied feeling some type a way about me still being involved with Babydoll after Babydoll let everybody know what was going on. It did make Latoya look hella bad though. Hustle family was talking all shit, the kids was all confused and embarrassed about the situation. The whole hood was talking about how fucked up that shit was. Her own family was talking shit about her ass.

They was all talking bout how scandalous I was for fucking with the bitch too but I was only doing what Latoya was allowing me to do at the end of the day. It's not like I was raping the damn girl. So it wasn't really nothin they could say to tear me down about the shit cuz I'm a nigga, and a nigga from na zone at that. Whose to say Hustle wouldn't've hopped down on Babydoll right away if it was me that had got killed? All it really take is for a bitch to give you the greenlight. Lets say she chose somebody else from the hood to give the greenlight to, whose to say they wouldn't've went just like I did. At least I was breaking bread with her ass. Hell most niggas I know would've simply fucked the bitch and kept it pushing so I aint really feel bad about the shit at all after a while.

"Nigga this aint the junkyard, why you keep bringin nis trashy ass bitch to my crib?" Babydoll said when she came outside to the parking lot to get the money I was dropping off.

"Girl shut cho weak ass up, this nigga gone do whatever the fuck he wanna do an you aint gone do shit but cry about it, boo who," Latoya replied knowing exactly what to say to make Babydoll feel stupid.

"Hurr baby damn, I aint got time for this type a shit. Yall do too much," I said before peeling off 500 dollars from the big knot of money I had then handing Babydoll the rest.

"Why you givin her all that when you finna take me shoppin," Latoya asked boldly with her face all frowned up obviously feeling some type a way about me handing Babydoll most of my money.

"Cuz I'm his wife, you just a lil bitch he stringin along for some pussy at the moment. Stay in yo lane. Oh an I need some money for the nail shop too," Babydoll said as she snatched one of the hundred dollar bills I had in my hand before walking off like a model with the money.

"That's why he jus fucked me twenty minutes ago an licked my pussy hella good bitch. I'ma fuck em again soon as we leave Fresh Image too," Latoya yelled out as Babydoll walked across the parking lot towards the door to our unit.

"Girl Fresh Image expensive as fuck, you aint gettin shit wit that punkass 4hunnit dollars foreal bitch fuck you!" Babydoll yelled back before opening the apartment door and going in.

"Whyda fuck would you take me shoppin wit 400 dollars an give yo dustyass girlfriend na rest of yo fuckin money. You makin me miss my muafuckin husband cuz this some straight bullshit. Nigga you jus a knockoff anyway tho you could never compare to him I swearda God," Latoya lashed out with tears running down her face as I pulled out the parking lot.

"Bitch shut the fuck up an crunch this pack down," I said handing her some perk tens. "Get that NyQuil out the glove compartment, I'm finna stop at this gas station right hurr an get some juice," I added knowing exactly what all I needed for her to shut the fuck up an stop crying.

"What the fuck is you doin," Babydoll asked annoyed when she called my phone a couple days later.

"Nothin baby im in na lab, whurr you at wit my pussy? Whatchu doin?" I replied pretending not to realize or already know why she sounded so upset.

"Shut the fuck up do you even miss me? You haven't seen or talked to me in two days," she said feeling pissed that she hadn't seen or heard from me since I left with Latoya again.

"Yeah I miss you baby you know that," I replied as Latoya walked up to me and straddled me in my chair after realizing I was on the phone with Babydoll.

"I want chu to fuck me like you did this mornin baby," Latoya said seductively in my ear right next to the phone so Babydoll could hear.

"So this bitch jus gone keep bein na reason Ion't see or hear from yo dusty ass?" Babydoll asked feeling salty as fuck.

"Baby shutup I just seen you yesterday you too muafuckin dramatic," I said tryna brush off how extra freaky Latoya ass was acting all asudden knowing she was just doing all that to piss Babydoll off.

"I didn't even talk to you yesterday an you'ont even give a fuck, then you always lettin nat bitch disrespect me just cuz she givin yo thirsty ass some pussy. It aint never that serious Dashon," Babydoll said as Latoya unzipped my pants and pulled my dick out. After she pulled my dick out she took off her shorts and panties then started twerking in my face like a stripper. By the time she start grinding down on my dick Babydoll had just hung up the phone knowing Latoya had my full undivided attention. Latoya grabbed the table in front of me and rode my dick until I nutted. So I wasn't really worried about Babydoll hanging up the phone at the time no way. I guess that was the last straw for Babydoll ass though cuz she showed up at my mama house like thirty minutes later looking sexy as fuck. She had on this lil skin tight black mini dress and some cute lil wedges with her hair all dolled up and shit. She came right downstairs in the basement whurr me and Latoya was once my dad let her in.

"Damn baby whurr the fuck you goin? What's this?" I said pulling her towards me playfully while looking her up an down. "You must be tryna get cho lil pussy licked asumn huh," I said smiling and impressed by the way she just popped up out a no whurr looking all grown and sexy and shit.

"I always want my pussy licked, that's the only reason you even know howda do it," she replied with a smile cutting her eyes at Latoya before kissing me softly on the lips.

"Baby what the hell dun got inta you? Why you actin all perfect alla sudden?" I asked even more turned on by how nonchalant she was acting with Latoya being over thurr too.

"I'm jus tired of not bein aroun you baby, so if this whurr you gone be this whurr I'ma be. If I'm yo rib I'm sposed to be wit chu right?" she answered looking in my eyes before briefly glancing over at Latoya. She was listening to every word Babydoll was saying and surprisingly speechless. "I'ma be hurr for you no matter what cuz I really do love you an I know you worth fightin for. That's why we been holdin on to each other this long baby. I'll never let go you never did," she added focusing her full attention back on me before I grabbed her face an kissed her. I had been wanting her to say that shit so bad. Everything she was saying was exactly what I wanted to hear so I was even more sure about how real the love we had for each other actually was. Hell I damn near forgot Latoya ass was even down thurr.

"Yeah she a good one baby cuz not a lota wives would let a bitch ride they husband dick like I just did," Latoya said with a smile throwing all shade at Babydoll of course.

"Well since I'm not ridin na dick myself til he actually put a ring on it bitches like you can do my dirty work for now. Then once he gimme his last name I'ma remind em how filthy I am myself... He already know tho, that's why he still keepin me aroun anyway duh," Babydoll replied with a chuckle seemingly unbothered even though she was pissed that Latoya was able to brag about riding my dick right before she popped up over thurr.

"Well whatever, I was jus ridin his dick right thurr whurr yall sittin while you was on na phone. I hope you don't mind," Latoya said rolling her eyes as she chopped up the dope on the plate in front of her.

"Was it better than nat one time I road yo dick in na back seat at cho mama house back when yall stayed on Labadie?" Babydoll asked with a smile, playin it off like she wasn't trippin off what Latoya had just said so Latoya wouldn't know how bothered she was by it.

"Why you remember that so well lil crazy ass girl?" I asked playfully grabbing her pussy while she sat thurr giggling on my lap. She was purposely walking down memory lane to remind Latoya about all the memories we made together while she was still with Hustle.

"Boy whatever, you'ont even remember which time I'm talm bout," Babydoll said playfully rolling her eyes as she blushed.

"Yeah iight, that night you was sposed to go to yo cousin party but cho fake ass jus ended up ridin my dick in na car? Then took yo tired ass right back in na house an went to sleep like I told you to do in na first place," I replied with a smile as Babydoll kept laughing just to annoy Latoya.

"Baby pay attention to what she doin cuz I'ma need you to help her," I told Babydoll as Latoya rolled her eyes and kept doing what she was doing without saying another word

"I gotta pee," Latoya said getting up from the table after sitting thurr completely quiet for about 25 minutes straight. "I'll be right back daddy," she said as she walked right over to whurr me and Babydoll was sitting then kissed me seductively on my lips. She was obviously just tryna get up under Babydoll skin since Babydoll seemed to be on such a high horse at the time I guess. Babydoll's blood was boiling after seeing Latoya kiss me like that but she still played it cool like it didn't really faze her. She was making me wanna keep her around me 24-7 like I used to whether I had Latoya with me or not.

Jessica Whitfield

SHAMELESS

"Waddup fool! whatchu got goin on? When you popin out? The streets callin nigga whurr ya at?" DonDon said playfully when he called my phone a couple minutes later.

"I'm ova hurr in na lab wit Babydoll an Latoya. We finna pop out ina minute tho, you at the crib?" I answered casually like having Babydoll and Latoya with me in the lab together was really no big deal.

"Yeah but hold on wait a minute what? You say you in na lab wit Babydoll an Latoya? Nigga you bullshittin aint no way," he replied with a smile tryna figure out if I was really serious about actually having both of them in the lab with me or not.

'Cumon bruh you know I'm slime foreva nigga Ion't do no fakin. We finna pop out tho so get some weed for Babydoll ass cuz I only got a blunt left. An have some blood on deck too cuz I got all tens on deck we finna be hurt," I said gassing him up so he would have everything setup and ready once we got thurr.

"Cumon Latoya lets finish this up real quick so we can go pull up on Don-Don nem. We aint even got no blood hurr an I'm tryna get high," I said when Latoya came out the bathroom muggin Babydoll. I knew getting Latoya high would put her in a better mood so I was tryna get over thurr with DonDon ass soon as possible.

"Who all goin?" she asked with a attitude hoping I aint plan on Babydoll coming along with us. The situation was jus a lil bit more shameful and embarrassing for her with Babydoll still being in the mix knowing what was going on I guess.

"We all goin baby damn jus help me get this shit done so we can slide out. I'm ready to shake shid we been down hurr all day," I answered not really giving a damn if she was comfortable with Babydoll going or not.

"So you jus gone let cho girlfriend tag along wit us everywhurr we go now?" she asked feeling offended by me including Babydoll in our usual day to day agenda all asudden.

"No you actually taggin along wit us cuz you been a fuckin charity case since Hustle died," Babydoll responded harshly as I rolled my eyes and ignored em both. I was feeling a lil irritated with the constant back and forth at that point. Babydoll finally coming around and coexisting with Latoya was definitely a step in the right direction. But it would've been a lot easier for me to deal with em both if they was to just be friends instead of constantly taking shots at each other.

"So jus cuz she suddenly decided to start followin us aroun everywhurr we go I gotta sit in na back now?" Latoya asked as Babydoll opened the front door and got in when we all walked to the car.

"Of course I get the front seat. Why would he pullup wit his bitch in na back just cuz Hustle left yo ass stragged out dependin on my nigga to drive you aroun?" Babydoll blurted out before I could even answer.

"Latoya get the fuck in na back I been wit chu all day baby damn," I said as I opened the driver's side door and got in.

"It 'ont matter if you been wit her ass all day or not. Whyda fuck would you pullup wit cho bitch in na backseat anyway? That shit jus lame as fuck. Hustle not drivin nis muafucka so she has no place in na front seat while I'm in the car that's jus common sense. Was I ever ridin aroun in na front seat wit Hustle while her or Bre was in na back seat?" Babydoll snapped reminding Latoya about how Hustle was fuckin with her home girl behind Latoya back out of spite.

"Bitch Hustle would never let a bitch disrespect me like I disrespect you, that's why you mad ho! That nigga knew not to have no bitch he was fuckin all in my house or in na car wit my ass. He kept them bitches in ney place an far the fuck away from me outta respect bitch, which is somethin yo nigga aint even got sense enough to do cuz heon't give a fuck about chu! You wish you had a nigga like Hustle but bitch you could never. That's why yo nigga been wantin to fuck me, he already know his bitch aint never been on na same level as Hustle's wit cho drove ass!" Latoya replied getting in the back seat and talking a million dollars worth a shit while she was at it.

"Bitch you the one hopped on my nigga dick five minutes after yo husband got kilt. You so busy tryna take my spot you'ont even realize how much of a embarrassment you is to Hustle for even marryin yo lil ratchit ass. You obviously already wanid my nigga weather he called himself wantin to fuck you or not. I'm pretty sure Hustle wanid to fuck me too but Hustle could've never fucked me bitch that's on my daughter. You want what I got, I never wanid Hustle that's probably why he aint like me. A muafucka couldn't pay me enough to make a damn fool outta my late husband like you doin yours bitch. An if I was scandalous enough to do some thirsty as shit like what the fuck you doin I woulda made Hustle stop fuckin wit chu altogether. Especially if I knew you wasn't givin na nigga no pussy and I was. I'm not even fuckin Dashon ass while you braggin about ridin his dick but can't get the nigga to jus leave me the fuck alone. Girl yo pussy trash, you really think I'm worried about yo wack ass when I'm really jus embarrassed for you bitch!" Babydoll yelled back feeling furious.

"Girl bye, yo nigga love the way this pussy feel that's why he'ont give a fuck about yo lame ass not fuckin him stupid. That's why he haven't married yo silly ass yet an never will. He aint gone do shit but keep doggin yo ass out an doin whatever the fuck he wanna do while you sittin hurr lookin stupid. At least my nigga actually married me at the end a the day bitch. He showl aint have me ridin aroun wit a bitch he fuckin lookin crazy," Latoya said calmly, suddenly acting all unbothered after realizing how pissed off Babydoll was getting about the shit she was sayin.

Babydoll was a lil more in her feelings about it though. She tried to keep clapping back but start feeling a lil more defeated the more her and Latoya went back and forth. "Bitch all it take is for me to fuck him an you garbage ho. My pussy been untouched for damn ner three years, you'ont even know what the fuck you up against. You could never take my nigga when it's all said an done bitch. All you can do is get some dick til I decide to hop back on it. I could make this nigga forget all about yo thirsty ass if I really wanid to tho

The Streets of St. Louis

bitch remember that," Babydoll said feeling a lil tempted to just go ahead and fuck me just to prove her point.

"Aye I'ma end up droppin both a yall bitches off cuz yall givin me a headache steady arguin n shit damn. All three of us grown as fuck, why we can't jus pull up stylin witout all that catty ass fightin yall constantly doin. Both a yall hella bad an I'm nat nigga so everybody need to jus sit back an chill. Catch a vibe baby, roll this blunt up an relax man yall jus need to pipe down an let me enjoy this shit," I said handing Babydoll the last lil blunt I had left with a swisher hoping the weed would calm they crazy asses down a lil bit so it wouldn't be so much tension in the air. "Foreal yall, this every nigga dream. I jus wanna flex on na whole city an have a good time damn. All yall gotta do is go wit the flow, have fun wit each other, an be sexy. Fuck all that fightin shit. It's two bad bitches an a boss pullin up in nis muafucka regardless a who in na front seat. We killin shit out hurr in these streets," I added gassin they asses up so they could start tryna get along.

"Ok daddy, you know I do whatever you say," Latoya responded sensually before kissing my neck and ear from the back seat really just to piss Babydoll off some more. Once we pulled up at DonDon crib Latoya hopped out the car carelessly just ready to get high off the perks.

"Wasup slime," DonDon greeted with a smile as me, Latoya, and Babydoll walked up the stairs and into a house fulla people. They was all staring at the three of us like they had just seen a fucking ghost or something. Nobody really spoke on the shit but everybody in thurr was most likely thinking the same thing.

"Wasup BabyD, you gettin hella skinny girl you used to be way thicker than nis what's goin on?" DonDon said sizing up Babydoll after realizing how much weight she had lost stressing over me and Latoya.

"I love bein skinny Don. It look better wit my height, it's cute right?" Babydoll replied tryna figure out if the weight loss made her look more like a barbie or more like she was falling off.

"I mean you always gone be cute Babydoll but of course you look better when yo hips an ass popin out. Yo waist line was already hella little so you aint really need to lose no weight," DonDon answered basically keeping it alla way ahunnit with her so she wouldn't keep dropping all that weight like she was doing.

"Kiss my ass Don I'ma fuckin model, all my jeans are a size seven now," Babydoll said proudly with a smile.

"Yeah Babydoll but you always kinda had more of a top notch stripper look to me," DonDon responded playfully making Babydoll laugh while putting her middle finger up at him.

"I guess you can tell whether a bitch gettin dicked down real good or not," Latoya chimed in with a smile as she sat down on my lap in front of everybody purposely making Babydoll uncomfortable.

"I need a cigarette or some weed," Babydoll said brushing all the shade Latoya was throwing off by changing the subject so nobody would notice how embarrassed she was feeling.

"Cigarette? Babydoll when na fuck you start smokin cigarettes? Yo ass dun changed allaway up on a nigga wasup wit chu? I jus smoked my last Newport, I got some weed tho," DonDon replied taking the bag of weed I told him to get out his pocket but feeling a lil concerned about how much Babydoll had changed since the last time they was around each other.

"You left them Newports in na car?" Babydoll asked hoping she had a reason to go outside and get some air cuz she was feeling a lil more overwhelmed than she expected, especially wit Latoya being so extra.

"Yeah bae they on na side a the door," I answered as Babydoll made her way down the steps and out to the car to grab em.

"Ay tell her to grab them rellos too," I told Don soon as it crossed my mind even though she was probably already heading back up by then.

"Whats wrong Babydoll? Why you cryin?" DonDon asked in a more serious manner than usual when he saw Babydoll wiping the tears from her eyes at the car.

"Don please don't tell nobody I'm out hurr cryin. I'm jus tryna pull myself together real quick cuz ion't even feel like I'ma be able to do this shit right now," Babydoll answered holding her hands to her eyes so the tears wouldn't run down her face.

"Naw I aint gone tell nobody, you'ont feel like you gone be able to do what tho?" he asked sympathetically.

"Ion't even know what I'm tryna do right now, I think I jus wanna prove that she can't jus take him away from me but she a lil more confident than I am right now for some reason. Plus it's kinda hard to feel like I really still got his heart when he pretty much a whole different person now. He be actin like he straight possessed a sumn. Ion't even know howda deal wit him no more an its breakin me down. This who I wanna spen na rest a my life wit I swearda God but the shit he got goin on wit her is fuckin crazy. An whyda hell it feel like don't nobody else think the shit crazy but me all asudden. I'm straight losin my fuckin mind tryna play inta this shit for him. Ion't even know howda act aroun him no more foreal. While this bitch jus seem to have his ass so figured the fuck out already, pullin him further away while I'm tryin my hardest to hold on," Babydoll vented as Don stood thurr listening intensively until she was finished talking.

"Okay Babydoll first of all you aint got no business bein less confident than Latoya ass trust me. Second of all you jus gotta let this shit play out. Yeah the shit weird as fuck an everybody know that but at some point Dashon gone come to his senses an realize how dope you is for even hangin in ner wit his ass thru all this. Latoya can't take that nigga away from you girl everybody know what type a bitch Latoya is. That's why they always clowin Hustle for marryin her ass. Dashon know damn well he not finna let chu go for no muthafuckin Latoya, you crazy as hell if you think he would. He just grievin right now believe it or not. An yeah he grievin in a fucked up ass way that I'm pretty sure you'ont understand but that's just what it is I swear. Stop all that cryin an jus be yoself. You always been different from otha girls Babydoll so he showl can't replace you, especially wit somebody like her remember that," DonDon said before pushing her bangs out her face so they wouldn't get wet with her tears. "Its gone be okay jus hang in ner," he added looking in her eyes sort a calming her down with his comforting words. He was almost tempted to try an kiss her at the moment cuz she was still so pretty even when she cried. But before he even had a chance to go for it I came right outside tryna see what the fuck was taking them so long.

"Aye don't be tryna pushup on my bitch Don. I'ma handle yo ass like a nigga on na street," I said playfully as Babydoll quickly pulled herself together.

"Cumon bruh, I know who da fuck she is nigga," DonDon replied with a smile before taking the Newport Babydoll was handing him then heading back upstairs with us.

"So what chu an DonDon ass was out ther talm bout?" I asked Babydoll once we left him and Tyresha crib later on that night. I was still feeling curious about what was taking them so long to come back upstairs with the rellos an shit.

"Mmm mmm they showl was outside together for a nice lil minute too," Latoya butted in insinuating that Babydoll and Don had something going on behind my back so I wouldn't trust Babydoll.

"I mean he was jus seein if I was okay. Hell it seem like Hustle death fucked my life up more than anybody's an we aint even like each other half the time," Babydoll answered rolling her eyes with her face all frowned up. She was hella annoyed that Latoya always seemed to have something to say.

"Yeah whateva, don't be goin ova thurr actin all sad an shit Babydoll. The first thing a muafucka gone do is tryda take advantage of yo lil green ass. Don't get DonDon ass fucked up playin. He think I'ma let'm off easy cuz he my potna but I'll lay his goofy ass down too," I said jokingly making Babydoll finally crack a smile.

"Yeah whatever Dashon, every female in na world jus not that easy. It's different types a bitches on nis earth, we not all straggs you know," Babydoll answered obviously throwing a lil shade at Latoya as Latoya rolled her eyes.

HEARTLESS

"Aye Cutthroat straight jus kilt Twin bruh," Rambo blurted out when he called my phone soon as I answered.

"Damn he hit Twin too? How you know that? When nis happen? I jus talked to Twin ass earlier man nat shit crazy," I replied feeling appalled by the new information and anxious to hear a lil more about the details.

"Cutthroat seen em come out the gas station on Jefferson, followed em off the lot then chased em down. He was wit that one bitch in na Infinity. She said when he realized Cutthroat was on his ass he took off cuz he aint have no thumpa on em. She say it was a whole high speed til Twin crashed out but after he crashed the car he got out an ran. That's when Cutthroat hit em up from na car then chased em down on foot. She said he got allaway up on em too, shot em right in na back a his head man," Rambo answered shaking his head sympathetically.

"Damn bruh, so what about the bitch he was in na car wit tho? You mean to tell me she seen all that an he aint feel the need to knock her ass off too?" I asked curious as to why he would leave her alive after witnessing him murder Twin like she claimed he did. "That aint soundin realistic at all to me bruh. How you know the bitch aint fulla shit?" I replied, questioning weather or not the whole story was even true at that point.

"That's what I was thinkin at first but she said she never got out the car an nem windows hella tinted so he aint even know she was in ner. Then she said he was in nat same burgundy Honda that white bitch he be fuckin wit got. She described exactly how the nigga look an all. Plus she say Twin said Cutthroat name when he first peeped him, she aint tell the police shit tho. That bitch terrified, don't want nothin to do wit nothin trust me she aint lyin," Rambo answered, reassuring me that what the bitch said happened was actually true.

"Pullup on me tho bruh. Muafuckas steady callin my phone I gotta answer this otha end," Rambo said still feeling drained from Hustle death but a lil more numb to Twin's cuz the deaths around us was getting more and more common. They was definitely way to close for comfort too.

"Say no mo, I'm finna pullup on you now. Whurr you at on G code?" I asked knowing nine times outa ten that's exactly whurr he was.

"Yeah bruh pull up," he answered before taking his other call. I was a lil skeptical about pulling up on Rambo with Babydoll in the car after what she said about her tryna suck the nigga dick that one day, but I decided to pull up on him wit her ass regardless. I was curious to see how she was gone carry herself around him anyway. I wanted to know if she was gone start playing games and acting all slutty around him just to make me jealous.

"Aye bruh, I wasn't gone say shit at first but Ion't like how you doin Babydoll homie. She stressin na fuck out," DonDon said when he called my phone soon as I answered. "You finna have to see me inna minute cuz I aint feelin nat shit straightup," he said playfully but seriously tryna let me know how fucked up Babydoll was behind the whole me and Latoya situation.

"Man fuck all that bruh why Cutthroat jus hit Twin ass too?" I replied knowing I was the first to tell'm the news cuz it wasn't the first thing that came out his mouth when he called.

"What chu mean he jus hit Twin. That nigga had jus left wit that one bitch like thirty minutes before yall pulled up, so when all this happen?" DonDon asked feeling completely caught off guard by what I was telling him.

"I guess soon as he left that muafucka shid ole girl told Rambo everything. She seen na whole demonstration an Cutthroat ass aint even know she was in na car. She said he chased em down, made em crash, then got out the car an finished his ass when he tried to hop out an run. Shot em right in na back a his head bruh," I explained as the phone calls finally start coming in on him and Tyresha line about the news.

When we pulled up on Gamble I looked over at Babydoll in a way that warned her not to fuckin play wit me before hopping out the car to holla at

Rambo. I aint even have to say shit cuz my eyes said it all so she never even looked in that nigga direction.

"Wasup bruh, this shit gettin crazy out hurr huh? Niggas straight spazzin out," I said shaking his hand to greet'm.

"Yeah man nat shit gettin way outta hand foreal. An Cutthroat ass had jus pulled up on me wit Savage earlier today. He wanid to holla at me face to face about that shit wit him an Hustle. It was kinda hard to look that nigga in na eyes knowin he did that shit to Hustle tho man. That shit jus fucked me up bruh, I aint wanna walk in an find my nigga slumped ova like that. I'll never get that image outta my head. Me an Cutthroat was bout as close as me an Hustle was before he got booked but that shit kinda make me feel like Ion't even know the nigga. I still told em I wasn't takin sides cuz I do need to stay up outta that shit tho. I already got too much goin on wit them tallaban niggas an Cutthroat jus way too close to home for me. I mean I do feel some type a way about what happened but I wouldn't go as far as tryna kill Cutthroat behind it. Not unless I felt like he was tryna kill me too.

"Now Twin den got kilt behind nat shit, Lil Beezy gone, this shit just all fucked up. It seem like everybody jus gone end up killin each other off outta anger tryna retaliate," Rambo vented feeling like it was absolutely no hope for any one of our asses cuz everybody we knew was so naturally misguided and fucked up in the head. "We already gotta duck these outside niggas shid now we duckin each other too," Rambo added feeling hopeless. I definitely felt whurr he was coming from though. So I basically just let him know he did right by keeping the peace with Cutthroat and advised him to just stay alert and out the way. The streets was more of a battlefield than ever with all the carless killin going on right under our noses. I mean it wasn't really nothing new but it did hit a lil different once Cutthroat killed Hustle for some reason.

"I heard you dun got real Hollywood on nigga slime," Chad said playfully once Chucky handed me the phone. I had went to my mama house later on that day and Chad had called from na joint. He knew more about what was going on than a nigga on the streets damn near. He never wanted to call my phone cuz he knew my shit was probably hot as fish grease fucking wit Hustle ass. But the rumors about me, Latoya, and Babydoll was so crazy he couldn't wait to verify what the fuck was goin on.

"You ah…you got a lot goin on out thurr don't chu son," he asked with a smile feeling a lil unsure about how to actually bring the shit up. The whole conversation was obviously finna be a lot more awkward and uncomfortable than he realized. Especially considering how close he was with Hustle and Latoya too.

"Man somebody get my oldest boy a helmet please, cuz this lil nigga crashed out so quick Ion't even think he ready to hit the pavement again! Dude rookied out," I said jokingly slick changin the subject before he could really even bring the shit up. I did miss his lil ugly ass though. With everything going on at the time I knew I needed a real street nigga I could trust around me watching my back like I had when he was out. I'm hella alert and observant on my own but I was always a lil more comfortable runnin the streets with a extra set of eyes looking out for me. Besides my hands was pretty much full dealing with Babydoll and Latoya asses.

Them bitches gave me one good three some then went right back to fighting everyday. Hell I had to get em both pissy drunk and spike Babydoll drink just to pull that off. It was lit as fuck though I can't even stunt. It all started when we pulled up on Rello nem one night. Latoya start acting all extra freaky knowing we was the center of attention whenever I had her and Babydoll with me at the same time. She decided to put on a show for they ass cuz Latoya loved being the center of attention anyway. Once she realized all eyes was on us she start kissing all on me while Babydoll was sitting on my lap. Then she start rubbin all up on Babydoll while we was kissing so everybody in the room was even more infatuated with what was going on. By the time her and Babydoll start kissing niggas was in that muafucka straight droolin I swear. I was the man in that bitch. Niggas start acting like I was a straight up Don or somethin. When I took the girls back home with me it really went down. Latoya start lickin Babydoll pussy with her ass all tooted up so I slid my dick right up in her pussy while she was doing it. Then I laid flat on my back and let her ride the dick while Babydoll sat on my face and got her pussy ate until she came. After all that went down they both fell asleep in my arms and everything was perfect. That is until I turned on my side facing Latoya when I got tired of laying flat on my back. Babydoll crazy ass felt like I turned my back to her cuz I wanted to be closer to Latoya when all I was really tryna do was get comfortable. Latoya just happened to be sleeping on the side I wanted to lay on tho so that was the end of that. It was still hella fun while it lasted.

"Man Ion't know what chu, Babydoll an Latoya got goin on out thurr but from in hurr that shit sound like a straight up movie I swear. Niggas in nis muafucka talkin my ear off bout that shit bruh wasup?" Chad said after laughing off the jokes I was making about him crashin out and leaving me in the trenches alone.

"I wish I was out man shit steady changin on a nigga bruh. Seem like the streets aint even na same no mo. Hustle gone, I'm steady hearin Cutthroat name floatin aroun behind nat shit. Twin gone, Cutthroat name all in na midst a that. Lil Bezzy dun got hit, they sayin Murder went ghost after that shit happened wit Hustle an aint no tellin what that nigga gone be on when he pop back out. I jus wanna come home bruh," Chad vented feeling concerned and unsure about if I would even be able to stay alive and out the way until he finally made it up out that muafucka.

"Yeah the streets jus fucked up right now bruh. Seem like Hustle shook the muafuckin ground when he left this bitch cuz shit jus been rocky ever since. Everybody all shook up an sketched out cuz you 'ont really know who da trust after that shit. The shit make you feel like you can't trust nobody. I be wishin yo ass was still out hurr too bruh. I'm out hurr by myself in na trenches fool," I replied as he held the phone fulla regret, ready to hop right back in the streets wit me regardless.

By the time he did get out my ass was already locked up though. I was coming home one night and some St. Louis County police officers pulled right up behind me soon as I turned in my driveway. I couldn'tve pulled off cuz they blocked the driveway and had me boxed in. So I hopped out the car an tried to hurry up an run in the house

"Freeze!" One of the officers yelled as I ran to the door in the pouring rain."Mr. Collins Freeze!" The other officer yelled, letting me know they already knew who I was and had most likely been sitting thurr waiting on me to pull up. "Hands up Dashon, do not reach in the bag, hands up!" One of the officers yelled with his gun drawn, pointing it directly at the back of my head. "Im not, my hands up!" I yelled after reaching for the doorknob forgetting it was locked. The officer without his gun drawn approached me wit caution. He had his handcuffs out ready to cuff me but I still tried to dip out on they ass.

It was rainin so hard at the time I slipped an fell in the mud soon as I tried to take off though. Man them officers beat my ass so bad I swear. I know for a fact they was finna put a bullet in my ass had Babydoll not came and opened the door. With the fully loaded gun and all the dope I had in the lil lacost bag I was wearing they had the perfect excuse to kill me. I knew they was gone take the opportunity to soon as they got done beatin my ass like they was doing so thank God Babydoll came to the door when she did.

She was hella scared so she started to just record em through the window but the way they was beatin me down she had to come make her presence known. "Step back in the house and close the door maam" one of the officers said to Babydoll when she opened the front door. "No sir im on my property in my house, I shouldn't have to shut my door. I wanna see what's goin on. This my yard, I have a right to do this.

Me standing hurr watching what's going on outside of my house is not stoppin yall from doin yall job. Why the hell is yall doin all this anyway? Just take the fuckin bag and cuff him, it's two of yall it shouldn't even take all that" Babydoll replied with her phone out ready to record anything they said or did at that point. "Maam this young man was resisting arrest and this is procedure so please step back in the house and let us do our job." One of the officers answered as Babydoll start recording the whole conversation.

"Ok well he's not resisting arrest now. He look like he hurt pretty bad so maybe yall should just take what yall want and cuff him instead of steady beatin him down like yall was just doin" Babydoll replied as the officers finally took the bag from around me then put me in the car. So Chad ended up out thurr in the trenches alone too.

It damn near broke me down when I face-timed Babydoll from the feds and she told me he had got himself killed the night before. He was posted up on Gamble at his new lil bitch crib at the time. She had just moved in the recently remodeled apartments on Gamble with her two lil twin boys. Chad fell for the damn braud soon as she gave his ass some pussy too. That nigga was out thurr playin step daddy, lickin the bitch pussy, kissin her all outside in front a everybody an all. She had his ass doin all type a shit he thought he would never do.

This one lil nigga was ova thurr on the set at his granny crib an Chad new lil bitch Tweety was steady sayin he had broke in her crib a couple nights before. So Chad got on some heavy shit an told the lil dude he had to shake. "Fuck you mean nigga? Iaint goin no whurr, iont give a fuck what that bitch talm bout. You aint got no proof bitch fuck you!" Dude responded clutchin his pistal as he talked "iight say no mo nigga" Chad replied before runnin in Tweety crib an grabbin his thumpa too. Powpowpowpowpowpowpow. Chad came right back outa Tweety crib bussin. The lil nigga he was goin back an fourth wit was already clutchin his shit waitin on somthin to pop off. So when Chad came out bussin like he did dude start bussin right back immediately. Hit Chad ass right in the side of his neck. So he died right thurr on Gamble at Tweety front door.

Babydoll said Heavy called her phone at like one o'clock that morning with the news and she hadn't been able to go back to sleep since. I knew it was finna be some bullshit soon as she answered the phone that day cuz it looked like she had been up crying all night. Her and Chad was never really a big fan of each other but she already knew telling me that shit was finna break my heart. She knew the shit was hella hard for me to deal with especially after getting indicted then sentenced to five years in federal custody.

Hell I was already stressed out enough not knowing if me an Babydoll could really even be separated for five years without drifting apart at some point. That was my biggest fear too cuz Babydoll was literally all I had. I knew losing her would've definitely been my breaking point. And after taking her through so much before I went down I wasn't even sure if she was gone ride it out with me or not. It was hella stressful tryna hold on to her ass from in hurr knowing I left her out thurr with a bunch of fucked up ass memories that was bound to cross her mind from time to time. All I could do was pray to God she remembered the good times we had and that real deal genuine love we shared. It was always hella solid even before all the bullshit. We obviously had something special or we would've never made it this far.

Me and Latoya drifted apart cuz the drama with her and Babydoll was getting a lil too out of hand. I kinda knew deep down that if I kept tryna force them to be around each other I would eventually lose Babydoll for good and end up with Latoya lookin stupid. That shit just wasn't gone work though. I knew damn well Latoya was way to fucked up in the head for me. She even ended up moving back in the house Hustle got killed in an aint no way I was finna be pullin up over thurr. I aint even wanna take her ass over thurr to clean that muafucka up for real.

"Take me to the house real quick so I can help my mama clean up ova thurr. She said she not cleanin Hustle blood up cuz she gettin too emotional an she not really tryna be ova thurr by herself no way," Latoya said soon as she got off the phone with her mama that day.

"So you really finna tryda live thurr again?" Babydoll butted in feeling like Latoya was outa her fucking mind if she actually went back to live in that house.

"Yeah, I want my kids to feel like they daddy still hurr," Latoya answered bluntly.

"That's not no good ideal Latoya, them kids not finna wanna live in na house they daddy got murdered in," Babydoll replied giving Latoya her honest opinion despite how much she hated her. "Yeah I'm not even tryna be up in nat muafucka so I know damn well they not," I added hoping she would reconsider.

"They'll be fine but I need you to go in ner wit me cuz I haven't even been ner since before I got locked up," Latoya said feeling like she needed me by her side for comfort. I definitely understood why though. Hell I felt like I needed Babydoll by my side goin back up in that muafucka. Latoya wasn't too crazy about Babydoll coming in too but I just needed the same comfort I had when I seen Hustle slumped over by the door that day. So when we pulled up to the house I turned the car off an took the keys out letting Babydoll know to come in the house too. Soon as we all went in I realized we had to face Latoya mama and hear what she had to say about everything that was going on for the first time. It was hella awkward too. Her mama came to the door and greeted us with the broom in her hand anxious to address the elephant in the room even though she didn't right away. So all three of us was hella uncomfortable knowing her mama was about to kick the conversation off at any minute.

"I did the kitchen an na bathroom Latoya. We gone hit the bedrooms together once you get up this blood cuz my lil heart just can't take all that now," her mama said still ready to talk about the situation at hand but tryna find a way to ease her way into it first. Latoya was so irritated and annoyed that she hadn't really said a word. She just start cleaning Hustle blood up off the floor quietly while Babydoll glanced around the room speechless herself.

"So yall know how this look right?" her mama finally blurted out breaking the silence and confronting the three of us like she had been dying to do since the moment we walked through the door. "Yall literally got the whole city talkin bout whateva this is yall got goin on. An maybe somebody can explain exactly what that is to me cuz Ion't be knowin what the hell to say when everybody be askin me about the shit," she continued urging us to clarify what was really going between the three of us once and for all.

"I mean I was under the impression that he was in a relationship wit her so I jus wanna know whurr you fit in to alla that an what role you sposed to play," she added directing the conversation to her daughter and demanding a explanation out of her first and foremost.

"Mama I'm grown, Ion't care what they steady talkin about. It aint even nobody business but mines so I really don't care," Latoya snapped, feeling even more annoyed about having to have this particular conversation with her mama.

"Well I'm pretty sure Hustle family feel like it's they business Latoya. Hell for all they know you had Dashon kill Hustle jus so yall could fuck aroun. Yall never know what people thinkin. You makin people feel like you never even loved Hustle by doin all this. They feel like you never was a true friend like he thought chu was, even tho he was closer to you than anybody. An people jus feel like you dun completely lost yo damn mind for allowin him to fuck wit her when yall been together for years an still is," her mama replied addressing all three of us again before she finished talking.

"Mama everybody already know Cutthroat kilt Hustle and Twin first of all. Second of all can't nobody tell me I aint love my damn husband but Hustle is gone now! He is never comin back so I need to deal wit this shit however I wanna deal wit it. I'm tryna move on wit my life the best way I can an be happy. I'm not finna be sittin aroun all sad an miserable cuz that's not gone bring Hustle back! Nobody knows how this shit feel so everybody can just kiss my ass! If Dashon makin me happy that's just what the fuck it is whether he was Hustle friend or not! Muafuckas just need to leave me alone an mind they fuckin business," Latoya lashed out in frustration as she continued to clean up Hustle blood.

Babydoll just listened without saying a word. Hearing Latoya express how she was feeling automatically put her mind in deep thought cuz for the first time she actually understood whurr Latoya was coming from. The fact that Latoya was so shameless about what was going on with me and her finally made sense. It still made Babydoll wonder how long I was gone be willing to keep playing Hustle role just to keep Latoya happy though. She felt like maybe I was tryna make Latoya happy for Hustle's sake. But that would mean she had to deal wit Latoya for the rest of her life if she really wanted to be with me cuz Hustle was gone forever. All Babydoll really wanted was for it to go back to just being me and her at some point. Everything would've be okay in her lil world as long as we fell back in love with the idea of spending the rest of our lives together again. But the whole conversation had her feeling like it was just never gone end up happening like that cuz I was never gone be willing to cut Latoya off.

When we left the house I took the girls to the beauty supply store and gave em both some money to get they hair done in a attempt to lighten the mood and cheer em up a lil bit. When they came back out Babydoll told me she needed sum more money cuz the kind of hair she picked was more expensive. So I gave her the rest of the money and she went back in the store to buy the hair. Now this is whurr the situation went all the way left. When Babydoll went back in the store Latoya hopped in the front seat. "I wanna sit up hurr wit chu. I'm kinda stressed out an Ion't really wanna sit in na back all by myself right now," she said grabbing my hand and placing it on her leg for comfort.

FIGHT TO THE DEATH

"Iight baby, I know it's been a long day for you. You can sit up hurr wit me for a minute," I said foolishly not realizing what the hell I had just gotten myself into by telling her that she could.

"Thank you baby…damn I forgot to steal some lip gloss while I was in ner hold on I'll be right back," she replied before getting out the car and going back in the beauty supply store. While she was still in the store Babydoll came back out and hopped right in the front seat like she always did. I knew it was finna be some bullshit right then and thurr.

"Baby let Latoya sit up hurr this one time. She jus had to clean up all Hustle blood an shit," I said hoping she would be a lil more sympathetic under the circumstances.

"Um no, why the fuck would I get in na back that's stupid. I'm not gettin in na fuckin back you got me fucked up," she replied getting all worked up immediately.

"You gotta get in na back. He said I could sit up hurr," Latoya said when she came back out to the car after opening the passenger's side door.

"Fuck you bitch make me!" Babydoll replied ready to go head to head for the front seat at that point. Latoya was too though, so she pulled Babydoll arm like she was finna drag her lil ass up out the car an that's when the whole fight kicked off. They both ended up in the back seat pulling each other hair and hitting each other as hard as they could. With all the built up animosity they had for each other it was damn near impossible to break it up too. I mean they was really going at it. I aint really know what the fuck to do cuz they was steady making a scene outside the damn store. I was scared somebody had already called the police about it so I just pulled off while they was still in the back seat fighting.

Hell I was just tryna hurry up and get away before the police even pulled up. I had way too much dope in the car at the time to be taking them type of chances. Plus I had a whole glock on my waist so aint no way I was stickin around with all that going on. I pulled over at the park around the corner to try an break the shit up again but they was really goin at it and was not finna let me stop em either. Luckily one of Latoya mama friends rode past and recognized who Latoya was then pulled over to help me out. I gave the bitch a hunnit dollars to drop Latoya ass off after we broke up the fight then headed back to my mama house so Babydoll ass could get back in her own car and the hell away from me too. Both of they asses had me stressed the fuck out that day. I just wanted to be alone after that shit.

"Go get cho hair done Babydoll," I said pulling up next to her car.

"So is you gone keep fuckin wit that bitch or what? Jus let me know now cuz if so you can kiss my ass straight up. I got a whole fuckin scratch on my face and my neck," Babydoll said looking in the mirror at the tiny scratches on the side of her face and neck.

"Girl aint nothin wrong wit cho ass. You can barely even see that shit. Get cho dramatic ass out my car Babydoll. You got the hair you wanid now go get it done damn. Let me go my phone steady ringin. I'm tryna focus on gettin nis money leave me the fuck alone!" I said harshly not giving a damn about nothing she had to say honestly.

"Bitch you is so fuckin disloyal, I fuckin hate chu! I hope you die wit that bitch!" she screamed before getting out the car and slamming the door behind her. After I pulled off I pulled up on Rello nem by myself for the first time in a lil while. I usually made sure I had Babydoll and Latoya with me when I did. But this time I pulled up on em to vent about how hard it really was to keep that shit up.

"Nigga you did what?" Rello responded appalled when I told him how the whole fight got started in the first place.

"I jus felt bad for her ass bruh, she had jus cleaned up all Hustle blood an shit. I was jus tryna make the bitch feel better foreal," I said in my defense before he got on my head about telling Babydoll to get in the back like a damn fool.

"Man you dead ass wrong for that shit I aint even gone lie to you bruh. Babydoll bad as fuck and she loyal. Latoya ass jus gone fuck whoeva wanna fuck her long as they got some money or sum dems. You can't put a bitch like Babydoll in na back for a bitch like that. Nigga you mus be smokin nat shit," Rello said playfully as everybody laughed.

"Shid I could fuck Latoya if I tried homie. I wouldn't even tryda fuck Babydoll lil ass cuz I know she aint gone go but I bet chu any money Latoya will tho," he added, still tryna put me up on game about how right he was about me being wrong. "If you'ont believe me I tell you what, bring em both to the crib tonight. I'ma have a lil kick back in nis muafucka. Jus pay attention to they body language bruh. Peep how Latoya be constantly eye ballin a nigga while Babydoll watchin every move you make an everything goin on aroun you fool. That's the bitch you want in na front seat an by yo side nigga," he explained letting me know he was gone shoot his shot wit Latoya just to prove his point. He figured he might as well get some pussy out her ass too since she was always slick giving him the greenlight every time she came around.

When I pulled back up on Latoya to pick her up I told her I was wrong for telling her she could get in the front cuz the whole fight could've been avoided if I hadn't. Rello made me feel like shit but I knew he was right about what he said. So I decided to pull up on Latoya first and let her know whurr my head was at not wanting to make her feel like I was just saying the shit to make Babydoll happy.

"You know I love you Latoya, I wanna make you happy an all but I'm already takin Babydoll thru enough by doin all this. I'm jus never gone put her in na back seat cuz even I feel like that's kinda crossin na line a lil bit. Not only that, this not even gone work if yall finna be puttin yall hands on each other cuz yall was puttin all three of us in harm's way. Hell if the police was to pullup on our ass wit all that goin on we all could go to jail. That's just too much drama for me. An Babydoll gone be aroun no matter what so I'ma need the two of yall to get along for this to work," I explained once she came out to the car and got settled. Surprisingly Latoya just sat thurr calmly listening to everything I had to say then cracked a peaceful smile when I was done.

"Ok daddy I'll be nice," she said softly looking prettier than ever then kissed me gently on my lips without saying another word. When we pulled up on Babydoll Latoya automatically got in the back seat before Babydoll even got to the car. That was her way of letting me know she was gone respect what I had said i guess. Babydoll came to the car looking like a real-life Barbie with her hair all fresh and perfect looking. But soon as she seen Latoya in the back seat her face frowned up instantly. She rolled her eyes annoyed with Latoya's presence and my obvious lack of loyalty to her. The last thing she wanted to do was start fighting again as cute as she was looking though. She just sat thurr quietly the whole ride unsure if I was really worth the amount of disrespect she had to deal with if she chose to keep holding on to our relationship. I knew I needed to get her alone and was banking on Rello to take Latoya off my hands so I could.

When we pulled up at Rello crib I finally realized how slutty Latoya was actin around him. Ion't know if she was tryna make me jealous for telling her Babydoll wasn't ever getting in the back or if she had already been acting like that and I just never noticed or paid attention. But either way she was definitely proving his point. So I pulled Rello to the side real quick and told him to hurry up and shoot his shot.

"You got a lil more than you can handle bruh. Lemme take one a they sexy asses off yo hands for the night, youon't need boffum," Rello said smoothly pulling Latoya over to him and setting her on his lap while Babydoll sat quietly on mine. I aint even gone lie I was a lil bit jealous watchin Latoya all on the nigga dick instead of mine cuz she was looking sexy as fuck that night. I knew she wasn't the one I needed to be worried about by then though. I was more worried about securing my relationship with Babydoll cuz she was definitely way more emotionless than usual. The fact that she hadn't said nothing since I picked her up let me know she was most likely just fed up with the bullshit to the point whurr she was finally ready to let me go.

"Yeah go spend some quality time wit cho wifey. You'ont pay her enough attention," Latoya said with a smirk tryna make me and Babydoll feel some type of way I guess.

"Iight we finna slide out then yall be safe, hit me up bruh," I responded before heading out with Babydoll unbothered.

"Don't tryda be all up in my face now jus cuz Rello took yo bitch nigga. Get cho fake ass on. Howda fuck you gone pull up on me wit that bitch when we was jus straight bangin ova the fuckin front seat," Babydoll said soon as I tried to kiss her once we got back to the house.

"First of all Babydoll, what the fuck did Latoya do soon as I pulled up? She got her ass right out an sat in na fuckin back seat like I told her to. Second of all Rello aint take shit, I specifically told the nigga to hop down on Latoya ass so I could be alone wit my bitch. The one I'ma be wit foreva an aint passin off to nobody. So you'ont even know what the fuck you talm bout you jus sayin some shit shutup an lay back," I said before pulling down her pants and panties with a grin knowing if I licked her pussy like she always wanted me to she wouldn't be mad no more. She never could resist me when I did that shit I swear. It always made it so easy to control her ass. Whenever I felt like she was on the verge of leaving me that's all I really had to do to change her mind. This time I drove her crazy with it though, I took my time and paid real close attention to her body language. Everytime I felt like she was finna cum I eased up off it just so she could last longer. I knew her body like the back a my hand by then of course. So soon as I felt like she was about to explode I stopped lickin and just start talking to the pussy softly while my lips rubbed tenderly against it teasing the nut til she begged me not to stop. I knew she would never leave my side and that was my peace. When we nodded off together that night I slept better than I had since the night Hustle died.

"I'm on G code bruh, pull up on me real quick man I need to holla at chu foreal. I can't talk ova the phone tho jus pull up," Lil Rodney said when he called my phone a couple hours later.

"Wasup bruh, you good? Whats goin on," I replied confused an still half sleep.

"Jus pullup bruh hurry up," he answered before hanging up the phone leaving me even more confused and curious as to what the hell must have happened. Babydoll was still knocked the fuck out so I snuck away without her even knowing (thank God). Cuz she would've swore up and down I was tryna duck off with Latoya ass or somethin. When I pulled up on Gamble I was certain that whatever happened definitely had to be serious tho. Lil Rodney had tears in his eyes which was something I thought I would never see based off his whole demeanor and how emotionless he always was.

"They dun kilt my nigga man, they straight kilt Rambo," he said soon as I walked up to him.

"You gotta be fuckin kiddin me, when? An who kilt em?" I responded feeling a lil overwhelmed with yet another nigga that close to me gettin killed all asudden.

"Jus now I guess shid his babymama called an told me he pulled up on na truck thinkin it was me but I sold the damn truck yesterday an got this," he said pointing to the all black hellcat Charger he pulled up in.

"It was them tallaban niggas bruh, they peoples cashed me out for that muafucka. Rambo never even knew that shit tho cuz it aint even cross my mind to tell em. Now I feel like it's my fault they got up on his ass like that… an it really kinda is. Rambo was stressin me out so I been duckin his calls an shit but that's somethin I should've let em know. I should've put em up on game soon as I sold that muafucka regardless of how mad I was at that nigga. I jus wasn't thinkin man but I do business wit them tallaban niggas bruh. That's why I was so mad Rambo kept trippin wit they ass, I still thought I had enough time to straighten nat shit out tho. Now they dun kilt Rambo an Ion't even know howda handle the situation no more," Lil Rodney vented knowing it wouldn't be wise to go wrong with the niggas but unsure if he could really just go on doing business with they ass like nothing happened.

"Look man, you jus gotta see what the fuck these niggas really on bruh. That shit wit them an Rambo was personal, I know that for a fact. But you'ont know if they'll get on sum back door shit thinkin you prolly finna hit they ass first or not. They know damn well yall was hella close so you gotta feel some type a way about the shit. You need to holla at dude wit the truck an see whurr the fuck that nigga head at foreal. He might tryda spin you, he might keep it ahunnit bout the shit, he might even get on sum heavy shit right off the bat. Either way you'll know whurr that nigga head at though. Once you got a clear understandin about that you can take it from ner. Now what all Rambo babymama say?" I asked after giving him my advise about how to handle the situation moving forward.

"She said he peeped the truck an was like (look at this nigga hurr, been duckin me all week). Then pulled up hittin na gas playin an shit, you know how Rambo is bruh," Lil Rodney explained feeling even more guilty and responsible for Rambo's death while telling me what happened. "She said once he realized it wasn't me he hit the gas an took off but the driver fired like six shots an hit Rambo in na fuckin head twice," he continued as the incident played out vividly in his head like he was actually thurr himself. "She said when he died his foot was still smashed down on na gas so she had to straight hop up out the car while it goin top speed before Rambo crashed into a buildin straight ahead," he added not leaving out a single detail as far as he knew.

I felt hella crushed listening to Lil Rodney tell me what happened but the feeling was so familiar that I aint even realize how heartbroken I really was behind the shit. It was more of a numb feeling that I had grown pretty much accustomed to at that point. "Look man, call the nigga wit the truck bruh. You gotta see wasup so you can know howda handle this shit. You jus need to know what they on. Rambo was my nigga too but I'm still not finna advise yo ass to go da war wit them niggas unless you got to. Life goes on, you either gone keep livin yo life or die behind nat shit. If you put cho own life on na line make sure it's because some niggas comin for you tho. Cuz Rambo aint comin back no matter what. That shit is foreva bruh," I explained bluntl urging him to handle the situation wisely rather than just reacting outa anger.

"This nigga straight callin me right now bruh! What the fuck I'm sposed to say," Lil Rodney blurted out in a panic looking down at his phone as it rang.

"Jus let em talk, put it on speaker," I said quickly, eager to hear what the nigga had to say myself.

"Wasup?" Lil Rodney said calmly after answering the phone and putting it on speaker so I could hear exactly how the conversation was finna go.

"Aye we gotta talk homie," Dude said ready to come clean about what happened so they wouldn't be to sketched out to keep doing business with each other I guess. He was fresh out the joint and them tallaban niggas had put up enough money for him to cash Lil Rodney out for that truck. Plus they gave the nigga a phone fulla geeks that was hooked on the shit Lil Rodney had. So he probably sat back and thought about how much the incident was gone affect his ass if Lil Rodney found out about what happened. He knew nine times out ten he would.

"I know you an nat nigga Rambo be rockin out or whatever but he jus pulled up on me wit some bitch on na passenger side an I hit his ass up. When I was locked up he kilt my lil brother man, my only brother an my mama only other son. He caused my family a lota pain when I was gone so when na opportunity presented itself I aint hesitate to take em out. That's jus not sumn I was willin to let slide, it aint no disrespect to you tho. I'm actually tellin you this shit outta respect cuz Ion't want chu to think I'm on no shiesty shit wit chu. I'm still about my money an Ion't want no bad blood between us in na midst of what we do. Cuz that'll fuckup a lota niggas cashflow you know what im sayin," Dude explained as Lil Rodney held the phone unsure about how to respond at the moment. I knew Lil Rodney was at a lost for words an didn't really know what to say so I muted the phone myself.

"It's all good homie, it is what it is," I said quickly before unmuting the phone so he could repeat what I said and end the conversation without getting off on a bad note. "You gotta watch them niggas now tho Lil Rodney," I advised warning him not to let his guard down around em cuz I knew they would always question whether he really just chunked it up and let it go or not. "I do feel like them niggas straight need you tho. So Ion't think you got to much to worry about long as you not lettin nobody know shit about cho operation. If you start feelin like a nigga tryna figure all that out jus cut the shit short altogether. That aint doin shit but lettin you know a muafucka tryna knock you out the box an takeover," I explained reminding him to stay cautious, observant, and alert no matter what. "Play it cool tho nigga. Dude obviously don't want no smoke cuz he showl called tryna explain hisself before the shit got back to you. Not even knowin you had already talked to Rambo babymama. Niggas know who the fuck you is but it's always a fuck nigga inna game tryna earn some stripes remember that," I preached as he nodded his head in agreement.

Them wasn't even the niggas he needed to be worried bout though. Nikki first baby daddy ended up killing Lil Rodney on some hating shit. They seen each other at the carwash one day and Lil Rodney aint think nothing of it. As far as he knew dude aint even have a problem with him. It was never supposed to be no beef between em and they never got into it with each other or nothin.

He knew dude was probably a lil jealous cuz he most likely still wanted Nikki and was fucked up about the fact that she had a son by somebody else. But Lil Rodney showed all love to his son too though. He definitely made sure both of they lil asses had everything they wanted and he never treated his son better than the other one. Every time dude picked up his son Lil Rodney had that lil nigga laced in all designer shit. Dude never had to buy his son no shoes cuz Lil Rodney made sure both the kids had every pair of Jays that came out plus any other shoes that was poppin at the time. He kept both of they hair cut and they both got whatever the fuck they asked for. Dude tried to play it cool when he seen Lil Rodney at the carwash looking like money. He shook his hand and everything but the envy was just way too real. He knew his son looked up to Lil Rodney and never really looked up to him which hurt dude pride like a muafucka. Not only that, when he seen him at the carwash that day he was looking all broke and dusty while Lil Rodney had on all drip, he was clean as a muafucka. He had on like eight thousand dollars worth a jewelry dressed in all white, getting the brand new white Cadillac Escalade he had just bought washed. So the embarrassment had to just be too much to bare especially after pulling off in a old ass Honda Civic with expired plates. He pulled that muafucka right around the corner then ran back up on the lot with a whole AR masked up soon as Lil Rodney got in the car getting ready to pull off. It was pretty much just Lil Rodney time to go though cuz dude lit up the whole car and Lil Rodney was the only one that got hit. He had a couple niggas with him at the time an they did start shooting back while dude was running back to that silly ass car but he still got away untouched. They could've hawked his ass down if Lil Rodney wasn't hit but they just rushed to the hospital instead hoping Lil Rodney would survive and recover.

Jessica Whitfield

TWO WAYS OUT

After I heard what happened I realized everybody was just leaving in they own lil way. The streets was basically letting us know that it was a million different ways to die by the guns that we lived by. It was literally a jungle out thurr and one wrong move would end yo whole world just like it is for the animals that live in the wild. Dodging all them bullets just wasn't as easy or common as it used to be for some reason. Even Heavy fat ass got right out gettin shot up by some random niggas jumpin fresh off the porch, but he aint get killed until of couple months ago. That was the hardest part of my whole bid damn near cuz he had everything in order just ready for me to come home and takeover.

After Chad got killed Heavy got the phones I left out thurr with him then ran his bands up like a muafucka. Chad aint really know how to handle all them people calling back to back but Heavy showl did. He put DonDon and Dre in position then found a whole new plug who put him on a whole nother level with the shit. He was able to just sit back and let DonDon and Dre work the phones after that cuz he was just serving weight. I mean big weight too, he had the whole city turnt up off the dope he was serving. He put Chucky ass back on once he jumped back in the streets. And DonDon nem had more money then they ever had. He even made sure Babydoll was straight for me. It aint start going down hill for him until Chucky ass got caught up and sent to the fucking feds. That was a big ass let down too cuz the last thing my mama wanted was for both of our asses to be up in this muafucka. After Chucky got booked Savage had Heavy nem rockin with some new niggas who was plotting on the whole gang. They knew they would eventually be able to take out Heavy, DonDon, and Dre with the help of Savage scandalous ass. So when the time was right they ended up taking all three of em out at once, incuding Heavy cousin Fatboy. He was the one who gave Heavy the plug in the first place. They trusted Savage cuz he was from na zone of course but Savage aint give a fuck about none of that shit. He jus wanted to take over and get the plug hisself really. He made sure he got Heavy, DonDon, Dre an Fatboy altogether one night and everybody but Don was dead on arrival once the cops pulled up. DonDon spent six hours fighting for his life at the hospital before he died leaving me with a million unanswered questions.

    I been locked up for damn near five years so I ain't really know too much of nothing for real. I just knew Heavy was the man out thurr cuz his name was ringing like a muafucka even in hurr. I aint know nothing about them new niggas Savage had him runnin with. An Babydoll was pretty much clueless too cuz I always made sure she knew not to stick around for too long whenever she pulled up. I just aint want her gettin caught up in the mix of shit. I never really wanted her in the mix when I was out jammin myself let alone wit Heavy nem. They had way more going on then I ever did. I mean them niggas was playin wit all bricks once Heavy got that plug. So they asses was on a whole different level with the shit. I was always worried about something happening to Babydoll cuz she was all I really had out thurr since the moment I got booked. I knew I wouldn't be able to handle it if she would've ended up dead or locked up like everybody else I was affiliated wit. Shid I still be on edge and paranoid when the damn girl miss my call. Especially after Chucky got booked on top of Heavy nem getting killed right when I'm finally on my way back home. That shit just make me feel like anything could happen even now. I was already worried about Babydoll tryna use DonDon ass to get back at me for fucking wit Latoya the whole time. That's another reason I wanted her to stay the fuck away from them niggas. The thought of another nigga touching her drive me crazy in this muafucka I swear. It made my time hurr a lot harder knowing she could use Latoya as a excuse to get even wit me by suckin DonDon dick or some shit outa spite. I wasn't really sure if she wanted revenge that bad or not but considering everything I took her through with Latoya ass showl made me wonder.

    Latoya ended up strung out on the same shit we made all our money off of. I heard she be experimenting wit a bunch of other drugs now too. So she basically just got to a point whurr the dems wasn't even enough for her ass no more. Cutthroat ended up getting locked up for the murder of Hustle and Twin right around the time I got booked for this fed case. We finally came face to face when we seen each other at St. Louis County Jail. This was right before I found out the feds was coming to get my ass too. St Louis County put you in a open area with other men and women when you first come in but everybody be in thurr for different shit. Some people be in thurr for lil petty traffic tickets or 24 hour holds and shit. Then it's people coming in thurr for murder and drug charges like us. They keep everybody in that same lil area with unlimited free phone calls until they figure out whurr you going though. You either bond out and get released from thurr or they take you upstairs whurr it's less freedom.

"You kinda hard to catchup wit aint chu," he said when he approached after spotting me from across the room.

"I find it hard to believe you was actually lookin cuz I'm not to hard to find. You aint have no problem findin Twin did you? What make me so different?" I replied not even able to look the nigga in the eyes knowing what he did to Hustle.

"I was lookin for Twin cuz he threatened my life. I was lookin for you so we could sit down an actually talk about what happened," he said taking a seat in the chair next to mine.

"Man I'll never understand why you did that shit to Hustle or Twin, so it really aint even shit for us to talk about foreal," I said looking straight ahead as I talked even though he had sat down right beside me.

"Well I did that to Twin cuz he made it clear that he wanid to kill my ass but wit Hustle it was more about respect," he said calmly disregarding the response I gave him about us not having shit to talk about.

"I wanid to kill you too, I just never spoke on na shit cuz I aint see no reason to," I said bluntly letting him know whurr my head was really at after hearing about what he did.

"I already knew you did homie. I know you bruh, been knowin you our whole life. Shid the only reason I aint pull up on you is cuz I aint wanna have to kill you first," he replied with a smirk unbothered by me letting him know that I wanted to kill him myself.

"I think you jus knew I was gone be the one to make you pay for what chu did to Hustle," I said finally looking him in his eyes.

"You was always the one I knew I would have to kill but never really wanid to for some reason," he said after given me a slight chuckle. "That's why I spared yo life just so you know. You know how many times I seen Babydoll car parked outside a DonDon crib?" he asked with his eyebrows raised before carrying on. "An Babydoll…man she so damn pretty, she nice too. I asked her for some change one day when I seen her at the gas station jus to see if she knew who I was but she was clueless. She jus handed me a dollar, told me to have a blessed day then walked to her car," he said with a evil grin basically letting me know he could've easily killed Babydoll too if he really wanted to take me down. Hell that would've been worse than just killing me for real. I sat thurr feeling hella bothered about him letting me know he had the opportunity to kill Babydoll without her ever even seeing it coming and felt bad cuz I never even showed her who he was.

"Quincy Johnson," the lady behind the desk interrupted before I was even able to respond.

"I'll see you on na other side one day bruh. Remember what I said," he added as he got up out the chair beside me and headed to the front desk so they could escort him upstairs.

Savage ended up getting locked up too. He just so happened to run into Chucky at the Justice Center while Chucky was down thurr waiting for the feds to come pick him up. They just throw a bunch of niggas in a cage and expect em to behave at the Justice Center. So soon as they put Savage up in that muafucka Chucky questioned'm about the shit that went down wit Heavy nem. Drako had found out who all had something to do with that shit soon as he got out and it aint take him long at all to spread the word about it.

"Thats on nem niggas for lettin nat shit happen hell I aint pull the trigger," Savage answered before Chucky just bombed off on his ass without letting him say another word. Chucky already knew he wasn't gettin out no time soon so he was quick to pop off on anybody. They say Chucky fucked Savage ass up in that cell. That lil nigga was in thurr trippin but he always been like that though I swear. He had just got grazed in his head tryna fight some nigga on the southside right before he got booked. My mama felt like maybe he needed to go sit down so he wouldn't end up gettin killed. She aint want him to go away for a whole five years after I just did damn near five in this muafucka myself though.

Yesterday I walked the yard reminiscing on the memories I shared with all my niggas that's dead and gone now and it took me way back to when I was a kid. Me and Chad had got caught stealing from the corner store one day so my mama got mad and told me I couldn't go outside. It was a nice summer day so everybody was out thurr live as fuck while I sat in the crib looking out the window pissed. "Get out the damn window lookin like a sad puppy boy. If ya ass wasn't down at that corna store stealin you'd be out thurr playin wit cha friends instead a stuck in na house now wouldn't you?" my uncle said unsympathetically when he came in the front room and seen me looking out the window sulking.

"I'm jus sayin, Chad got caught stealin too but he still playin outside," I said as I sat down on the couch with a attitude and folded my arms.

"Cheer up nephew, you live an you learn. Everybody mama don't give a damn about whether they son gone do right or not but yours do. You aint really missin nothin out thurr no way. One day you gone look up an all them lil niggas gone be dead or locked up. So you better learn howda stand alone cuz they not always gone be aroun an you can bet cho ass on nat," he said as I rolled my eyes never realizing how right he was until now cuz once I walk out these doors tomorrow I stand alone…..

ABOUT THE AUTHOR

Jessica Whitfield was born and raised in St louis. She had a baby at 16 and dropped out of school so being street smart was simply the only way to survive. With a high school education it was a struggle to live the life that she wanted so she basically relied on her looks to get by. She was always drawn to strip clubs and has always been infatuated with the entire industry. Working at the strip club was her comfort zone but she never had the nerve to get on stage and dance. She would always pride herself on being able to use her looks and personality to collect money there even though she admired the dancer's confidence too. After meeting the love of her life, the strip club industry wasn't really where she wanted to be anymore, so she found herself getting wrapped up in the life that he lived. She started writing The Streets of St. Louis in 2018 and didn't complete it til 2021. In the meantime, she moved from one house to another, survived the pandemic, gave birth to the son she always wanted, and lost her only brother to gun violence just minutes away from her home. Telling this story is something she feels like she was born to do despite everything that seemed to slow down the process of completion. Her ultimate goal is to turn this book into a tv series.